ROUTLEDGE LIBRARY EDITIONS: COMPARATIVE EDUCATION

Volume 14

EDUCATION IN EAST AND WEST GERMANY

EDUCATION IN EAST AND WEST GERMANY

A Bibliography

VAL D. RUST

Routledge
Taylor & Francis Group
LONDON AND NEW YORK

First published in 1984 by Garland Publishing, Inc.

This edition first published in 2018
by Routledge
2 Park Square, Milton Park, Abingdon, Oxon OX14 4RN

and by Routledge
711 Third Avenue, New York, NY 10017

Routledge is an imprint of the Taylor & Francis Group, an informa business

British Library Cataloguing in Publication Data
A catalogue record for this book is available from the British Library

ISBN: 978-1-138-54113-9 (Set)
ISBN: 978-1-351-00358-2 (Set) (ebk)
ISBN: 978-1-138-54413-0 (Volume 14) (hbk)
ISBN: 978-1-138-54496-3 (Volume 14) (pbk)
ISBN: 978-1-351-00462-6 (Volume 14) (ebk)

Publisher's Note
The publisher has gone to great lengths to ensure the quality of this reprint but points out that some imperfections in the original copies may be apparent.

Disclaimer
The publisher has made every effort to trace copyright holders and would welcome correspondence from those they have been unable to trace.

EDUCATION IN EAST AND WEST GERMANY
A Bibliography

Val D. Rust

GARLAND PUBLISHING, INC. • NEW YORK & LONDON
1984

Library of Congress Cataloging in Publication Data

Rust, Van Dean.
Education in East and West Germany.

(Reference books In international education ; vol. 1)
(Garland reference library of social science ; vol. 202)
Includes indexes.
1. Education—Germany—Bibliography. I. Title.
II. Series. III. Series: Garland reference library
of social science ; v. 202.
Z5815.G3R88 1984[LA722] 016.37'0943 83-48216
ISBN 0-8240-9050-0 (acid-free paper)

Printed on acid-free, 250-year-life paper
Manufactured in the United States of America

CONTENTS

FOREWORD

This series of annotated bibliographies of education in selected nations and regions is designed to provide a resource to scholars, students, and a variety of other professionals needing to understand the place of education in a particular society. The format of each volume is similar yet each contributor has had the freedom to adjust the common outline to reflect the peculiarities of their particular nation or region.

Each contributor to this series is a scholar who has devoted his professional life to the nation or region he has been assigned. Without exception they have not only studied the educational system in question, but they have lived and travelled widely in it. In short, they are exceptionally knowledgeable about their subject.

Every volume in the series begins with an extended essay about the nation's educational enterprise—its history, development, problems, etc. Following this essay is an annotated bibliography, broken into major categories, of the most important and accessible books, articles, dissertations, etc. published in English.

Since this series is designed to be a useful research tool, the editor and contributors welcome suggestions for future volumes as well as ways in which this series can be improved.

Edward R. Beauchamp
University of Hawaii

PREFACE

We have undertaken in this volume to provide the English speaking world with a comprehensive record of published English language materials which focus on education in the Federal Republic of Germany (FRG), and the German Democratic Republic (GDR). These two nations have a common historical origin and it was only after 1945 and the end of World War II that they have undergone processes of development from opposing ideological points of departure. In the past three decades dramatic divergence in values, life styles, and schooling can be seen between the two Germanies. In spite of this, we have chosen to include in one volume the major books, articles, dissertations, etc., on both countries, because all Germans continue to share a cultural heritage that permeates life. Further, much of the material reviewed here is historical in nature and appropriately belongs to the literature of both national groups.

We are aware of one major obstacle in dealing with the two Germanies. While abundant English language materials are available about the Federal Republic of Germany, a dearth of material exists on the German Democratic Republic. We run some risk, therefore, of implying an imbalance in terms of activities and contributions which the two Germanies promise to the researcher and student. This certainly has not been our intent and the imbalance that is evident in terms of cited references reflects a political condition rather than pedagogical qualities.

The book has two major sections. In the first section we have provided an introductory essay which sketches the role of education, formal and nonformal, in the two Germanies. Not only have we outlined various facets of the educational system and placed them in some socio-historical context, but we have attempted to provide the reader with research assistance. We outline library and archival holdings that are available to the researcher, and we discuss trends as well as lacunae in educational research.

The second section consists of an annotated bibliography of English language materials. A relatively large English language literature is available which sheds light on general or specific issues connected with education in East and West Germany. Illustrative of this would be no less than 1088 citations indexed in the ERIC files between 1972 and 1982.

One of the greatest weaknesses in the literature is the lack of availability of prepared bibliographical collections. In fact, prior to this publication, no comparable document has been available to the English speaking world. Those few bibliographical collections that are at hand, are either restricted to specific topics or are abbreviated in scope. It has been necessary for researchers to undertake their own search of materials, usually beginning with more general retrieval options, such as the card catalogue of libraries, ERIC, or the United States Library of Congress Union catalogue.

It is important to explain how we have compiled references in our study and the criteria we have used in selecting references for certain of the chapters. Of particular importance is the date of publication. We have chosen to apply different quality criteria to two time periods: pre-World War II, and 1945-1982. The only materials published prior to 1945, which have been included in this study, are those materials which remain crucial to a general understanding of German education. The basis used to make such a judgment is whether the material was cited in some post-1945 publication on education in Germany.

A more inclusive policy has been exercised regarding materials published in the period following World War II, although certain quality control decisions were made for materials. One of the major criteria used was the availability of a reference in a research library. The author has spent considerable time at the libraries at UCLA, the University of California, Berkeley, the University of Southern California, and the University of Utah. If a particular manuscript or journal was unavailable for review or annotation at these libraries, it was usually not included in this manuscript. Our rationale for this policy was that this document should serve as a resource tool for the student and researcher, and if a document is generally unavailable, it would serve little purpose to list it. The consequence of this decision is that approximately three percent of identified citations have not been included.

More specific criteria for inclusion were used for certain chapters. An extensive and rich literature from the social sciences is available to the educational researcher. It would have taken us far beyond the intent of this volume to provide an extensive bibliography of social, political, economic, anthropological and historical studies that would be relevant to education. Our criterion for inclusion was simple. Any social science study cited in an educational study between 1945-1982 was included here. This method of selection has the singular advantage of reflecting studies that have actually been helpful enough to the educational researcher to have been cited. A good balance is reflected in studies of historical significance as well as contemporary social science works on both Germanies.

The chapter on philosophy of education posed additional difficulties. Only a very few studies that describe themselves as focusing on German philosophy of education are in existence.

It is obvious, however, that the philosophical and pedagogical ideas of a large number of Germans have been published in translation. These scholars have also been the focus of attention by English speaking scholars. We have chosen to be extremely selective in our coverage of specific individuals. That is, we have chosen to include only those individuals who typically are highlighted in texts on the history of German educational thought, and we have usually included only those works that are on education rather than on more general philosophy. Obviously, such distinctions are impossible in many cases. The philosophers are clustered according to the conceptual orientation of their time period. Significantly, almost none of the contemporary philosophical works has been translated into English. The reader will, consequently, find a void with regard to men such as Theodor Ballouff, Otto Friedrich Bollnow, and Josef Derbolav.

An extensive literature is avaiable about administration, organization and essentially every level of education in West Germany. Information about East Germany is very spotty. In the last decade a limited number of more general studies on education in East Germany have been published, which have helped to provide some sense of what has happened since the German Democratic Republic came into existence. Most of the information prior to that has come from government sponsored sources, which reflect hostile sentiments toward traditional Germany and the West, and which also reflect the pervasive ideology of the regime.

The single category having by far the largest collection of references is that of higher education. In fact, 40 percent of the references are in this category. Upon reflection, this should not be surprizing. Most publications come from people in higher education and we would assume that these scholars would tend to focus on that aspect of education with which they are most familiar. Once again, the greatest higher education attention has been given to West Germany, but the East has its share of treatment, even though the reader will find several subsections with no references in them.

Following the bibliography, we have listed three indexes. The first is a journal index, where at least one appropriate citation has been found. Approximately 400 such journals are listed. The second is an index of authors cited in the manuscript. The third is an index of the various sections and subsections as well as other topics in them.

I wish to express appreciation to Hugh Stocks, who assisted in formatting the script program in the computer. Jorge Nakamoto served as a student Research Assistant in the project. The UCLA Graduate School of Education graciously made funds available from its University Opportunity Fund to cover most of the word processing costs. I have reviewed all of the references cited in the study and take personal responsibility for all of the annotations made.

INTRODUCTION

HISTORICAL ROOTS

German education traces its origins, as do the schools throughout Europe, to the monastic or church schools of the Middle Ages. These schools were not general in any meaningful sense, but were intended to provide those given the priesthood with the tools to carry out their duties, especially to read and interpret the scriptures. The oldest specific type of institution that has maintained continuous existence since the Middle Ages is the university.

The university has been at the pinnacle of formal education since the end of the Middle Ages. In fact, the oldest institutions of higher learning came into being in the twelfth and thirteenth centuries at Paris, Bologna and Salerno. In German speaking areas, the universities emerged for the first time in the fourteenth century under charters from sovereign princes and cities at Prague (1348), Vienna (1384), Heidelberg (1385), Cologne (1388), and Erfurt (1392).[1] The major function of the university was to prepare clerics, although humanism extended itself, with its cultivation of worldly professions. Four major faculties of study became the norm: theology, law, medicine, and letters. The faculty of letters focused on the seven liberal arts which had carried over from ancient Greece. This was especially evident in the newer humanistic universities such as Freiburg (1456), Tuebingen (1477), and Wittenberg (1502). In conjunction with the Reformation and counter-Reformation, universities with even more modern programs came into being at Marburg (1582), Koenigsberg (1544), Jena (1558), and Wuerzburg (1582).

The Age of Enlightenment witnessed the establishment of Halle (1694), and Goettingen (1737) universities. Of course, even the oldest adjusted their structures and programs to the newer thinking. Whereas the previous institutions had been based on the Aristotelian concept that knowledge is generated from deductive processes, the new mode accepted induction as

---

[1] For an historical overview, see Abraham Flexner. **Universities: American, English, German**. Oxford: Oxford University Press, 1930.

legitimate. That is, it was assumed that knowledge can be obtained through experience and experimentation. Of course, even the oldest universities modified themselves so that they took on the form of the newer institutions. However, they all retained a classical form and the changes that had occurred throughout the centuries had not yet altered the basic character of the university.

The major function of the first grammar school, known in Germany since the sixteenth century as the **Gymnasium**, was to prepare young men for university study by giving instruction in Latin, since Latin provided a universal medium of communication for the learned classes. Of course, they provided other important functions such as boys' choirs for church services. In fact, through the eighteenth century secondary schooling and the church could be considered a unity with the **Gymnasium** providing a service function to the church and the university. From the time of the Renaissance, the **Gymnasium** represented a resurrected school of antiquity, where both physical and mental faculties were developed through classical languages, poetry and fiction, philosophy, and character training. The basic form of the **Gymnasium** was set early in its development and its form remained through several centuries. Even the budding scientific influence of the seventeenth and eighteenth centuries had almost no impact on the **Gymnasium**. The so-called **Realien** which represented physical reality or knowledge of the tangible world had minimal influence on the **Gymnasium**; the so-called **Ritterakademie** (academy for noblemen) actually posed the major competition for the classical school, but it was reserved for the sons of nobility and included, along side classical studies, new languages, history and geography, and military studies such as riding and fencing.

The laity played almost no role in these activities, although school-like arrangements existed as early as the thirteenth century which provided basic skills for certain segments of society. Writing craftsmen, for example, who ran establishments to aid people in preparing letters, bills of sale, and other documents, would take young people into their care as apprentices so that they might become contributing members of the guild.

It was not until the Reformation, however, that the notion of education for all people became common. This occurred initially among Protestants and was related to salvation rather than vocation; eventually, the value of education permeated Catholic lands as well. This religious impulse was translated into secular schooling regulations in specific German states. The first important regulations were the Saxon School Code of 1528 and the Wuerttemberg School Code of 1559. The latter provided for the establishment of vernacular primary schools in every village for both boys and girls emphasizing basic skills as well as music and religion. Control of schools and instruction was, of course, retained by the church. Most of the North German states eventually followed the Wuertemberg model.

In the seventeenth century a further educational impulse can be seen coming out of the rationalist, liberal and humanitarian beliefs that all people have the capacity to learn and become learned. The Enlightenment belief that even simple people could become self-sufficient thinkers, contributed to the adoption of the 1642 Gotha and the 1658 Magdeburg School Codes, which brought both elementary and learned studies under quasi-secular control.

The Period of Absolutism witnessed further control of schooling by civil authority. Friedrich the Great is credited with having established the first primary school law for the entire state of Prussia with his 1763 **General-Land-Schul-Reglement**, which required all children from five until thirteen or fourteen to attend school and master basic skills and undergo religious and political indoctrination.

The basic intent of modern public schooling and academic studies was set during the revitalization period following the defeat of the Prussian army by Napoleon at Jena in 1806. The Prussians retained the schooling tasks which had been carried on in traditional German elementary schools (including basic skills, religious and moral indoctrination, and enlightened learning in the vernacular). In addition, the school was transformed into an instrument for the development of a patriotic and loyal citizenry to the Prussian state.[2] Religious instruction remained a foundation stone for the German culture, and it was incorporated as one element in the trinity: God, Child, and Fatherland. Studies in language, history, music and religion came to be viewed as instruments through which children would become loyal to the Prussian state.

In Prussia, the first fundamental shift in the role of the **Gymnasium** took place during the revitalization period in the early years of the nineteenth century. The new philosophical thinking of Herder, Humboldt, Fichte and others was to shift the classical studies away from Latin to Greek as the richer and more fundamental language. More importantly, however, was a shift in task or aim. The **Gymnasium** was no longer to be mainly a cleric related institution but was to prepare educated personnel to fill civil service positions for the incipient modern bureaucracy.

Of course, this changing role had been perceived somewhat earlier in some of the smaller German states. Weimar declared as early as 1733 that the **Gymnasium** would cease being an institution only for theologians, physicians and lawyers. It was to

---

[2] Wilhelm Flitner. **Die Vier Quellen des Volksschulgedankens**. Stuttgart: Ernst Klett Verlag, 1963.

take on the task of serving God and the Fatherland, by preparing leaders for the state, military, economy, administration, and commerce, as well as choir masters and school masters.[3]

The state intervened at many levels to structure and tailor the **Gymnasium** to its needs. Prussia adopted the leaving examination (**Abitur**) in 1788, which formalized the qualifications necessary for the student to move from the Latin school to the university. State determined **Gymnasium** teacher qualifications were set during the first half of the nineteenth century. The curriculum of the school was also formalized. Significantly, it was built on a neo-humanistic or classical foundation, especially the Greek language, literature, and thought, rather than having specific vocationally oriented courses.

The modern university, as we understand it, took form in the nineteenth century and was also an outgrowth of the revitalization period after the French had defeated the Prussians. Universities which had previously been seen as "autonomous corporations in a hierarchical, semifeudal society of privilege and tradition," were fundamentally altered to take on "a new position within the emerging modern state and bourgeois society."[4] Many of the older institutions were closed or reformed as an actual theory of the university emerged through the efforts of such men as Humboldt (1767-1835), Fichte (1762-1814), and Schleiermacher (1768-1834). The theory included the idea of a learned class that was independent but which, through philosophy and science, would assist the state in transforming the entire society. The learned class would possess the freedom to pursue, without self-interest, whatever avenues of learning that showed promise. With science at their foundations, the universities at Berlin (1810), Breslau (1818), and Bonn (1818) set the model for all of university study in the German speaking world.

It is crucial to understand that the Germans not only included **Naturwissenschaft** (natural science) as a science but **Geisteswissenschaft**, which deals with the world of the mind, culture and spirit. Consequently, in spite of its reorientation toward science, the university retained an allegiance and a commitment to liberal education. The spiritual and the material were all considered to be legitimate and necessary aspects of scientific study.

---

[3] Fritz Blaettner. **Das Gymnasium**. Heidelberg: Quelle und Meyer, 1960, p. 38.

[4] Charles E. McClelland. **State, Society and University in Germany: 1700-1914**. Cambridge: Cambridge University Press, 1980, p. 103.

In spite of the deeply mystical elements of science study, the crowning achievements of German higher education were seen by the external world in its practical achievements. The Prussian victories over Austria in 1866 and France in 1870 awakened the world to the emergence of Germany as a world power, and this power was seen to be connected to its educational commitments. The number of faculties in the university were expanded to eventually include such fields as economics, social sciences, agronomy, veterinary medicine, and forestry. In addition, an impressive array of technical institutes, business schools, and mining academies came into being.

During the nineteenth century, German educational institutions at all levels gained a stature unparalleled in the Western world. One of the main features of that period was the stream of educators and social reformers who migrated to Germany to see first hand the school system, that Henry Barnard claimed "has attained a degree of excellence which has attracted the attention of statesmen and commanded the admiration of intelligent educators in every part of Christendom."[5]

In our discussion so far we have focused on the increasing involvement of the state in schooling. We do not wish to imply that the German state authorities were responsible for designing the total structure of education in Germany. Often, it simply formalized what had become a social fact. For example, the introduction of natural science in education came about largely through initiatives outside the **Gymnasium** and university. As early as 1652 the **Academie Naturae** had been established at Leipzig where scientific papers were published. In 1700 the Berlin **Societas Regia Scientarium** also came into existence. This later became the **Deutsche Academie der Wissenschaft** and served as a forum for informal meetings, collected and shared research manuscripts, and aided generally in scientific studies and experiments.

Schools having a science component were also established. In 1694 August Hermann Francke began to establish schools intending to instill a sense of faith and knowledge based on Pietism. These schools also drew modern languages as well as practical and natural sciences into their curricula. In 1747, Julius Hecker established the first **Realschule** which was the forerunner of the practically oriented middle schools that followed in the nineteenth century. Johannes Bernhard Basedow established the **Philanthropinum** in 1774, which also introduced practical studies. Although these schools usually placed great emphasis on Latin instruction, mainly because that was what

---

[5] Henry Barnard. **National Education in Europe**. Hartford: Case Tiffany and Co., 1854, p. 87.

most people thought a school did, they, nevertheless, broke from the classical tradition and focused their curriculum on the natural sciences. Under the influence of philanthropists, these schools multiplied throughout the century, and as the modern world began to take form in Europe, the better **Realschulen** even gained some parity with the more prestigious **Gymnasia**.

In 1832 Prussia declared that **Realschulen** could qualify the young for specified middle-level civil service positions. In 1859, a distinction was drawn between those **Realschulen** with and without Latin. The Latin based schools were eventually renamed **Realgymnasien**. A second kind of **Realschule** also developed called the **Oberrealschule**. This school type came from the old technical schools (**Gewerbeschule**) of Prussia, and in 1877 they were transformed to provide both a general education and a professional education. In 1882 they were given the new name with accompanying status and rights.[6] In 1901 both the **Realgymnasium** and the **Oberrealschule** were finally given the same formal status as the classical **Gymnasium**, at least in that their graduates qualified for university study.

Vocational education is another case in point. Prior to the nineteenth century it took place almost entirely within the framework of practical experience under the tutelage of a master craftsman. The major economic enterprise in Europe had been the guild. In the guild, the neophyte practiced with the master for up to seven years before moving on to the next stage of competence, that of the journeyman. Finally, if worthiness was demonstrated, he too was allowed to become a master. Schooling and civil involvement in the process were almost totally missing. Two factors led to the introduction of vocational schools. First, the industrial revolution with its factory system led to a breakdown of the guild system. Second, as primary schooling became universal, the young were deprived of engaging in extended direct, participation as an apprentice. The first vocational schools were so detached from real life experiences, however, that they failed to satisfy their intended purposes.[7]

Finally, in 1897, the German state intervened with a regulation mandating that the youth must be at a work station for all but one day a week. On the off-day the youth would be in school and receive theoretical training. The state dictated the length of time the apprentice would be in service (usually three years), and this was to take place upon completion of compulsory primary schooling at age 14.

---

[6] Blaettner, 1960, p. 294.

[7] Karl Abraham. **Der Betrieb als Erziehungsfaktor**. Freiburg: Lambertus, 1957.

The education of women is still another case in point. In speaking of traditional schooling, we refer almost exclusively to males. This is not to imply that education for girls did not occur, but it took place within the confines of the home and the household. It was not until the Age of Enlightenment that men like Pestalozzi popularized the idea of general education and the possibility that everyone had the ability for general learning, that some attention was given to schooling young women.

Through the efforts of women and enlightened men, schools were opened in increasing numbers to young girls in the nineteenth century. The main interest of these reformers was that a parallel system of education be created that would give females a vocational and political status comparable to that of males. Initially, the schools which were established were copies of the schools for boys, but eventually schools which addressed themselves to what was considered to be the peculiar condition and needs of females took form. These included not only elementary schools but general and vocational secondary schools, institutions of higher learning and academies, and they remained largely under private sponsorship through the century.[8]

By the end of the nineteenth century, almost all forms of education had been consolidated under secular authority. However, this authority remained decentralized and under control of the various states. Even with the unification of German states through the foundation of the North German Confederation in 1867 and the establishment of the Second German Empire in 1871, the German states continued to exercise cultural autonomy.

It was not until the collapse of the Second Empire at the end of World War I and the writing of the Weimar constitution that the Republic came to participate with state and local entities in governing primary and secondary schooling, including vocational education. The Weimar Republic also signaled the first stages of a formal movement toward a unified or comprehensive schooling process. In the past, the masses and elites had enjoyed separate educational experiences. Those who attended the **Volksschule** (peoples school) had little opportunity to transfer to the learned schooling process. Private tutoring and special preparatory institutions supplied the young elites with the schooling necessary to enter the higher schools. Until this time the sharp social class divisions were strictly reinforced by the school system.

---

[8] Susanne C. Engelmann. **Die Erziehung des Maedchens.** Leipzig: Quella, 1929.

The social revolution, which led to the Weimar Republic, signaled the first attempts to break down the dualistic structure. This was a natural outgrowth of the New Education Movement, which was both indigenous in nature and worldwide in scope. The major focus of the movement was toward education, in both its formal and informal dimensions. Informally, the youth movement came into full bloom in the decade just prior to World War I. This was largely a youth inspired, youth led movement that emerged in a number of communities. Eventually, these groups bound themselves together to form an association dedicated to propogating folk music, folk dancing, friendship and exchange of views.

The more formal dimensions of the movement began as a series of isolated school reform projects. Each reformer resorted to his own mode of expression, and his theoretical and philosophical base often took on a distinctive character. There was no united movement and, in fact, many critics of certain trends were the leaders of other reform undertakings. Hermann Nohl noted four primary educational trends which emerged in the pre-World War I phase: (1) The Country Home Schools (**Landerziehungsheime**), which were boarding schools in rural areas, (2) The Art Education Movement, (3) The movment for self-directive character training, and (4) The Activity School Movement (**Arbeitsschule** Movement).[9] A major thrust of the entire movement was the comprehensive or common school (**Einheitsschule**), and the Education Law of 1920 (article 146) stipulated that a four year common school was to become a reality by 1925. Teacher backgrounds also became common for the first time in that all **Volksschule** instructors were required to pass the **Gymnasium** leaving examination. Prior to this time, **Volksschule** teachers were products of the **Volkschule** who had gone on to a special teachers seminar that was not connected with conventional higher education.

Secondary schools now consisted of four nine year forms, each having identical rights: **Gymnasium, Realgymnasium, Oberrealschule**, and the **Deutsche Oberschule**. The last form just mentioned had been established in 1925 in Prussia and focused on German studies rather than classics, science, or modern languages. In addition, a six year middle school existed to prepare those of a middle class status. Further, young people who completed compulsory schooling and went on to become apprentices were required to attend theoretical training one day a week at a vocational school (**Berufsschule**) until they had reached the age of eighteen.

---

[9] Herman Nohl. **Die paedagogische Bewegung in Deutschland und ihre Theorie.** (6th ed.) Frankfurt a/M.: G. Schulte-Bulmke, 1963.

The movement toward a common school was not able to take full form before National Socialism overwhelmed the German state with its intention of establishing a Third German Empire, which was to last 1000 years. Schooling was totally centralized by the National Socialists, who remolded the educational process and curriculum to suit their needs. These needs included the inculcation of character or a sense of "orderliness, obedience, comradeship, leadership and above all receptivity to the National Socialist Weltanschauung"[10] It also focused on physical fitness. The press of National Socialism permeated every facet of life. The mission of schooling was redirected, and young people were organized into Hitler youth groups which served to control and dictate their out-of-school activities. Thus, character and physical fitness took priority over intellectual development and academic achievement throughout Germany until the collapse of the German military forces in 1945.

THE OCCUPATION PERIOD

At the end of World War II, the allied powers joined in a single voice at Potsdam in declaring that German education was to undergo a thorough process of denazification, followed by the democratization of the country. This process would permeate all facets of German society. An extensive adult education program would be initiated. The universities would undergo definite democratization, and the schools would devote themselves to the transformation of future generations of German citizens.

The immediate problem of conducting school seemed formidable indeed. Most of the teachers were thought unfit, most of the school buildings were destroyed or damaged, and most of the remaining undamaged textbooks were declared unfit for use. Because Germany had been partitioned into four zones of occupation, controlled by France, Great Britain, the U.S.A., and the U.S.S.R., each zone began to impose quite distinct governing policies, standards, and processes of denazification, as well as democratization.

---

[10] Arthur Hearnden. **Education in the Two Germanies.** Oxford: Basil Blackwell, 1974, p. 28.

For expedient reasons, all allied powers quickly turned the schooling task over to the Germans themselves. One unique feature seems to have characterized the Russian practice. Whereas all other allies were as thorough as they could be in terms of screening National Socialist sympathizers out of the more important positions, the Russians dictated that only those Germans sympathetic with communism were to be placed in policy making positions. The Western allies were less discriminant and mainly focused on the negative side of the process. Consequently, the Russians were successful in implementing a school structure that deviated radically from the traditional German system.

The structure which emerged in the Soviet Zone of Occupation was an eight year common school with provision for two further years for the majority of students before they entered vocational studies. A four year scientific branch beyond the eight year school, existed for those going on to higher studies. All schools, including the common school, were to end with a leaving examination.[11]

Illustrative of the reconstruction efforts was the work done in the Russian zone to fill 60,000 teaching positions. Since the old guard could not be relied upon, authorities drew **Neulehrer** from the ranks of the working class and put them through an eight month training program. Over 15,000 began teaching during the 1945/46 school year and another 25,000 in 1946/47. Fully two-thirds of all teachers in 1946 were **Neulehrer** (new teachers).[12] A significant higher education innovation was adopted immediately after the war. In an attempt to break down the elitist nature of the university, the Russians and their East German collaborators established a three year "worker and peasant faculty" which provided bridge courses to the university for those inadequately prepared to take advantage of university study. Professors were expected to curtail a good share of their normal research and lecture time in order to channel their energies to this new faculty.[13]

---

[11] Frederic Lilge. "German Educational Reforms in the Soviet Zone of Occupation." **Harvard Education Review**, 18 (Jan., 1948), 35-46.

[12] Karl-Heinz Guenther and Gottfried Uhlig. **History of the Schools in the German Democratic Republic, 1945 to 1968.** Berlin: Volk und Wissen Volkseigener Verlag, 1973, pp. 28-30.

[13] Mina J. Moore-Rinvolucri. **Education in East Germany.** Hamden, Conn.: Archon Books, 1973, p. 97.

The Occupation Period

Americans approached reconstruction with a fervent missionary spirit and a naive notion that the Germans would benefit from an American model of education. Robert Lawson characterizes the descriptions of reorganization efforts as reading "like a school reorganization plan drawn up by devoted American teachers and citizens for the children of their own community."[14] The missionary zeal of the Americans actually worked to their disadvantage for the Germans rejected most of their recommendations as being alien and dysfunctional. This is not to imply that some reform proposals were not implemented, but these were usually those which had general professional support in the American zone itself.

The British probably had the least impact on educational reforms. In fact, their policy appeared to be no policy at all as they concentrated on informal relations and local action. One could probably also conclude that, from an American vantage point, the British were not inclined to impose a system on the Germans that did not exist in Great Britain itself. Selectivity, structural divisions, and class distinctions were as prevalent in Great Britain as in Germany.

The French did have success, albeit in a somewhat different direction than most Americans wished. They did not alter the traditional school structure so much as try to democratize by imposing a curricular emphasis on French language and culture. Consequently, the Western powers allowed the pre-National Socialist educational structure to reassert itself, while in the Soviet zone a fundamental structural change became the norm.

In spite of the differences that were emerging in the various zones of occupation during the first two years after the war, the occupational powers continued to try and coordinate their activities. As late as June 25, 1947, the Allied Control Council issued a ten point program intended to serve as educational guidelines for zone commanders.

1. There should be equal educational opportunity for all.
2. Tuition, textbooks and other necessary scholastic material should be provided free of charge in all educational institutions fully supported by public funds which cater mainly to pupils of compulsory school age; in addition, maintenance grants should be made to those who need aid. In all other educational institutions including universities, tuition, textbooks and necessary material should be provided free of charge together with maintenance

---

[14] Robert Lawson. **Reform of the West German School System, 1945-1962**. Comparative Education Dissertation Series No. 4. Ann Arbor: University of Michigan, 1965.

grants for those in need of assistance.

3. Compulsory full-time school attendance should be required for all between the ages of six and at least fifteen; and thereafter, for those pupils not enrolled in full-time educational institutions, at least part-time compulsory attendance up to the completed age of eighteen years.
4. Schools for compulsory school attendance should form a comprehensive educational system. The terms 'elementary education' and 'secondary education' should mean two consecutive levels of education, not two types or qualities of instruction which overlap.
5. All schools should lay emphasis upon education for civic responsibility and a democratic way of life, by means of the content of the curriculum, textbooks and materials of instruction and by the organisation of the school itself.
6. All school curricula should aim to promote understanding of and respect for other nations, and to this end attention should be given to the study of modern languages, without preference for any language.
7. Educational and vocational guidance should be provided for all pupils and students.
8. Health supervision should be provided for all pupils and students. Instruction should also be given in hygiene.
9. All teacher education should take place in a university or a pedagogical institute of university rank.
10. Full provision should be made for effective participation of the people in the reform and organisation as well as in the administration of education.

Done at Berlin, 25 June 1947.[15]

EAST AND WEST GERMANY

The radical difference in schools that emerged in the East and West during the occupation period is indicative of the general divergence between the Soviet zone and the three Western zones. The breach between the two areas finally led to the establishment of the Federal Republic of Germany, which consisted of the territory of the three Western zones. On June 23, 1949, a Basic Law was adopted which gave great power to the eleven states of the Republic: Baden-Wuerttemberg, Bavaria, Berlin, Bremen, Hamburg, Hessen, Lower Saxony, North Rhine-Westfalia, Rhineland-Palatinate, Saarland, and Schleswig-Holstein. The Basic Law stipulated that education and child care was the right and responsibility of parents.

---

[15] Official Bulletin of the Allied Command, Berlin, No. 8

The Republic was to be responsible for overseeing education although it delegated to the states the responsibility to establish and run the school system. Private schools were allowed to exist although they were to be approved by the state. Most of the states remained quite conservative in terms of the schooling structure which they adopted. The city states of Berlin, Bremen, and Hamburg chose to adopt the most innovative systems. For example, Berlin adopted a six year common school structure and a nine year compulsory school period.

The rest of the Federal Republic generally adopted a less radical structure, which consisted of a four year common school experience after which children would be channeled into one of three streams. Most of the children would remain at the **Volksschule** until their eight year compulsory schooling requirement was satisfied. This school was intended to provide the mass of the people with the foundation education, including civic and social skills, before they entered into the vocational education stream. The **Real-** or **Mittelschule** provided a six year program which was to serve as preparation for the middle level positions in business, industry, and management. The nine year **Gymnasium** led to the leaving examination and the right to engage in higher education studies.

It is remarkable that such a high degree of consensus was achieved among the states. The various states were very independent, although they formed a Standing Conference of Ministers of Education in 1948. This group sought to coordinate their efforts in such a manner as to avoid too much dislocation between one state and another.

In response to the Western decision to form a Federal Republic, the Soviet zone declared itself an independent state on October 7, 1949, and a 1946 law regulating education in the occupied zone formed the basis of a new educational law. The five states, which were located in the Russian zone were abolished and the country was divided into fifteen administrative regions, including the capitol city of East Berlin. There were: Rostock, Schwerin, Neubrandenburg, Potsdam, Frankfurt an/Oder, Cohbus, Madgeburg, Halle, Erfurt, Gera, Suhl, Dresden, Leipzig, and Karl-Marx-Stadt. However, education remained, as it has been from the beginning of the occupation period, under central authority.

From the beginning of the two Germanies, distinct systems of education existed. In the next decade, we observe the two systems becoming even more distinct from each other. The reasons are complex, but largely attributable to the identification of the Federal Republic of Germany with the West, and the German Democratic Republic with the socialist states of Eastern Europe.

The Federal Republic took the major brunt of criticism for the attrocities which had been perpetuated by the National Socialists. In the East, which was run by communists who had been persecuted along with the Jews during the Nazi period, the leaders perceived themselves as liberators from the tyranny of National Socialism and were able to avoid any identity with it. Those in the West suffered humiliation, whereas, those leaders in the East expressed no sense of guilt.

Those in the West chose to grasp onto the few cultural traditions for which they could claim pride. Having been the undisputed education leaders of the world throughout the Modern Age, the West Germans turned to the traditional school as one means of preserving those positive elements of their cultural tradition. The leaders of state in the East were not concerned with preservation so much as reconstruction and the transformation of society toward a socialist model.

The East German task was by far the more difficult and required an approach that has been interpreted by some as unjust and ruthless. Whereas the attitude that characterized traditional schooling in Germany was academic excellence, the East Germans were intent on making the development of socialist education and society their highest priority. Such a shift in priorities was especially difficult for educators to accept. The teaching profession took for granted that there must be thorough training, high motivation, and outstanding achievement. Those who failed to demonstrate these qualities had traditionally been screened out of the system in a decisive manner. However, adherence to those traits of academic excellence were not widely shared by those who were not members of the elite classes. This was explained away in that those of the working classes were described as being victims of sustained exploitation and it would be necessary that they be given preferential treatment in the school over those who demonstrated academic excellence.

The idea of an extended common schooling experience was also antithetical to the German schooling tradition. It was difficult for many to understand how excellence could be insured if everyone was to participate in a common schooling experience.[16] It was also difficult to understand how the school could retain high standards while fostering the all-round development of the personalities of all youth. Other innovations added a further burden to the East German task. All private schools, including religiously sponsored institutions, were abolished, and in all schools, boys and girls were to be taught together.

---

[16] Hearnden, 1960.

Innovations were also under way at the universities. The academic year was extended to ten months, a basic philosophy course became mandatory for all, consisting mainly of Marxist notions of political economy and historical materialism. Further, every student was required to spend some time in industrial and agricultural work.

In the West, democratizing activities, such as student government, were simply grafted on to the traditional structure, which valued discipline, self control, and perserverence. In fact, the major changes which took place in the West had little to do with the reform of the school structure. For example, in 1955, an agreement between the ministers was reached regarding such issues as school holidays and the grading system, while no decisions were made that affected the different types of institutions.

During the first decade of the Federal Republic of Germany, some progress was made toward democratizing the school system, when the so-called "alternative route" (**zweiter Bildungsweg**) was inititiated in the mid-fifties, which allowed young people who had learned a trade to gain eventual access to the university. It was, however, necessary for the student to move through the vocational school, then the technical school, or through evening studies for the **Abitur**, before being admitted to the university.[17]

The first major reform proposal to come on the scene in West Germany was the so-called **Rahmenplan** of the **Deutscher Ausschuss fuer das Erziehungs- und Bildungswesen** in 1959. Even this plan did not challenge the tripartite division of the school system, but it did recommend the introduction of an observational period (**Foerderstufe**) or a two year period following the four year common school after which a decision would be made as to which of the schools the child would finally be placed.[18]

Meanwhile, the East Germans concentrated their energies on internal reforms of the schooling process, as well as extending the common school experience beyond eight years. Following the example of the Soviet Union, which revived the Marxist notion of polytechnical education in the early fifties, the Socialist Unity Party (SED) began forcing its will on the teaching profession which continued to stress academic excellence and the continuation of the four year **Oberschule** which maintained many

---

[17] Rudolf Lengert. **Das Schulwesen in der Bundesrepublik Deutschland**. Sieburg: F. Schmidt, 1963.

[18] A. O. Schorb. **Fuer und Wider den Rahmenplan. Eine Dokumentation**. Stuttgart: Ernst Klett Verlag, 1963.

features of the upper level of the traditional **Gymnasium**.

At the beginning of the school year in 1958, polytechnical education was formally introduced into compulsory schools. It consisted of a ten year general education program intended to provide the German Democratic Republic with the personnel necessary to live and be productive in a technological-industrial society. The curriculum concentrated on ideological orientation, natural science, as well as technical exposure and training. The school was divided into two levels: the lower level consisted of grades 1-4, and the upper level consisted of grades 5-10. At the completion of the ten year school, pupils entered vocational training, or a two year program of studies leading to university study after a one year period of practical work. A major innovation was the practice of sending pupils in grades seven through ten to a school-associated industries or training centers for one day each week, where they were to participate in instruction and work experience in socialist production.[19]

After further refinements of the system, including the introduction of a small number of specialist classes and schools to train for professions needing a high degree of mathematics and science, a school law was passed on February 25, 1965, which set the framework for elementary and secondary education in East Germany.[20]

In 1968, a tertiary education reform was also instituted in East Germany. Until that time, universities had retained their traditional structure of faculty boards presided over by a Dean. Each field often resembled a barony-type arrangement with the professor dictating from on high. This structure was abolished in an attempt to facilitate communication and encourage cross-fertilization. Faculties were abolished and universities were joined with other institutes of higher education. All were brought under the control of a Minister of Higher Education. Sections replaced faculties, each with a director appointed for three years, who worked with a team of professors, teachers, and students. The systems that were set up in the 1960's have held firm until this day. We shall describe them in greater detail in the next section of this essay.

We can see that the East Germans have had a consistent and stable policy since the end of World War II. Their attempt to forge a new Germany was seen by them as being based on the

---

[19] Margrete S. Klein. **The Challenge of Communist Education: A look at the GDR.** New York: East European Monographs, 1980.

[20] **Education and Training in the German Democratic Republic.** Germany: Staatsverlag der Deutschen Demokratischen Republic, 1966.

following facts:

(1) The educational system of the German Democratic Republic is based on the fact that the past has been overcome, that the lessons which were learned from the suffering and experiences of our people in two world wars were decisively applied, whereby the social roots of fascism, imperialsim and militarism were eliminated forever.
(2) In the educational system of the German Democratic Republic the best and most progressive ideas of humanist thinkers and educationists from the times of the bourgeois revolution were realized and further developed.
(3) In the educational system of the German Democratic Republic these progressive bourgeois ideas were connected with the educational ideas and experiences of the German and international socialist working class movements from Karl Marx to the present and with the ideas of Marxism-Leninism.
(4) The educational system of the German Democratic Republic developed in the period of the anti-fascist democratic order and in the process of our fundamental social change so that it could cope with the new requirements that arose when the fundamentals of socialism had to be established and that are now made by the allround construction of socialism.[21]

At the same time the West Germans continued to engage in band-aid reform measures. The situation in West Germany finally reached a crisis point in the mid-sixties, as the country suddenly found itself to have the most conservative system of education of any major country in Europe. The publication of a small book by Georg Picht in 1964, entitled **Die deutsche Bildungskatastrophe** (The German Educational Catastrophe) provided a label to the situation. In the book he argued that the economic miracle of the post-war period had blinded the West Germans to the fact that they had fallen behind the other countries in their ability to produce qualified educated personnel. The media turned the "educational crisis" into a cliche that was on everyone's lips. The crisis was intensified by projections of educational experts. The OECD, for example, projected that the Federal Republic would be last among the thirteen European OECD countries in terms of the number of secondary school leavers it would produce (eight percent of an age level) between 1970 and 1980.[22]

---

[21] **Education and Training**, 1966, pp. 10-11.

[22] Dahrendorf, 1965, p. 41.

In 1965, an agreement was reached between the state governments and the central government to establish a German Council of Education (**Bildungsrat**). Its purpose was to deal with the crisis and draw up plans for restructuring the educational system. In 1970, the Council submitted a comprehensive plan for reform having the following recommendations:

> Compulsory education beginning at five, and lasting ten years; establishment of a leaving certification (**Abitur I**) for the middle school, with the intention - and hope - that it would be obtained by most pupils;horizontal stages in the educational system from elementary to further education; a secondary stage I concludes the basic education of all pupils, secondary stage II leads, with numerous variations to **Abitur II** - the minimum requirement for university admission - and to initial vocational qualifications.[23]

While the plan envisioned by the **Bildungsrat** could best be satisfied within the framework of a comprehensive school, it was also recognized that the plan was politically viable only if it could be achieved within the tripartite structure that already existed. The major issue had to do with the number of students that were to qualify for the **Abitur** and was not whether the **Gymnasium** should lose its status position. Thus, the **Gymnasium** was allowed to continue to be the selective school, and the **Realschule** was allowed to be more selective than the **Hauptschule**, but all three schools were allowed to award the intermediate qualification (**Abitur I**), which gave access to upper secondary education.

With a few modifications the above plan gained joint approval by the heads of the federal and state governments in an Overall Education Plan, adopted in 1973. This plan was based on the following principles:

(1) The development of an education system which - making allowance for overall social developments - caters for the entitlement to promotion and development of individual talents, inclinations and skills, and qualifying persons, thereby, to shape their personal, professional, and social life on their own initiative.
(2) Equality of opportunity and efficiency level complement and condition each other and are realizable through curricular reform as well as differentiation and individualization of the educational programme.
(3) Democratic cooperation and responsibility must promote the discernment and understanding of all concerned.

---

[23] Helga Thomas. **Innovation in Education: Germany.** Paris: Organization for Economic Cooperation and Development, 1971.

(4) Academic basic training assures professional mobility and, consequently, better social opportunities. Apart from integration into the economic process, individuals must be encouraged to participate in the process of "life-long learning" towards creativity, spontaneity, responsible behavior and self-determination.[24] Structurally speaking, the systems of West and East Germany differ radically at specific junctures. Our intent in the remainder of this essay shall be to contrast the two Germanies with regard to preschool, elementary and secondary school, vocational education, higher education, teacher training, and general adult education.

SCHOOLING LEVELS AND TYPES

PRESCHOOL

The striking differences between East and West are immediately manifest when we look at preschool programs. East Germany has become one of the leaders of the world in terms of its commitment to state run programs for preschoolers. It obligates itself to care for all babies over twenty weeks old, and at ten weeks if mothers are students or in some training program. This care extends from 6:00 a.m. to 6:00 p.m. or 7:00 p.m. to accommodate the work schedule of mothers. Even those doing shift work can place their babies in children's homes if their schedule does not coincide with that of the creches. The adult baby ratio is about six to one. In 1979, 60.3 percent of all children up to the age of three were being cared for in the creches, and this figure is rising.

From the age of three, children are placed in state sponsored kindergartens where they remain until they begin compulsory schooling. In 1979, 92.3 percent of all children in this age group were attending the kindergartens.[25]

---

[24] Hans-H. Wilhelmi. "The School System in the Federal Republic of Germany." **Bildung und Wissenschaft**, No. 12-79 (e), 1979. Published by Inter Nationes at Bonn-Bad Godesberg, p. 156.

During the past decade more and more combined creches and kindergartens have come into existence to insure continuity and uniformity of development of children.

In contrast, West Germany remains committed to the ideal that the child remain in the home during its early years. The state recognizes, however, that no child can be brought up by parents alone, and so it has provided assistance of many kinds. This assistance, however, has not been a part of the general schooling program. In fact, kindergartens have traditionally not even been the responsibility of the Ministry of Education; instead, the Ministry of Health has overseen these institutions. Consequently, they have conventionally been seen as substitutes for healthy home environments rather than enriching components of normal growth and development.

The state rarely even sponsors kindergartens. At least two thirds of all institutions are private. Further, as the number of kindergartens increases, we find that they do not contribute to a reduction of social contrasts. A child of a middle class, professional parent is twice as likely to attend kindergarten as a child of low income, working mothers, and if these children attend some institution, it will likely be a daycare center specifically designed to take care of them rather than provide an experience that might prove socially integrative.

In the last decade, some steps have been taken to incorporate preschooling into the broader educational system, but this has touched off such controversy that the plan has not been implemented. One consequence has been in inclusion of different classes that deal with children of differing physical, intellectual, and social states. Based on the recommendations of teachers, physicians, and psychologists, children might enter school before they are six years old, if they can demonstrate that they are ready. Other children may not be placed in the regular beginning class at all, but may begin in a transition or special education class.[26]

---

[25] **Development of Public Education in the German Democratic Republic**. Berlin: Ministry of Education, Ministry of Higher Education, State Secretariat of Vocational Education, 1981, p. 16.

[26] Hans G. Lingens and Barbara Lingens. **Education in West Germany: A Quest for Excellence**. Bloomington: Phi Delta Kappa Educational Foundation, 1980, p. 18.

Schooling Levels and Types

COMPULSORY GENERAL SCHOOLING

Whereas West Germany has retained the more traditional form of schooling, reflecting sharp social divisions, East Germany has adopted an integrated compulsory school. On the one hand, West German children attend a common school (**Grundschule**) for four years (six in Berlin), after which they are channeled into one of three quite different schools: the four or five year upper elementary school (**Hauptschule**), the six year middle school (**Realschule**), and the nine year grammar school (**Gymnasium**). On the other hand, almost all East German children attend a ten year common school (**polytechnische Oberschule**).

It is necessary to consider internal divisions before gaining a complete picture of the structure. East German common schools are divided into three levels with the following grades: 1-3, 4-6, 7-10. The lowest level corresponds roughly to the West German common school, and in fact, it was four years in duration until the past two years. The East German middle level corresponds roughly with the so-called "orientation stage" in West Germany, which means that even though children are already separated into separate schools, the programs of study remain similar enough so that lateral transfer from one school to another is possible without loss of time.

The upper level of the East German common school remains integrated in terms of external structure, but there is some internal differentiation. The trend in West Germany has been to move toward integration in terms of external structure, but to retain divisions by differentiating internally. Certain international comparisons of industrialized countries continue to conclude that, in spite of integration efforts, the Federal Republic of Germany continues to retain a higher rate of social selectivity than any other industrialized country.[27]

A good example of the integration difficulties in West Germany would be the slow development of the comprehensive school (**Gesamtschule**), which typically comprises grades five through ten. This school has received enormous play in the public press, among educational theorists, as well as with policy makers. The comprehensive school was to be Germany's answer to the social divisions that existed between secondary institutions. However, as of 1978, less than three percent of all secondary

---

[27] Helga Thomas. **Innovation in German Education**. A CERI Technical Report. Paris: Organization for Economic Cooperation and Development, 1971.

pupils had been placed in these institutions, and a large percentage of these were in so-called "cooperative comprehensive schools" which simply amounted to having the upper elementary, the middle, and the grammar schools all on the same campus.

The program differences and similarities between East and West are significant. We might recall that the pre-war emphasis of the German elementary school as toward a "folk-oriented curriculum." Of course, it included basic skills training, but its main emphasis was on building an identity with and an allegiance to the Fatherland. Elements of this socialization focus continue to exist, but the trend in both East and West has been toward more scientific specialized subject matter study. In the West, children are quickly weaned from a single home room teacher and by the third grade over two thirds of their program of studies is spent with subject matter specialists in mathematics, music, art, religion, and physical education. In the East, approximately two thirds of the lower level curriculum is devoted to German and mathematics, and children are also exposed to fundamental concepts about nature and society. A distinctive element of the program of studies would be a concerted East German attempt to integrate schooling with socially useful work. At the lower level this is translated into manual instruction and gardening.[28]

When we move beyond the first three or four grades, it is difficult to compare schooling experiences precisely because the West German youth are dispersed in different institutions. In East Germany, all courses in grades four, five, and six, except an optional one hour needle work class in grades five and six, are mandatory. Children continue taking courses in German and mathematics, drawing, music, sport, but pupils also begin natural and social science instruction. The work related program also shifts gradually from manual training and gardening toward productive work.

In the last four years additional programs are added, specifically related to production. A course in polytechnical education is taken each year as well as productive work and socialist production. In grades seven and eight, this takes place at so-called polytechnical centers, which are special facilities connected with enterprises. In the last two years, the young are systematically exposed to ten different fields of work. Usually this consists of exposure and labor under real working conditions.

In sum, a student leaving the ten year East German school would have taken a program of studies almost identical with that of every other pupil, which would include ten years of German, mathematics, drawing, music, and sport; six years of Russian,

---

[28] Klein, 1980.

history, biology, and geography; five years of physics; four years of chemistry, civics, and a second foreign language; as well as ten years of polytechnical and labor related experiences.

The secondary program in the West is not so easily described. The West Germans attempt to provide all children, regardless of ability or institutional affiliation, with a solid general education. Beyond this, the program a child engages in is reflected in the particular institutional aims. The upper elementary school attempts to prepare young people for the world of work. In this respect the program is not dissimilar from the program in East Germany, although the tone is quite different. We recall that all East German youth are engaged in the same course of studies, and almost no differentiation of any kind takes place until grade seven, whereas in the West it is already evident that the children at the upper elementary school are destined for vocational rather than general educational purposes.

Still another difference is ability grouping from the very beginning, at least in terms of mathematics and foreign languages. At the end of the upper elementary program, young people receive a leaving certificate, which allows them to undertake various types of continuation schooling or apprenticeship programs.

The middle school, as its name implies, is intended to prepare young people for middle level vocational competence. The intention is that these young people will assume leadership positions in the more practical professions. Besides receiving a general education, the pupils receive some foundation in areas such as agriculture, commerce, industry, and public service. A heavy compulsory program is imposed on the students, but in grades seven and above, a wide range of optional subjects, taken according to skill, aptitude and inclination, are made available in mathematics/science, languages, economics/social studies, and technical studies.

Pupils who complete the middle school, qualify to enter the upper level of the grammar school, senior technical schools (**hoehere Fachschulen**) or to engage in business and administrative training, while attending a vocational school.

The grammar school in West Germany continues to provide the foundation for academic excellence. It is presently divided into two levels. Level I (grades 5-10) (**Abitur I**) leads to middle level school qualification, while Level II (grades 11-13) (**Abitur II**) provides the capstone for university preparation. Whereas the East German school is characterized by integration, the grammar school has become more and more differentiated. Since the turn of this century, young people entered schools that provide foci in classical studies (languages and literature), natural science and mathematics, or modern languages. In recent years, still other streams have been added so that pupils can now concentrate on such subjects as social studies, economics and business, fine arts and performing arts, sport, and educational sciences.

At the beginning of the program all students take certain required subjects including religion, German, the first foreign language, mathematics, social studies, geography, music and art. Extensive differentiation then begins in grade seven and continues through the rest of the program. Concerted attempts have been made to facilitate transfer possibilities. In theory, a young person is able to do this, but subjects may have to be made up before the pupil can proceed with an alternative program.

We would make one final observation pertaining to attendance ratios. Traditionally, in West Germany, over 80 percent of the young people attended the upper elementary school. This was still approximately 70 percent as recently as 1960; however, by 1978, this figure had dropped to approximately 40 percent. This means that a greater percentage of young people than ever before were taking advantage of the possibility of attending a school that provided greater economic and social rewards. The middle school figures, for example, shifted from 11 percent of all 13 year olds in 1960 to 24 percent in 1978, and the **Gymnasium** grew from 15 percent in 1960 to almost 25 percent in 1978.[29]

SECONDARY EDUCATION LEVEL II

Two major options are open to young people in the two Germanies after they complete their general compulsory schooling. Those who are qualified may enter educational institutions leading to university study; others may enter vocational and technical training. It is at this level that the educational systems in the two Germanies once again converge. The coveted prize awaiting the academically gifted is the secondary school leaving certificate (**Abitur**). This is obtained in two ways in the East. Pupils who complete the ten year school may be admitted to a two year program in extended school classes (**erweiterte Oberschule**), or to a three year vocational education program "with **Abitur**." The outcome of the latter option is that young people possess both the **Abitur** and vocational competence in some field. The number of youth qualifying for extended school classes is relatively small and only about one pupil in seven (15

[29] Hans-H. Wilhelmi. "The School System in the Federal Republic of Germany." **Bildung und Wissenschaft**, No. 12, 1979.

percent) passes into this stream, and an even smaller number take **Abitur** classes in vocational schools.[30]

In the West, the upper level (**Oberstufe**) of the **Gymnasium**, including some **Gesamtschule** programs, prepares young people for the **Abitur**. This is a three year program, however, which means that the time required for university qualification in the West totals at least thirteen years. At this stage, grade levels are replaced by a series of courses providing basic and specialized study. All students are required to study (a) language/literature, (b) social sciences, and (c) mathematics/natural sciences, but they engage in in-depth study of specific subjects. A recent innovation has been the special grammar school (**Fachgymnasium**), which provides a very similar possibility as the vocational program "with **Abitur**," in the East.

In spite of the fact that expanding numbers of young people are obtaining the **Abitur**, it remains a relatively exclusive figure. For every person in the **Oberstufe** at the **Gymnasium**, at least fifteen are engaged in vocational training.[31] It is possible, of course, to obtain the **Abitur** by attending night school or taking the second educational track, via technical school, but these routes place enormous hardship on the growing numbers of youth resorting to them.

The second option open to youth in both Germanies is vocational and technical education. To the foreigner, this is very confusing because there are so many branches available and so many ways of learning a certified skill. To the German, however, the scheme is usually quite rational. Those young people in the West wishing to learn a trade after the ninth or tenth year of compulsory general schooling have two major possibilities. First, they can become apprentices in programs lasting from two to three and one half years in length. This option is selected by two out of every three young people preparing for a trade. Apprentices must attend a vocational school (**Berufsschule**) for one or more days a week, where they receive theory and general education instruction. Second, they can attend a full time vocational school, usually for one or two years. This time counts as a part of the apprenticeship training, which occurs after the schooling period.

The above arrangement is very similar to that in East Germany. One major difference is that apprentices must attend vocational school two full days each week in East Germany as opposed to one in West Germany.

---

[30] **Development of Public Education**, 1981.

[31] **Development of Public Education**, 1981, p. 24.

A wide range of other schools are available, mainly to pupils who have completed vocational training. These schools qualify students to extend competence in their field or even to move from vocational to technical to academic pursuits.

Students in both countries are also able to engage in preparation for advanced technical study. In the East this training starts either as a continuation of vocational training or directly after completing the ten year school. In the West, students usually enter the **Fachoberschule** at the conclusion of the vocational training or following the completion of the **Realschule** or Level I of the **Gymnasium**, where they remain until twelve years of schooling have been completed.

THE DISADVANTAGED CHILD

Both Germanies make provision for the education and training of young people who are physically, mentally, or emotionally unable to benefit from normal education. Both countries endeavor to provide learning environments that will equip the young to work productively in the normal programs or at least move them in that direction. Typically, all but the most severely disadvantaged children actually work on the same curricular program as normal children. The special provision is that they move at a slower rate. Special schools exist in both countries for specific handicaps, such as blind or partially blind, deaf or partially deaf, etc.

A special condition exists in West Germany that does not involve psychological handicaps so much as cultural handicaps. Since shortly after World War II, at a time of severe labor shortages, guestworkers came to Germany from Southern Europe and now comprise approximately twelve percent of the labor force. In communities where guest- workers are concentrated as many as 30 percent of all births are of foreign parents. The impact of these young people on the schools has been dramatic and traumatic. German officials are faced with the dilemma of trying to provide a German education to these young people or to prepare them to return to their parent's homeland. Further, regardless of the approach taken, language barriers are often so great that 60 percent of these young people are forced to repeat classes. Special preparatory classes and courses in German are offered. The home country may even provide a teacher to schools where a national group is concentrated so that they can get some touch of Yugoslav, Turk, or Spanish social studies and language training. The problems attending this issue are far from being solved; in the meantime, productivity of the educational program continues to suffer.

TERTIARY EDUCATION

Many types of institutions fall in the category of tertiary education. In West Germany, the universities, technical universities (**technische Hochschulen**), and specialized institutions of university standing, such as medical or theological colleges provide programs of the highest status. In addition, one finds a full array of teachers colleges, art and music academies, technical colleges, and comprehensive higher education institutions.

In East Germany, very similar kinds of institutions exist, except that comprehensive higher education institutions have not come on the scene. In fact, the traditional divisions in tertiary education appear to be far greater in the East than in the West.

One of the important understandings an American must keep in mind when looking at higher education in both Germanies, is the traditional separation between scientific and technical pursuits. Even in East Germany, where the integration of practice and theory has received such great play, there remains a separation between technical colleges and universities. Curiously, this separation clearly reflects traditional status distinctions. Whereas in the West, schools of advanced technology have gained university status, in the East they remain vocationally oriented focusing on the practical application of theoretical and scientific knowledge, rather than its generation. They are even considered to be feeder institutions to university study rather than co-partners in higher education.

We do not wish to imply that East Germans have moved away from their basic ideological orientation at the tertiary level. They simply have failed to struggle and experiment with new institutional mechanisms for achieving their aims.

In West Gemany, these distinctions have clearly broken down. Indicative of the breakdown is the emergence of two new institutions of higher learning. Comprehensive institutions of higher learning (**Gesamthochshulen**) have appeared during the past decade, and they attempt to combine the functions of the university, teachers colleges, technical colleges and specialized colleges into one institution. By 1981, one of these institutions had been established in Kassel in the state of Hesse and five had been established in Northrhine-Westphalia at Essen, Duisburg, Wuppertal, Paderborn, and Siegen. A total of approximately 60,000 students are in attendance. The urgency for higher education reform at the outset of the 1970's, which led to their establishment, appears to have subsided and no plans are under way to expand the number; however, they have established enough precedence to eventually impact on the entire system of higher education. For example, they admit students who have not completed the **Gymnasium,** and, in fact, young people who complete technical school (**Fachoberschule**) are eligible for admission. This means that the school career of such pupils is one year less than the thirteen years required for the **Abitur**. These students are eligible to follow study courses along side the ex-**Gymnasium** students.

The second innovative institution to come on the scene has been the technical college (**Fachhochscule**). Most of these came into existence betwen 1969 and 1971, and represent an upgrading of the engineering schools and technical schools for business, social studies, industrial design and agriculture. They are somewhat related to the community college short-cycle notion, usually offering a three year program of studies for students who have completed the technical school (**Fachoberschule**).

Students who are enrolled will have a wide range of compulsory and optional courses. All programs require students to engage in practical experience, usually taken during vacations or special "semesters of practical training" (**Praxissemester**).

In East Germany, the **Gesamthochscule** has not yet come into existence, although the university provides many of the branches offered in them. In both Germanies, the university remains the pinnacle of the educational system.

The conventional route to the university or college is the **Abitur**. As we have mentioned, there is an alternative route to the university via vocational, technical, and engineering schools. Other admissions criteria are also applied. For example, if the pupil in East Germany has gone directly to the extended secondary school after the ten year school, he or she must engage in one year of social service prior to being admitted to university study. Even after fulfilling the **Abitur** and social service criteria, the student is not yet guaranteed admission. Consideration is also given to social background. Although the figure shifts greatly from year to year, it is estimated that approximately 55 percent of entering students are the children of workers and cooperative farmers.

We recall that after the war a workers and farmers faculty was set up to provide prerequisite training for university study. This was gradually phased out and in 1978, a striking new initiative was undertaken. Because so many young people were entering the university with no practical experience in the field of study they had chosen, a one-year pre-university practical course was initiated for applicants in technical, agricultural, economic and medical branches, if they had had no previous vocational experience.[32]

The program of study for East German university students lasts from four to five years (six for medicine). Every student must study Russian and one other foreign language for two years. Adding this to polytechnical school Russian, we find that all students will have nine years of Russian language. Marxist-Leninist study is also required as is physical education. It would probably be fair to generalize that the traditional emphasis on teaching and research continues to dominate university studies, but it has shifted from an emphasis on pure, theoretical research to practical, applied research, related to real needs of industry, the military, farming, or commerce.

One striking innovation in East Germany is the full-scale adoption of correspondence courses. A good number of students are working full-time in some job and they are guaranteed 36 to 48 workdays of paid leave per academic year to engage in their studies. Toward the end of their program, they receive up to three months additional time off to complete and prepare to defend their thesis or dissertation.

In the West, the major admissions problem facing the universities is the increasing numbers of young people who qualify for study. According to tradition, a young person is able to undertake any field of study that person wishes, regardless of the type of secondary schooling experience that person had. As the university has shifted from an elite to a mass institution, it has become necessary to restrict the number of young people entering specific fields of study. This is known as the **Numerus Clausus** procedure which allows the university to determine capacity while actual selection is based on the relative performance of students on the **Abitur**.

West German students who enter the university, are lodged in faculties and the duration of studies varies from four to six years. One of the major issues confronting the university has been pressure to set a specific time period in which students are to finish their studies. This is looked at as a money saving device and would also open up more places for the multitude of students wishing to get in.

We recall that universities were largely under the jurisdiction of the state, but as new structures have taken shape, involvement of regional and Federal forces has become imperative. The relationship of these levels is formally an outgrowth of the 1973 Federal plan which aims to organize a "permeable system of graduated, inter-related study courses and final qualifications"

---

[32] The Development of Education, 1981.

by amalgamated institutions, which are legally independent but which are highly integrated. That is all well and good, but the universities have chosen to retain their independence by resisting major changes.

TEACHER EDUCATION

Except for teachers of preschools, teacher education is considered to be a part of tertiary education in both Germanies. Because of its importance to the system of education, we have reserved a special section for it. The profession is accorded great status in these countries, although there remain social and financial distinctions in teachers in the various types and levels of institutions.

A much closer relationship exists between licensure and credentials in the Germanies than is the case in America. Teachers at all levels and in both the public and private sectors must satisfy specific credential requirements before they are allowed to practice their profession. We shall describe the basic elements of these requirements in this section.

Preschool Teacher Education

Traditionally, those who wished to teach preschools have been able to attend special institutes following the ten year school in the East or after gaining the middle level leaving certificate in the West. Training now consists of a three year program, which certifies for a craft level certificate. In the West, candidates must have an additional year-long practical experience before certification is granted. Also, attempts are being made to upgrade the level of training, at least in the West, by setting up programs at teachers colleges and even at universities.

Elementary School Teacher Education

Teachers of lower and upper elementary school in the West and teachers of grades 1-4 of the ten year school in the East would be most comparable in terms of status and training. The training takes place at a teachers training college and consists of general education and education science courses, as well as specialized study such as German, mathematics, and sport. Teachers colleges have traditionally been separate and distinct from universities. In recent years in the West, the trend has been to integrate them with universities. This has been accomplished in many states, but they often remain physically separated and their faculties and programs have not yet become fully accepted by university personnel.

Schooling Levels and Types

Whereas the Western program is three years in length (four in Bremen for upper elementary teachers), in addition to one to three years of practical experience, the Eastern program is four years. We might also mention that upper elementary teachers in the West are identifying themselves more and more as specialist teachers rather than generalists, who teach all subjects. In this respect, they are becoming more like the teachers of the middle and secondary schools.

Middle and Secondary Teacher Preparation

A distinction remains between **Realschule** and **Gymnasium** teachers in the West, and we must, therefore, treat them separately from each other, as well as separately from the upper level of the East German ten year school and the extended secondary school.

Realschule Teachers: In the West, future **Realschule** teachers complete three years (four at Bremen) of study at the university and then transfer to the teachers college for three additional semesters of practice oriented study. At the university, these students study two subjects in some depth as well as general education. Because this study takes place at the university it is highly academic and is taken together with students who are not planning to teach. Practical and education science courses are restricted to the teachers college program, which takes place at the end of the study period.

Gymnasium Teachers: These teachers must complete at least four years of university study in addition to three semesters of practical training. Often, university study extends for six or seven years during which time the student concentrates on two subjects. University study includes philosophical and pedagogical studies. Practical training consists of a supervised practice teaching experience as well as attendance at a pedagogical seminar conducted by the school district.

Upper Level Polytechnical and Extended Secondary Teachers: In East Germany, future teachers of grades 5-10 and grades 11-12 of the extended secondary school study either at universities or at advanced educational colleges, which are distinct from teachers colleges. Students spend four years concentrating on two subjects as well as taking courses in the social sciences and philosophy (mainly Marxism-Leninism) and pedagogical studies. In contrast to West German secondary teachers, practical experience is tightly integrated with academic subjects and extends throughout the university experience.

Vocational and Technical School Teacher Preparation: In West Germany, different qualifications are necessary, depending on the type of vocational or technical school in question. Vocational school teachers are generally divided into two types. The more academic oriented teachers must complete four years of university study, one year of specialized training, and teacher training. The more practice oriented teachers are qualified practitioners but have also taken further training at a technical school, as well as teacher training.

Those teachers at senior technical schools must have the same qualifications as **Gymnasium** teachers or have natural science degrees from the university. In addition they have several years of actual professional experience.

In East Germany, teacher training for technical and vocational education takes place in technical colleges. Those who teach the science courses are trained at the technical university or technical colleges. The ministry dictates that this training be uniform with regard to teaching methods.

In-Service: One of the major distinctions between East and West is the in-service education policy. Whereas, in the West, the tradition still holds that teachers reach full qualification at the beginning of their careers, in the East, teachers engage in programs of professional renewal related to Marxism/Leninism, pedagogy, psychology, teaching methods, and specialized subject matter knowledge. In the West programs exist for further development, but they are primarily of a voluntary nature and are for those who wish to improve themselves.

ADULT EDUCATION

Three factors can be cited for the extensive adult education programs that can be found in both Germanies. First, a long tradition of adult improvement has existed in German speaking countries. Second, a dramatic impulse came from the post-World War II reeducation era. Third, advanced industrialism brings with it an inherent need for continual education and renewal. An additional factor is very evident in East Germany. Communist authorities have been intent on transforming German society toward the development of socialist personalities.

Because of the felt need to alter the German personality in the East, adult education has had a greater visibility and has reached greater portions of the population than has been the case in the West. The programs in the East also show a greater, all-encompassing nature than exists in the West. Obviously, a monolithic, centralized authority is required to develop such a system. In the West, adult education programs are much more pluralistic and diverse, addressing a wide variety of educational goals. These have taken some form through legal mandates which define adult education as following six basic categories: (1) non-vocational education with a final certificate, mainly qualifying for university study, technical school, etc.; (2) vocational training, including in-service training, professional advancement, retraining, or rehabilitation; (3) political education; (4) recreational creative courses; (5) parent and family education; (6) individual education.[33]

The delivery system for adult education is quite similar in both countries. It includes correspondence courses, evening courses, university extension, and programs organized by unions, social organizations, scientific groups, churches, industrial and commercial enterprises.

YOUTH GROUPS

Any discussion of education in Germany would not be complete without some discussion of youth groups which serve to support the more formal elements of education. Germany has a long tradition of youth groups. Earlier, we mentioned the youth movement at the turn of this century as well as the Hitler youth movement. Today, we observe extensive opportunities for young people in both Germanies although their character and aims differ.

In the East a series of youth groups corresponding closely to those in the Soviet Union touches the lives of a high percentage of the youth. Children of ages 6-9 are called young pioneers. They are usually led by a trained pioneer leader, who is a tutor in the local school. They wear a blue scarf and a badge bearing the initials JP (**Junge Pioneere**) which is set on a blue background with three leaping yellow flames and the motto "be ready." Their flag shows a picture of their badge on a blue ground and has the inscribed motto: "For Peace and Socialism Ever Ready."

Children of ages 9-14 belong to the Thaelmann Pioneers. They are provided with club and sports facilities connected to the local school, as well as some 116 local pioneer houses throughout the Republic. There is no compulsion for young people to frequent these houses but they provide an extensive

[33] Renate I. Mreschar. "Adult Education in the Federal Republic of Germany," **Bildung und Wissenschaft**, 6-76(e), 1976, published by Inter Nationes.

array of purposeful, absorbing activities for the youth. Members are also given places in pioneer holiday camps, where youth go during school vacation.

Young people of ages 15-25 belong to the Free German Youth (**Freie Deutsche Jugend**). Their uniform is a blue shirt or blouse worn with dark trousers or skirt. Their badge has the letters FDJ inscribed with a blue background and a rising sun.

Membership requires evidence of "a high sense of social awareness, a high standard of ethics and morality, and good standards of discipline and responsibility."[34] Within the framework of the political ideology of the country, those who fail to adhere to the above standards face ejection from the group and are prevented from enjoying the social and political advantages of membership.

The whole tone and structure of youth groups is quite different in West Germany. There is no centrally organized structure which coordinates and directs the groups. The following groups are listed for illustrative purposes: German Sports Club Federation, Workers Union Youth, Association of German Catholic Youth, Protestant Youth of Germany, YMCA, YWCA, Socialist Youth of Germany, German Rural Youth, German Friends of Nature Youth, German Mountain and Hiking Association, and the Boy Scouts. These represent but a small portion of all the organizations available to youth. Because they are so disparate in purpose, there is little possibility or interest in coordinating their efforts. It would also be impossible to compare the degree of participation in the organizations in the East as opposed to the West. It is possible to conclude that it is considerable in both countries.

---

[34] Moore-Rinvolucri, 1973, p. 75.

ADDRESSES OF RESEARCH INSTITUTES

A number of research institutes exist in the Federal Republic of Germany and the German Democratic Republic which are engaged in educational research. We have listed the more important ones below.

EAST GERMANY

Akademie der Paedagogischen Wissenschaften
der Deutschen Demokratischen Republik
Otto-Grotewohl-Strasse
DDR 108 Berlin
Tel.: (00372) 237 or 230

Haus des Lehrers
1020 Berlin
Alexanderplatz

Forschungszentrum fuer Technische Lehr- und
Lernmittel, Sektion Berufspaedagogik
Technische Universitaet Dresden
Mommsenstrasse 13
8027 Dresden

Institut fuer Fachschulwesen der DDR
Annabergerstrasse 119
PSF 441
9010 Karl-Marx-Stadt

Institut fuer Hochschulbildung an der
Humboldt-Universitaet zu Berlin
Otto-Grotewohlstrasse 17
108 Berlin

WEST GERMANY

Arbeitsgemeinschaft fuer Hochschuldidaktik e. V.
Rothenbaumchausee 32
2000 Hamburg 13
Tel.: (040) 448532

Arbeitskreis Grundschule e. V.
Schloss-Strasse 29
6000 Frankfurt a/Main 90
Tel.: (0611) 771047

Bundesinstitut fuer Berufsbildung
Fehrbelliner Platz 3
1000 Berlin 31

Tel.: (030) 86831

Deutsches Institute fuer Fernstudien (DIFF)
Bei der Fruchtschramme 6
7400 Tuebingen
Tel.: (07071) 26028

Deutsches Institut fuer Internationale
Paedagogische Forschung (DIPF)
Schloss-Strasse 29/31
6000 Frankfurt a/Main
Tel.: (0611) 771047

Deutsches Jugendinstitut
Saarstrasse 7
8000 Muenchen
Tel.: (089) 381831

FEoLL--Forschungs- und Entwicklungszentrum fuer
Objectivierte Lehr- und Lernverfahren
Rathenaustrasse 69-71
4790 Paderborn 1
Tel.: (05251) 601

Georg-Eckert-Institut fuer
Internationale Schulbuchforschung
Rebenring 53
3300 Braunschweig
Tel.: (0531) 340841

Geschaeftsstelle der Bund-Laender-Kommission
fuer Bildungsplannung und Forschugsfoerderung
Peterberg 18
5300 Bonn
Tel.: (0228) 54020

Hessisches Institut fuer
Bildungsplanung und Schulentwicklung (HIBS)
Bodenstedtstrasse 7
6200 Wiesbaden
Tel.: (0621) 3420

Informationszentrum fuer Fremdsprachenforschung
(IFS)
Liebigstrasse 37
3550 Marburg/Lahn
Tel.: (08421) 382141

Institut fuer Arbeitsmarkt- und
Berufsforschung der Bundesanstalt fuer
Arbeit(IAB)
Regensburgerstrasse 104
8500 Nuernberg
Tel.: (0911) 171

Addresses of Research Institutes

Institut fuer Didaktik der Mathematik (IDM)
der Universitaet Bielefeld
Postfach 8640
4800 Bielefeld
Tel.: (0521) 1065045

Institut fuer Film und Bild in Wissenschaft
und Unterricht
Bavaria-Film-Platz 3
8022 Bruenwald/Muenchen
Tel.: (089) 64971

Institut fuer die Paedagogik der
Naturwissenschaften (IPN) an der Universitaet Kiel
Olshausenstrasse 40-60
2300 Kiel 1
Tel.: (0431) 8803120

Landesinstitut fuer Curriculumentwicklung,
Lehrer-fortbildung und weiterbildung
Goerlitzerstrasse 3
4040 Neuss
Tel.: (02101) 13041

Landesstelle fuer Erziehung und Unterricht (LEU)
Schwabstrasse 43
7000 Stuttgart 1
Tel.: (0711) 66841

Max-Planck-Institut fuer Bildungsforschung
Lentzeallee 94
1000 Berlin 33
Tel.: (030) 8295201

Paedagogische Arbeistelle des Deutschen
Volkshochschulverbandes
Holzhausenstrasse 21
6000 Frankfurt a/Main
Tel.: (0611) 554338

Paedagogisches Zentrum
Uhlandstrasse 31
1000 Berlin 31
Tel.: (030) 86871

RPZ (Regionales Paedagogisches Zentrum)
Bahnhofsplatz 7-9
6550 Bad Kreuznach
Tel.: (0671) 25404-5

Staatsinstitut fuer Schulpaedagogik (ISP)
Arabellastrasse 1
8000 Muenchen
Tel.: (089) 92141

Chapter 1

BIBLIOGRAPHIES

GENERAL BIBLIOGRAPHICAL SOURCES

1. "Comparative Education Bibliography." **Comparative Education Review.**

The **Review** contains a regular bibliography of all articles in approximately twenty journals. The **Review** seeks to add journals to those regularly covered, so there is some variation in the journals covered over time. A small number of these journals are in languages other than English. The October, 1980, issue (Vol. 24, No. 3) listed the following journals:

British Journal of Educational Studies
Canadian and International Education
Chinese Education
Comparative Education
Compare
Convergence
Higher Education
European Journal of Education
International Education
International Review of Education
Minerva
Oxford Review of Education
Presence Africaine
Prospects
Revista de Educacion
Revista Latinoamericana de Estudios Educativos
Slavic and European Education Review
Soviet Education
Vergleichende Paedagogik
Western European Education

There is no category specifically related to either of the two Germanies in the bibliography, although the European category is broken down to Eastern Europe, the Soviet Union, and Western Europe.

2. **Deutsche Nationalbibliographie.** Leipzig: Deutsche Buecherei.

Published since 1931, it is a union catalogue of literature published in both German states and literature published in the German language in foreign countries. The bibliography is published yearly by the **Deutsche Buecherei** in Leipzig, which has served as the national archive for German literature since 1913. In its acquisition program are included the complete German literature, including university publications, translations of German works published in other countries and literature about Germany and important people of all German speaking countries.

3. **Deutsche Bibliographie: Halbjahres-Verzeichnis.** Frankfurt a/M: Deutsche Bibliothek. Published every six months.

The semi-annual catalogue is divided into two parts. The main part is an alphabetical title catalogue and the second part is a subject index. It is published by the **Deutsche Bibliothek** in Frankfurt, West Germany, and was created in 1946 by an agreement of the city, the West German Book Traders Association, and the British and American military authorities. In 1969 it was converted into a legal federal institution with claim to deposite copies from the Federal Republic. Its aim is the same as that of the **Deutsche Buecherei** in Leipzig, East Germany, acting as the central agency for the registration of all new publications.

4. **Educational Resources Information Center (ERIC).**

ERIC is a nationwide American information network for the dissemination of educational information. The ERIC system was begun in 1965 and by 1966 eleven clearinghouses had been established. The first issue of **Research on Education** was published in 1966. Of greatest value to the researcher is the computer search service. Although foreign materials were not adequately indexed in the beginning, they are becoming more and more complete. The most inclusive descriptor to use for this data set would be the term **Germany**. No less than 1088 references were indexed from 1972/June 1982.

5. **National Union Catalogue.** Washington, D.C.: Library of Congress.

The **National Union Catalogue** contains in its present printed version a photoreduced copy of every Library of Congress card plus copies of cards from over 1,100 North American Libraries. It would be of great help to the educational researcher in verifying titles of works, directing the researcher to the actual location of works, and assisting in bibliographical compilations. The third reason is especially valuable here, because of the lack of bibliographies on special educational topics in Germany.

PUBLISHED BIBLIOGRAPHIES

6. Apanasewicz, Nellie. **Education in Eastern Europe: An Annotated Bibliography of English Language Materials, 1965-1976.** Washington D.C.: U.S. Department of Education, 1980.
East Germany is covered on pages 31-34.

7. "Bibliography: Education of Minorities." **World Year Book of Education**, (1960), 361-91.

8. "Bibliography of Lifelong Education." **The World Year Book of Education**, (1978), 301-311.

9. Dulac, Claude. "Educational Finance (Primary-Secondary Levels) Bibliography." Division de l'education, des sciences et de la culture. Ottawa, Canada, November, 1978.
An extensive bibliography which includes a few citations relevant to West Germany.

10. Gougher, Ronald L. "Comparison of English and American Views of the German University." **History of Education Quarterly**. 9 (Wint.,1969), 447-79.
An extensive bibliography is included.

11. Henderson, James C. "Some sources for the study of German education." **British Journal of educational studies**, 9 (Nov, 1960), 48-56.
Bibliographical references, mainly in German.

12. International Bureau of Education, Geneva.
Series of data publications on specific subjects. More than 300 publications in the series. 1927-present.

13. **International Yearbook of Education.**
Geneva: International Bureau of Education, 1933 to date.

14. **World Year Book of Education**.
University of London Institute of Education and Teachers College, Columbia University. 1932-40 and 1948 to date.

Chapter 2

SOCIAL SCIENCE STUDIES RELEVANT TO EDUCATION

HISTORICAL STUDIES

GENERAL

15. Barraclough, Geoffry. **Origins of Modern Germany.** Oxford: Blackwell, 1966. 2nd. Edition.

This historical account covers a wider ground than is found in most recent histories of Germany. The author attempts to uncover the original factors governing modern Germany by going back to Mediaeval Germany and giving considerable attention to the German states and their governments at various periods of time in relationship to other states in Europe. Little attention is given to schooling and education.

16. Bruck, W. F. **Social and Economic History of Germany from William II to Hitler: 1888-1938.** Cardiff: Oxford University Press, 1938.

Bruck writes a book which is both historical and theoretical in terms of economics.

17. Clapham, J. H. **The Economic Development of France and Germany: 1815-1914.** Cambridge: The University Press, 1921.

18. Dill, Marshall Jr. **Germany, A Modern History.** Ann Arbor: University of Michigan Press, 1961.

Dill writes a succinct history of Germany which stresses the last century. It is not intended to be a scholar's book but is addressed to the general educated public. Little attention is given directly to schools and education in this book.

19. Gillis, John R. **Youth and History: Tradition and Change in European Age Relations, 1770-Present.** New York, Academic Press, 1979.

20. Holborn, Hajo. **A History of Modern Germany.** New York: Alfred A. Knopf, 1969, 3 vols.

A history covering the Reformation to the end of World War II, this provides a comprehensive overview of this period, including not only political and constitutional history but social and economic considerations as well.

21. Kohn, Hans. **The Mind of Germany.** New York, Charles Scribner's Sons, 1950.

Kohn writes an intellectual and political history by concentrating on selected individuals and themes, such as Goethe, Friedrich Schlegel, Father John, Heinrich Heine, Richard Wagner, Friedrich Nietzsche and Rainer-Maria Rilke, placing them in their socio-economic context. He feels that contemporary Germany has lifted itself out of its authoritarian past and has become democratic.

22. Masur, Gerhard. **Imperial Berlin.** New York: Basic Books, 1970.

Traces the history of Berlin giving extensive attention to Social and Cultural Factors. Chapter Six is titled: "Writers, Journalists and Scholars," where special attention is given to the University of Berlin.

23. Pascal, Roy. **The Growth of Modern Germany.** London: Cobbett Press, 1946.

This small volume traces the emergence and growth of German nationalism to Hitler's reign. He focusses on the undemocratic and militaristic features of German society.

24. Passant, E. J. **A short History of Germany, 1815-1945.** Cambridge: University Press, 1960.

This is a brief history of modern Germany which traces both political as well as cultural developments. It is intended for the general reader.

25. Pinson, Koppel S. **Modern Germany.** New York: Macmillan, 1959.

This book provides a history of Germany during the past two centuries and attempts to provide a synthesis of political and cultural history. Because German thought is so crucial to education, this provides an important contextual work for educators.

26. Reinhard, Kurt. **Germany: 2,000 years**. New York: Frederick Ungar, 1962. 2 vols.

Attempts to present a comprehensive statement of political and cultural history of Germany, beginning from prehistory. Cultural history includes sections on music, literature, art, scholarship and education, with commentaries on the major fields of study, such as sciences, philosophy, historiography,and arts and crafts, when appropriate. An important contribution.

27. Valentin, Veit. **The German People**. New York: Alfred Knopf, 1952.

This is a comprehensive history of the German people, tracing their origins and following their course until the collapse of National Socialism. Slight attention is given to cultural factors.

28. Villard, Oswald G. **The German Phoenix**. New York: Harrison Smith and Robert Haas, 1933.

This is a history of the German Republic, a picture of events that led up to the rule of the National Socialists. Villard gives great attention to social and cultural elements; Chapter Eleven is titled "The Republic, Youth, and Education."

PERIOD RELATED STUDIES

IMPERIAL GERMANY

29. Dawson, William Harbutt. **The German Empire: 1867-1914, and the Unity Movement**. New York: Macmillan, 1919, 2 Vols.

Dawson attempts to provide a general history of the German Empire. He makes no claim that his is an objective account, and actually stresses that it is written from a British standpoint.

WEIMAR REPUBLIC

30. Clark, R. T. **The Fall of the German Republic: A Political Study.** London: George Allen and Unwin Ltd., 1935.

Clark attempts to profit from the mistakes made in allowing the Weimar Republic to fall and examines why this occured. It is a political study or political history.

31. Eyck, Erich. **A History of the Weimar Republic** (trans. by H. P. Hanson and R. G. L. Waite). Cambridge: Harvard University Press, 1962, 2 Vols.

This is a translation of a work originally published in German in 1953. It is written by one who both participated as a jurist in the Weimar Republic and took time to ponder what happened.

32. Rosenberg, Arthur. **A History of the German Republic** (trans. by I.F.D. Morrow and L.M. Sieveking). London: Methuen and Co, 1936.

Traces the brief history of the Weimar Republic. His German volume ends at 1930 but he provides a brief epilogue in this English version for the succeeding four years.

NATIONAL SOCIALISM

33. Bracher, Karl D. **The German Dictatorship.** New York: 1972.

Includes an account of the ideology of National Socialist education, found on pages 247-272.

34. Heiden, Konrad. **A History of National Socialism.** New York: Alfred Knopf, 1935.

Heiden traces the roots of National Socialism and terminates the study as it is at a high point in German popularity.

35. Lichtenberger, Henri. **The Third Reich** (trans. by Koppel S. Pinson). New York: Greystone Press, 1937.

Although this is a translation from the French, Professor Lichtenberger has given additional materials in discussing the historical background that led to the Third Reich. He does give some attention to education, even though his focus is elsewhere.

36. Mosse, George L. **The Crisis of German Ideology: The Intellectual Origins of the Third Reich**. New York, Grosset and Dunlap, 1964.

Mosse maintains that the Germans were captured to such an extent by an ideology of unity and the **Volk** that they lost sight of civilized law and civilized attitudes. In this historical analysis, Mosse sees education and youth playing an important role.

37. Mosse, George L. (ed.). **Nazi Culture: Intellectual, Cultural and Social Life in the Third Reich**. London: W.H. Allen, 1966

A number of documents related to National Socialist culture are provided. These refer to the family, womanhood, the social reality, racism, Nazi heroes, science, Christianity, workers, shopkeepers and a number of other categories. An impressive number of documents about schools, the university, youth groups and school texts are included.

38. Pollack, James K. and Homer Thomas. **Germany in Power and Eclipse**. New York: Van Nostrand, 1952.

A political science study of Germany during the war years giving a historical account of government and administration and political movements with further sections on the various states and provinces which make up the whole of Germany. Education is briefly referred to at times.

OCCUPATION AND RECONSTRUCTION

39. Foundation for Foreign Affairs. **Field Report on the French Zone in Germany**. Pamphlet No. 1, Washington D.C., 1946.

This small pamphlet lays out the economic and political situation in the French Zone.

40. Gimbel, John. **A German Community Under American Occupation: Marburg 1945-52**. Stanford: Stanford University Press, 1961.

This is a case report on the occupation of Marburg for seven years after World War II. Of primary interest is the political thinking of the Americans, who tried deliberately to direct the course, and the Germans, who responded to produce an effective disillusionment of these forces. Attention is given to school and university affairs.

41. Knapper, Marshall. **And Call It Peace.** Chicago: University of Chicago Press, 1947.
An account, by an English military officer, of the collapse of Germany, the planning of operations and the attempts of the occupation forces to begin denazification. Great attention is given to reeducation.

42. Lichtfield, Edward H. (ed.). **Governing Postwar Germany.** Ithaca: Cornell University Press, 1953.
A collection of essays dealing with (1) the evolution of Postwar governments, (2) levels of governments, (3) Processes of Government, (4) Functions of Government, and (5) Politics. Alonzo G. Grace has written an essay on education in this collection.

43. McInnis, Edgar, Richard Hiscocks and Robert Spencer. **The shaping of Postwar Germany.** New York: Frederick A. Praeger, 1960.
A collection of essays giving factual historical information, which is then analyzed in the final chapter. The focus is largely on military/political affairs.

44. Nettl, J. P. **The Eastern Zone and Soviet Policy in Germany: 1945-1950.** London: Oxford University Press, 1951.
In his important study of Soviet policy, Nettl unfortunately devotes little attention to schools and education. His is a political and economic study.

45. Pollack, James K. and James Meisel. **Germany under Occupation.** Ann Arbor: George Wahr, 1947, (revised edition, 1949).
The authors provide materials and documents which are intended mainly to be of use to political scientists. These focus on all four zones of occupation.

46. Prittie, Terrence. **Germany Divided.** Boston: Little Brown and Co, 1960.
This book is still in the spirit of German reeducation, focussing on military issues, such as rearmament, postwar political issues, such as reunification, and attitude issues, such as authoritarianism.

47. Zink, Harold. **American Military Government in Germany.** New York: Macmillan, 1947.
This is an important document showing the structure of the Occupation forces, its aims and roles. Significant attention is given here to denazification, education and democratization.

CONTEMPORARY STUDIES

GENERAL

48. Dornberg, John. **Schizophrenic Germany.** New York: Macmillan, 1961.
A journalist, Dornberg attempts to characterize the complexities of Germany, which, though changing, retains some of its terrible past. Of special interest to educators is chapter 11, "The Fault of the Schools," where he argues that a democratically oriented educational system is a basic prerequisite for Germany's spiritual rehabilitation and reconstruction.

49. Grosser, Alfred. **Germany in our time: A political history of the Post War years.** London: Penguin, 1974.

50. Tempel, Gudrun. **The Germans: An Indictment of my People.** New York: Random House, 1963.
This small book is a collection of notes which the author wrote in Paris, which represent a self-examination which she has carried on since the war.

EAST GERMANY

51. Baylis, T. A. **The Technical Intelligentsia and the East German Elite: Legitimacy and Social Change in Mature Communism.** Berkeley: University of California Press, 1974.
Explores the political profile of a new social stratum in European communist society: the technical intelligentsia. A major section is devoted to the education of the new intelligentsia in East Germany.

52. Childs, David. **East Germany.** London: Frederick A. Praeger, 1969.
Provides a broad overview of East German political, economic, and social life. Childs' main thesis is that East Germany does not fit the stereotypes usually given it. To him, it is much more complicated. Chapters on education, mass media views of Great Britain and America, and the role of women, are especially noteworthy for educators.

53. Dornberg, John. **The Other Germany.** Garden City, New York: Doubleday, 1968.
The book has a political and economic focus with an extensive discussion of leaders such as Walter Ulrich and Erich Honecker. A full chapter on education is included and titled, "The Proprietors of Tomorrow".

54. Hangen, Welles. **The Muted Revolution: East Germany's challenge to Russia and the West**. New York: Alfred A. Knopf, 1966.
A collection of vignettes of East German life by a newspaper and radio correspondent, it is not intended to be a definitive history or scholarly analysis but a series of personal impressions.

55. Hanhardt, Arthur M. Jr. **The German Democratic Republic**. Baltimore: Johns Hopkins Press, 1968.
This is a part of a series of studies on the building of communist party states as a loosely structured community or system. It attempts to outline both the integrative and unique features in East Germany.

56. Holm, Hans Axel. **The Other Germans: Report from an East German Town** (trans. from Swedish by Thomas Teal). New York: Pantheon Books, 1970.
This is a picture of people living together in a small East German town. It focusses on specific people, but also describes a week-end at a hotel, an advertisement page of a newspaper, the mayor's office and other aspects of life, including a section on a teacher and a verbatim third-grade lesson.

57. Keefe, Eugene K. and others. **Area Handbook for East Germany**. Washington D.C.: U.S. Government Printing Office, 1972.
This is one of a series of handbooks prepared by the Foreign Area Studies Program of American University. One of the thirteen chapters is devoted to education.

58. Legters, Lymann Howard (ed.). **The German Democratic Republic: A Developed Socialist Society**. Boulder, Colorado: Westview Press, 1978.

59. Ludz, Peter C. "Discovery and 'Recognition' of East Germany." **Comparative Politics**, 2 (July, 1970), 681-92.
A review article of recent literature by D. Childs (1969), J. Dornberg (1968), F.H. Hartmann (1965), L. Hornsby (1966), and J.E. Smith (1969), dealing with East Germany.

60. Ludz, Peter C. **The German Democratic Republic from the Sixties to the Seventies: A Socio-Political Analysis**. Cambridge: Center for International Studies, Harvard University Press, 1970.

61. Smith, Jean E. **Germany Beyond the Wall.** Boston: Little, Brown and Co., 1969.

A first-hand account of life in East Germany is given. Its purpose is to provide some insights into a nation that is prosperous, growing and raising an already impressive standard of living. Chapter 8 is devoted to education.

62. Sontheimer, Kurt and Wilhelm Bleeck. **The Government and Politics of East Germany** (trans. by U. Price). London: Hutchinson, 1975.

This book attempts to give a comprehensive picture of the political, social and economic system of East Germany as well as its foreign policy. Written by West Germans, it denounces the tragedy of separation. Chapter 7 is titled "The Educational System."

63. Steele, Jonathan. **Inside East Germany: the State that Came in from the Cold.** New York: Urizen Books, 1977.

This is an attempt to show, in the special case of East Germany, that communism and even communist parties in Eastern Europe are not carbon copies of the Soviet System. The chapter "Social Services from Cradle to Grave," gives some attention to education.

64. Stopler, Wolfgang F. **The Structure of the East German Economy.** Cambridge: Harvard University Press, 1960.

65. Zimmerman, Harmut. "The GDR in the 1970's." **Problems in Communism**, 27 (Mar.-Apr.,1978), 1-40.

WEST GERMANY

66. Baker, Kendall L. and others. **Germany Transformed: Political Culture and the New Politics.** Cambridge: Harvard University Press, 1981.

67. Conradt, David. "West Germany, a Remade Political Culture." **Comparative Political Studies**, 7 (July, 1974), 222-38.

The author looks at evidence of survey archives and concludes that political development has taken place in West Germany.

68. Dahrendorf, Ralf. **Society and Democracy in Germany.** London: 1968
A sociological analysis of German society, it is a comprehensive study which looks at a multitude of facets which are interrelated, with a focus on the democratic nature of German society, or the lack thereof. He gives rich attention to education and the schools.

69. Dornberg, John. **The New Germans: Thirty Years After.** New York, Macmillan, 1976.
A correspondent for American newspapers and magazines covering both East and West Germany, Dornberg provides a journalistic account of present day Germans in contrast to those immediately after the war. He argues the Germans have overcome their major deficiencies and are a "cured" people. Extensive references to education are made.

70. Keefe, Eugene K. and others. **Area Handbook for the Federal Republic of Germany.** Washington, D.C.: U.S. Government Printing Office, 1975
This is one of a series of handbooks prepared by the Foreign Area Studies Program of American University. It gives major consideration to social categories but also looks at economic and national security issues. Several education related sections are included.

71. Merelman, Richard M., and Charles R. Foster. "Political Culture and Education in Advanced Industrial Societies: West Germany and the United States." **International Review of Education**, 24 (1978), 443-65.
The authors suggest that political alienation is a normal outcome of the incompatibility between egalitarian goals and social inequalitites in democratic systems. Comparisons between the United States, a stable democracy, and West Germany, an emergent democracy are made.

72. Nist, Joan S. "Trends in German Youth Literature." **The ALAN Review**, 8, 1 (Fall, 1980), 7.

73. Pribic, Rado. "Young People's Literature in the Federal Republic of Germany." **Journal of Reading**, 24 (Jan., 1981), 304-07.
The author explains that one in ten books in the world is written in West Germany and the four major themes in children's books are: terrorism, minorities, careers, and personal problems.

74. Rist, Ray C. "The Guestworkers of Germany." **Society**, 15 (Jul./Aug., 1978), 81-90
The paper discusses the social conditions in which guestworkers and their families live in West Germany and the social policies and programs instituted by the government in response to these people.

75. Rist, Ray C. **Guestworkers in Germany: the Prospects for Pluralism**. New York: Prager, 1978.
There are three parts to this comprehensive study, the third part concentrating on the education of the guestworker child. After discussing the general policies and programs, Rist focuses on two cases: the Bavarian and the Berlin. The author is pessimistic about the condition of the guestworker improving in Germany.

76. Ryder, A. J. **Twentieth-Century Germany: From Bismarck to Brandt**. London: Macmillan, 1978.
The author sees great continuity in the German condition through the various changes that have occured in the twentieth century.

77. Verba, Sidney. "Germany, the Remaking of Political Culture." In Lucian W. Pye and Sidney Verba (eds.). **Political Culture and Political Development**. Princeton: Princeton University Press, 1965.
Verba points out that changes in the German culture are due as much to social forces as to the specific impact of war and the post-war era. He provides public opinion data showing German people resist anything that would upset their ordered lives.

78. Wallenberg, Hans. **Report on Democratic Institutions in Germany**. New York. American Council on Germany, 1956.

79. Wells, Roger Hewes. **The States in West German Federalism**. New York: Bookman, 1961.
A study of federal-state relations from 1949 to 1960. He examines this relationship mainly from the state level.

Chapter 3

PHILOSOPHY OF EDUCATION

PERIOD RELATED PHILOSOPHICAL STUDIES

PRE-WORLD WAR II

80. Kneller, George F. **The Educational Philosophy of National Socialism.** New Haven, Yale University Press, 1941.
An important assessment of German educational philosophy of National Socialism, why it occured and how it adapted to German traditions.

81. Roman, Frederick William. **The New Education in Europe: An Account of Recent Fundamental Changes in the Educational Philosophy of Great Britain, France and Germany.** London: George Routledge and Sons, 1924.

INDIVIDUAL PHILOSOPHERS AND CONCEPTUALIZERS

NEW HUMANISTS IN THE CLASSICAL PERIOD

A. Humboldt, Wilhelm von

82. Humboldt, Wilhelm von. **Humanist without Portfolio: An Anthology of the Writings of Wilhelm von Humboldt** (trans. by M. Cowan). Detroit: Wayne State University Press, 1963.
Includes a section on education on pp. 125-144.

83. Thomas, Carla R. "Philosophical Anthropology and Educational Change: Wilhelm von Humboldt and the Prussian Reforms." **History of Education Quarterly**, 13 (Fall, 1973), 219-229.
Discussion of the role of Humboldt in revitalizing Prussian education following the defeat of the Prussians by Napoleon at Jena in 1806.

CLASSICAL IDEALISTS

A. Kant, Immanuel

84. Franklin, Edward. **The Educational Theory of Immanuel Kant**. Philadelphia, J. B. Lippincott, 1904.

85. Kant, Immanuel. **The Educational Theory of Immanuel Kant** (trans. and edited by E. F. Buchner). Philadelphia: J. B. Lippincott, 1904.

86. Kant, Immanuel. **Kant on Education** (trans. by A. Churton). London: Kegan Paul, Trench, Truebner and Co., 1899.

87. Kant, Immanuel. **Foundations of the Metaphysics of Morals** (trans. by L. W. Beck). New York: Liberal Arts Press, 1959.

B. Fichte, Johann Gottlieb

88. Fichte, Johann Gottlieb. **Addresses to the German Nation** (trans. by R. F. Jones and G. H. Turnbull). Chicago: Open Court Publishing, 1922. Fichte, Johann G.

89. King, Willis Lorenzo. **The Philosophical Foundations of the Educational Theory of Johann Gottlieb Fichte**. Ann Arbor: University Microfilms, 1961.

90. Turnbull, George H. **The Educational Theory of J. G. Fichte**. Liverpool: The University Press of Liverpool, 1926.

C. Hegel, G.W.F.

91. Luqueer, Frederic Ludlow. **Hegel as Educator.** New York: Macmillan and Co., 1896.

92. MacKenzie, Millicent. **Hegel's Educational Theory and Practice.** London: Swann, Sonnenschein and Co., 1909.

OTHER CLASSICAL THINKERS

A. Herbart, Johann Friedrich

93. Dunkel, Harold B. **Herbart and Education.** New York: Random House, 1969.

94. Dunkel, Harold B. **Herbart and Herbartianism; an Educational Ghost Story.** Chicago: University of Chicago Press, 1970.

95. Dunkel, Harold B. "Herbart's Reply to Jachmann's Review of his 'General Pedagogy.'" **History of Education Quarterly**, 9 (1969), 234-52.

96. Eckoff, William J. (ed. and trans.). **Herbart's ABC of Sense Perception and Minor Pedagogical Works.** New York: D. Appleton and Co., 1896.

97. Herbart, Johann Friedrich. **The Science of Education: Its General Principles Deduced from its Aim and the Aesthetic Revelation of the World.** Washington D. C.: University Publications of America, 1977.

98. Herbart, Johann Friedrich. **Letters and Lectures on Education** (trans. by H. M. and E. F. Felkin). London: Sonnenschein, 1898.

99. Herbart, Johann Friedrich. **Outlines of Educational Doctrine** (trans. by A. F. Lange). New York: Macmillan, 1901.

100. Compyre, Gabriel. **Herbart and Education by Instruction.** London: George G. Harrop, 1908.

B. Froebel, Friedrich

101. Downs, Robert Bingham. **Friedrich Froebel**. Boston: Twayne, 1978.

102. Froebel, Friedrich. **Autobiography** (trans. by E. Michaelis). Syracuse: C. W. Bardeen, 1889.
Includes a bibliography of early works on Froebel.

103. Froebel, Friedrich. **The Education of Man**. Washington, D.C.: University Publications of America, 1977.

104. Fletcher, S. and J. Welton. **Froebel's Chief Writings on Education**. New York: Longman's, Green, and Co., 1912.

105. MacVannel, John Angus. **The Educational Theories of Herbart and Froebel**. New York: Teachers College, Columbia University, 1905.

106. Snider, Denton J. **The Life of Frederick Froebel**. Chicago: Sigma Publishing. 1900.

CRITICS OF THE INDUSTRIAL AGE

A. Nietzsche, Friedrich

107. Kaufmann, Walter Arnold. **Nietzsche, Philosopher, Psychologist, Anti-Christ**. Princeton: Princeton University Press, 1974.

108. Nietzsche, Friedrich. **The Future of Our Educational Institutions**. London: George Allen and Unwin, 1909.

THE NEW EDUCATION ERA THINKERS

A. Dilthey, Wilhelm

109. Rickman, H. P. "Dilthey and the Philosophy of Education." **International Review of Education.** 8 (1963), 336-43.
Dilthey belongs to the class of great philosophers and educators. His major contribution to the philosophy of education in Germany is assessed.

B. Spranger, Eduard

110. Spranger, Eduard. "The Role of Love in Education." **Universitas**, 2 3 (1958).

111. Spranger, Eduard. **Types of Man; The Psychology and Ethics of Personality** (trans. by P. J. W. Pigors). Halle: M. Niemeyer, 1928.

CONTEMPORARY PHILOSOPHICAL THOUGHT

A. Habermas, Juergen

112. Foster, W. P. "Administration and the Crisis in Legitimacy: A Review of Habermasian Thought." **Harvard Education Review**, 50 (Nov., 1980), 496-505.

113. Habermas, Juergen. **Toward a Rational Society: Student Protest, Science and Politics** (trans. by J. J. Shapiro). Boston: Beacon Press, 1970.

114. Habermas, Juergen. **Legitimation Crisis** (trans. by T. McCarthy). Boston: Beacon Press, 1975.

115. Habermas, Juergen. **Knowledge and Human Interests** (trans. by J. J. Shapiro). Boston: Beacon Press, 1971.

116. Mezirow, V. "Critical Theory of Adult Learning and Education." **Adult Education**, 32 (Fall, 1981), 3-24.

B. Heidegger, Martin

117. Heidegger, Martin. **Discourse on Thinking** (trans. by J. M. Anderson and E. H. Freund). New York: Harper and Row, 1959.

118. Heidegger, Martin. **What Is Called Thinking?** (trans. by F. D. Wieck and J. G. Gray). New York: Harper and Row, 1968.

119. Heidegger, Martin. **What Is Philosophy?** (trans. by W. Klubock and J. T. Wilde). London: Twayne Publishers, 1958.

Chapter 4

HISTORY OF EDUCATION

GENERAL HISTORIES OF EDUCATION

120. Cubberley, Ellwood P. **The History of Education.** London: Constable and Co., 1920.
Chapter 22 is titled: "National Organization in Prussia."

121. Eby, Frederick and Charles F. Arrowood. **The Development of Modern Education.** New York: Prentice Hall, 1942.
The authors have special sections devoted to German reformers during the eighteenth century, the nationalization of German education, the formation of the German school system, Herbart, Froebel, and other educators.

PERIOD RELATED GENERAL EDUCATION STUDIES

EARLY AND MIDDLE NINETEENTH CENTURY

A. National Systems of Education Take Form

122. De Hovre, Frans. **German and English Education: A Comparative Study.** New York: Charles Scribner's Sons, 1917.
The author looks at the "soul of modern Germany" and German education, then he looks at the "soul of England" and English education. Finally, he compares English and German education. His basic orientation is that German education is based on the national principle and that it is above all intellectual in nature.

123. Reisner, Edward H. **Nationalism and Education since 1789.** New York: Macmillan Co., 1923.
The book deals with nationalism in France, Prussia, England, and the United States.

B. Prussia Serves as a Model to the World

124. Bache, Alexander D. **Report on Education in Europe.** Philadelphia: Lydia R. Bailey, 1839.
Includes several chapters on all levels of education in Prussia, and certain aspects of education in other German areas.

125. Barnard, Henry. **National Education in Europe: Being an Account of the Organization, Administration, Instruction and Statistics of Public Schools of Different Grades in the Principal States.** Hartford: Frederick B. Perkins, 1854.
Gives great attention to education in various German states.

126. Mann, Horace. "A Preliminary and Critical Account of European Education." **The Common School Journal**, 6 (1844), 2-12.
An abstract of the Seventh Annual Report.

127. Mann, Horace. **Seventh Annual Report of the Secretary of the Board.** Boston: Dutton and Wentworth, 1844.
Mann reports on education in several European countries, including Prussia.

128. Stowe, Calvin E. **Report on Elementary Public Instruction in Europe Made to the Thirty-Sixth General Assembly of the State of Ohio.** December 19, 1837.

IMPERIAL GERMANY

129. Alexander, Thomas. **The Prussian Elementary Schools.** New York: Macmillan, 1918.
The study attempts to demonstrate that the elementary school has been fashioned to make spiritual and intellectual slaves of the lower classes. Published at the end of the first world war, it is written with a flavor of conflict and hostility.

130. Bruen, Hanan. "The Impact of Social and Political Factors upon the Teaching of History in the Secondary Schools of Imperial Germany and the Weimar Republic." Unpublished Ph.D. dissertation, University of Chicago, 1961.

WEIMAR REPUBLIC

A. General

131. Ahmad, Zia Uddin. **System of Education: England, Germany, France and India.** Calcutta: Longmans, Green and Co., 1929.

Looks at 25 different aspects of German education on pages 85-168.

B. The German Youth Movement

132. Becker, Howard. **German Youth, Bond or Free.** London: K. Paul, Trench and Trubner, 1946.

This study, by a sociologist, is in the spirit of the German reeducation thrust; however, it focuses on the German Youth Movement and includes a large section on education.

C. Experimental Schools and a New Pedagogy

133. Alexander, Thomas and Beryl Parker. **The New Education in the German Republic.** New York: John Day, 1929.

The New Education Movement is the European version of the progressive education movement. The authors provide a broad panorama of the movement, including chapters on the Youth Movement, youth hostels, sports and recreation, as well as discussions of specific schools that emerged in the period. A final section is devoted to a general discussion of the movement, its status and prospects.

134. Kellerman, Fritz. **The Effect of the World War on European Education.** Cambridge: Harvard University Press, 1928.

Special attention is given in this volume to Germany, with reference to World War I and the New Education Movement.

NATIONAL SOCIALISM

135. Beard, Charles A. "Education Under the Nazis." **Foreign Affairs**, 14 (April, 1936), 439-40.
Beard finds the Nazis have destroyed independent research, frank consideration of conflicting views, open discussion, judicial temper, and things which mark liberal education generally.

OCCUPATION AND RECONSTRUCTION

PLANNING FOR RECONSTRUCTION

136. Council for a Democratic Germany. "A Plan for the Reconstruction of the German Educational System." **School and Society**, 62 (Dec. 29, 1945), 435-436.
A brief plan to democratize the German system by a council sponsored by the American Association for a Democratic Germany.

137. Engelmann, Susanne Charlotte. **German Education and Re-Education**. New York: International Universities Press, 1945.
The book deals with education in Germany under three different political systems prior to the end of World War II. Its purpose is to set the stage for understanding so that educational reconstruction might take place in a more rational and wise manner and avoid the mistakes made in these periods to rebuild the schools, not only in Germany, but all of Europe.

138. Evans, Frederic. "The Re-Education of Germany." **Political Quarterly**, 16 (Mar., 1945), 21-30.
Evans anticipates the defeat of the Nazis and speculates about what must be done to re-establish law, the dignity of the individual and the rights of society.

139. Fraenkel, Heinrich. "Is Hitler Youth Curable?" **New Republic**, 11 (Sept. 18, 1944), 335-37.
Anticipates the collapse of the Nazis, and after giving some evidence of the failure of Nazi schools, he says there is still hope for reeducation although it must be done by the Germans themselves it it is to succeed.

140. Martin, Kingsley. "The Re-Education of Germany." **Political Quarterly**, 15 (1944), 135-147.
Refers to the Gods of power and terror, cruelty and magic, worshipped by pre-Christians, which have taken hold in Germany, and which must be rooted out by the Germans, themselves, with international support of these efforts.

141. Newman, James R. "How we Began the Re-Education of Nazi Germany." **American School Board Journal**, 112 (Feb., 1946), 33-34.
Outlines a chronology of events in three phases: July 10-Aug. 15, 1945; Aug. 15-Oct. 8, 1945; Oct. 8-Dec., 1945.

142. Peiser, Werner. "Goethe's Educational Philosophy and the Re-education of the German Youth." **Education**, 65 (Sept., 1944), 3-8.
Looks to Goethe as an example to follow in the reeducation of the German nation.

143. Specht, Minna. **Education in Post-War Germany**. London: International Publishing Co., 1944.
Anticipates the reeducation period following the war.

144. Specht, Minna and Alfons Rosenberg. **Experimental Schools in Germany**. London: Westminster Press, 1945.
In the spirit of educational reconstruction in post-war Germany.

145. Wilson, William. "Educational Approach to the Problems of Germany." **The Texas Outlook**. 28 (Nov., 1944), 8-19.
Wilson anticipates the reeducation process that must take place after the war.

THE ZONES OF OCCUPATION

THE BRITISH ZONE

146. Birley, Robert. "Education in the British Zone of Germany." **International Affairs**, 26 (Jan., 1950), 32-44.
After recounting what has taken place, he concludes it is simply too early to determine if the reeducation program has been successful.

147. "Education in the British Zone; the Vocational School." **Times Educational Supplement**, 1629 (July 20, 1946), 343.

148. Friedmann, Wolfgang. **The Allied Military Government of Germany--A Study of Educational Factors and Traditions.** London: Kegan Paul, 1947.
The author worked with the British military government and makes a critical appraisal of the reeducation program. Although it looks at the allied government, it is particulary helpful in understanding the British role.

149. Hare-Scott, K. "Education in Berlin." **Times Educational Supplement**, 1634 (Aug. 24, 1946), 400.

150. Hearnden, Arthur (ed.). **The British in Germany: Educational Reconstruction after 1945**. London: Hamish Hamilton, 1978.
This is a collection of papers arising mainly from a 1975 conference on British education policy in early post-war Germany. Others were subsequently added to provide a comprehensive view.

151. Lawson, Robert F. "English Approach to Educational Reorientation in Postwar Germany." **Comparative Education Review**, 8 (June, 1964), 58-64.
His account of the English reeducation efforts indicates that the British were more respectful of German education traditions and were not as persistent as Americans.

152. Nicholls, A. J. "The British Impact on German Education: A Triumph for Commonsense or a Missed Opportunity." **Oxford Review of Education**, 4 (1978), 125-29.
A review essay where the author reacts to Arthur Hearnden's study of British reeducation efforts after W. W. II.

153. Simmons, M. M. "Education in the British Zone of Germany." **Educational Record**. 29 (Oct., 1948), 423-27.

THE FRENCH ZONE

154. Bidwell, Percy W. "Emphasis on Culture in the French Zone." **Foreign Affairs**, 27 (1948), 78-85.
The French expect the Germans in their zone to support themselves economically, but they have an active and positive program of reeducation.

155. Willis, F. Roy. **The French in Germany: 1945-1949.** Stanford: Stanford University Press, 1962.
While pointing out that the French Zone has been described too often by its critics, this study attempts to look at the effect of French occupation in view of the growing rapproachment of the two countries. Chapter 8 is devoted to "Denazification and Re-education."

156. Wiskemann, Elizabeth. "French Foundations in Germany: Mainz and Saarbruecken." **Times Educational Supplement**, 1937 (June 13, 1952), 509.
Describes French influence on the Universities in the French Zone.

U.S.A. ZONE

157. Benton, William. "The United States Mission Reports on Education in Germany." **American Teacher**, (Feb., 1947).
Benton points out the emphasis of the U. S. Mission on developing democracy through the schools.

158. Christofferson, A. C. "Educational Reconstruction in Land Hesse, Germany." **Educational Forum**, 13 (March, 1949), 313-319.
The author outlines the traditional system then discusses the ten principles the U. S. government uses in rebuilding the schools. He indicts the selectivity of German education.

159. DeLong, Vaughn R. "School Reform in Land Hesse." **School Board Journal**, 117 (Oct., 1948), 39-40.
Focus on the traditional streaming program of German schools, and a call for integration. Lists the ten principles of democratic education formulated in the American Zone.

160. **Education and Cultural Activities in Germany Today.** Frankfurt: U.S. Office of the High Commissioner for Germany, Office of Public Affairs, 1950.
This represents a rich collection of reprints from the **Information Bulletin**, a monthly magazine of the U.S. High Commission.

161. "Educational Progress in the American Zone in Germany." **School and Society**, 64 (July 20, 1946), 36-7.
The report summarizes recent reports on reeducation.

162. Goodykoontz, Bess. "Teachers and Children in German Schools." **School Life**, 29 (July, 1947), 3-6.
Report of visits to rural and city schools and impressions gained as a member of the U. S. Education Mission to Germany.

163. Goodykoontz, Bess. "U. S. Education Mission Report." **School Life**, 30 (Oct., 1947), 10-12.
The report outlines the major recommendations of the U. S. Mission to Germany, which consisted of 10 persons, who spent five weeks in Berlin and the American Zone.

164. Grace, Alonzo G. **Basic Principles of Educational Reconstruction in Germany**. Frankfurt: U. S. Office of the High Commissioner for Germany, Education and Cultural Relations Office, 1948.

165. Grace, Alonzo G. "Germany Needs an Intellectual Airlift." **Texas Outlook**, 34 (May, 1950), 8-9.
Looking at Germany after five years of reeducation, he maintains that educational reconstruction will continue to require the best scholars and leaders of the United States.

166. Grace, Alonzo G. "Islands of Democratic Ferment in Germany." **American Scholar**, 19 (July, 1950), 341-52.
This is an apologist statement, maintaining that the lack of American intellectual, spiritual, and cultural achievement in Germany, as painted by the media, is not as bleak as usually described. Indeed, the process is simply a long and difficult one and there are signs of progress, such as the Chiemsee Conference on Education, youth organizations, self help programs, international work camps, work-study programs, Frankfurt-University of Chicago Experiment, the American Institute, the Nauheim Resolutions, community councils, etc.

167. Hocking, William E. **Experiment in Education**. Chicago: Henry Regnery and Co., 1954.
Takes critical stock of American attempts to reeducate Germany following World War II, and asks what we may have learned from these efforts. His concern is the arrogance any nation possesses as it assumes it can or should interfere with something as fundamental as education in another country. It is an important study, an essential study of the intentions, the process, and the outcomes.

168. Hopkins, L. Thomas. "Educational Progress in Germany." **Teachers College Record**, 51 (Oct., 1949), 14-21.
Reports on changes that have occured between his visit in 1947 to the American Zone, and a return visit in 1949. He concludes that little "progress" has been made and that Germany may never become truly democratic.

169. Huebener, Theodore. "Reform in German Education." **German Quarterly**, 26 (May, 1953), 150-153.
A brief account of the American reeducation effort.

170. Huebener, Theodore. "Have the German Schools been Democratized?" **Modern Language Journal**, 36 (Mar., 1952), 115-19.
He sees progress being made but notes that the Germans themselves must work out their own salvation. Because of the heterogeneity of the Germans, the effects of American influence are uneven.

171. Johnson, Philip G. "Secondary Education in the Schools of Germany." **School Life**, 30 (Oct., 1947), 12-14.
A brief report indicating the selectivity of secondary schools, entrance criteria, and training of teachers.

172. Koopman, G. Robert. "Freedom's Stake in German Education." **Education for National Security**. Official Report of the American Association of School Administrators, 1953. Washington, D. C.: AASA, 1953.

173. Landeen, William M. "United States Policy in the Re-education of Germany." **Institute of World Affairs Proceedings**, 23 (1947), 141-49.

174. "Lessons on the Air: School Broadcasts in the U. S. Zone." **Times Educational Supplement**, 1758 (Jan. 8, 1949), 21.

175. McClure, Worth. "The Educational Battle in Germany." **Phi Delta Kappan**, 32 (Jan., 1951), 207-208.
Claims Americans are loosing the battle in Germany where another generation of "blind followers" is being raised up.

176. Mayer, Herbert C. "German Education Can be Saved." **School and Society**, 74 (July 7, 1951), 1-3.
Claims that Americans have already lost the battle to change German education, but he argues we may win a second round and appeals for us to do so.

177. Newman, James R. "The Second Phase of Denazifying German Schools in Greater Hessen." **American School Board Journal**, 112 (August, 1946), 32-33.
A follow-up to his earlier report, giving quantitative data about the different types of schools in Hessen.

178. Pilgert, Henry P. **The West German Educational System.** Frankfurt a/M.: U. S. Office of the High Commissioner for Germany, Historical Division, 1951.
This study is primarily about U.S. policies and programs in Germany relating to formal education. It points out that denazification was only emphasized in 1945 and 1946, and since that time a positive approach was stressed. His conclusion is that while the old authoritarian culture continues, a steady movement away from this problem has been noted.

179. Pitt, Felix N. "Education Mission to Germany." **America**, (Jan. 18, 1947).
Pitt gives a full commentary on the contents of the Report submitted by George F. Zook, who chaired the U. S. Mission to Germany.

180. Prakken, Lawrence W. "American Educational Policy in Germany." **Education Digest**, 13 (Oct., 1947), 1-5.
Describes the organizational structure of the American occupation in terms of education, as well as basic policy.

181. Pundt, Alfred. "Re-educating the New Germany." **Journal of Higher Education**, 19 (Oct., 1948), 350-360.
Account of the post-war period with special attention being given to higher education in Bavaria. He feels the occupation mission of democratization has failed so far, but expresses hope.

182. Roemer, Joseph. "German Textbooks in the U.S. Zone of Germany." **Peabody Journal of Education**, 28 (May, 1951), 346-52.
Discusses the changes made in textbooks since the war.

183. Russell, William F. "Teaching Germans to Teach Themselves." **Foreign Affairs**, 27 (Oct., 1948), 68-77.
Assesses the American Military Government aims of (1) keeping order, (2) putting Germany back on its feet to carry on alone, (3) changing Germany from a world menace to a peaceful country. He asks how much reeducation can contribute to these aims.

184. Schneeweiss, Margarete L. "German Schools and Democracy." **Modern Language Journal**, 34 (Feb., 1950), 111-25.
One of the more thorough accounts of reeducation, its basic threads, why it is being implemented, and why it is being resisted.

185. Shafer, Susanne M. **Postwar American Influence in the West German Volksschule.** Ann Arbor: University of Michigan, 1964. Comparative Education Dissertation Series No. 3.

186. Schuster, George N. "American Occupation and German Education." **American Philosophical Society Proceedings**, 97 (1953), 159-62.
Assesses American reeducation since the war and concludes that the results are neither spectacular nor meager.

187. Strevell, Wallace H. **School Fiscal Policy Study, U. S. Zone of Germany**. Berlin: Office of the U. S. High Commissioner, Education and Cultural Relations Division, 1950.

188. Tone Fred H. and Hans Warninghoff. "Bremen School Reform." **Educational Forum**, 14 (Mar., 1950), 331-37.
The authors claim that Bremen has come as far as any Western German state in its school reforms. They contrast the old and new systems, suggesting difficulties in the new reform.

189. **United States Education Mission to Germany**, George F. Zook, Chairman. Washington D. C.: U. S. Government Printing Office, 1946.
Ten prominant educators were sent to Germany in the Summer, 1946, for the purpose of observing and evaluating the educational program of the U. S. Military Government. This is their report, and it served as a framework for subsequent reeducation policy of the U. S.

190. von Glahn, Gerhard. "Some Aspects of German Education in the U. S. Zone of Occupation." **Science Education**, 33 (Feb., 1949), 7-13.
A general statement of reeducation efforts is given.

191. Wrinkle, William L. **Prewar German Education and the Objectives of the U. S. Education Program in Germany.** Frankfurt a/M.: Office of the U. S. High Commissioner for Germany, Division of Cultural Affairs, Office of Public Affairs, 1952.

192. Wrinkle, William L. **Postwar Changes in German Education**. Frankfurt a/M.: Office of the U. S. High Commissioner for Germany, 1951.
Wrinkle provides a detailed list of changes, listed according to the state, in German education in 24 categories.

193. Zook, George F. "Japan and Germany: Problems in Re-education." **International Conciliation**, No. 427. New York: Carnegie Endowment for International Peace, 1947. pp. 2-40.
In this volume one finds summaries of the United States missions to Japan and Germany, with a good introduction by the author.

THE THREE WESTERN ZONES OF OCCUPATION

194. Fraenkel, Heinrich. "Education in Germany." **New Statesman and Nation**, 31 (May 11, 1946), 334; 31 (May 25, 1946); 31 (June 8, 1946), 441.
After two months in the three Western zones and two weeks in Berlin, Fraenkel reports the efforts being made to institute the **Einheitsschule** in the East and other activities. His focus is largely on the pupils and students.

195. Grace, Alonzo G. **Basic Elements of Educational Reconstruction in Germany**. Washington, D. C.: American Council on Education, 1949.
Points out that reconstruction must continue and provides a blueprint for that work.

196. Grace, Alonzo G. "Education in Occupied Germany." **Phi Delta Kappan**, 31 (Mar., 1950), 305-09.
Outlines basic efforts of reconstruction but appeals to nongovernment agencies to become involved.

197. Grimme, A. "German Educational Reconstruction." **The New Era**, 27 (July-Aug., 1946), 167-168.
A statement by an educational administrator in Hanover, who explains what the Germans are trying to do to deal with reconstruction at all levels of education.

198. Holtzclaw, Katherine. "Germany Needs Modern Home Economics." **Practical Home Economics**, 26 (May, 1948), 312-14.

199. Keohane, Robert E. "Dilemmas of German Re-education: Reflections upon an Experiment Noble in Purpose." **The School Review**, 62 (Oct., 1949), 405-415.

A reflective, self critical appraisal of the reforms imposed on the Germans and a call for us to give the Germans even more control over affairs than is now the case. He stresses the most serious gap: Social Studies in elementary school.

200. Lawson, Robert F. **The Reform of the West German School System."** Ann Arbor: University of Michigan, 1965. Comparative Education Dissertation Series, No. 4.

201. Lorey, August L. "Memorandum on a Report by Irving R. Kuenzli entitled 'Trade Unions and Public Education in Western Germany.'" **Harvard Education Review**, 21 (1951), 1-13.

A review of the reaction of Hesse teachers to Kuenzli's report in which he advocates reorganizing German education along the lines of the American system. The contrast in points of view are very clear.

202. McKay, Llewelyn R. "The 'New Look' in West German School." **History of Education Journal**, (Summer, 1956).

Outlines the historical structure of the German school system and points out that it still prevails. He gives eleven points of reform under way.

203. Snyder, Agnes. "Glimpses into German Schools." **Science Education**, 32 (Oct., 1948), 233-38.

Looks at housing, materials, food, teaching and teachers, and discusses the problems involved in giving education back to the Germans.

204. Snyder, Agnes. "Elementary Education in Occupied Germany." **National Elementary Principal**, 26 (June, 1947).

She gives a personal glimpse of her experiences in schools themselves for six months. She stresses the need to democratize.

205. Zuckermann, Stanley B. "Education in Germany Today: an American Appraisal." **Progressive Education**, 32 (Nov., 1955), 173-175.

Describes the problems involved in overcoming the authoritarian nature of German education. Expresses gratitude for being an American.

U.S.S.R.

206. Frankel, Heinrich. "Behind the Iron Curtain, the **Einheitsschule.**" **Times Educational Supplement,** 1691 (Sept. 27, 1947), 514; 1692 (Oct. 4, 1947), 528.

207. Lilge, Frederic. "German Educational Reforms in the Soviet Zone of Occupation." **Harvard Education Review,** 18 (Jan., 1948), 35-46.
Constrasts American and Russian policies and practices. He finds the Russians much more effective, if also more coercive, in their reform endeavors.

208. "Schools in the Soviet Zone: A West German Report." **Times Educational Supplement,** 1892 (Aug. 3, 1951), 621.
Review of a West German Teachers Trade Union booklet on schools in the Soviet Zone, as represented in official documents.

Chapter 5

ORGANIZATION AND STRUCTURE OF EDUCATION

GENERAL

EAST GERMANY

209. Bodenman, Paul S. "Education in the Soviet Zone of Germany." **School Life**, 41 (Dec., 1958), 14-17.
This is a descriptive account of the educational system in East Germany in general.

210. Bodenman, Paul S. **The Educational System of the German Democratic Republic**. Washington: U.S. Department of Health, Education and Welfare, 1975.
This pamphlet gives an overview of the entire system of education in East Germany.

211. **Children in the GDR**. Berlin: UNICEF-GDR National Committee, 1979.
Four of the chapters describe formal education, involvement in the pioneer organization, health care of children, and leisure pursuits for all children.

212. **Development of Education in the German Democractic Republic**. Berlin: Ministry of Education, Ministry of Higher Education, the State Secretariat of Vocational Training, 1981.
This booklet provides a survey of educational policy, educational institutions at various levels, cooperation between educational institutions and society at large, teachers and educational science.

213. **Education for Today and Tomorrow** (fourth revised edition). Dresden: Verlag Zeit im Bild, 1973.

214. Grant, Nigel. **Society, Schools and Progress in Eastern Europe**. Oxford: Pergamon, 1969.
The first section provides a general educational overview of Eastern Europe. Chapter 2 of the second edition focuses on East Germany.

215. **The Educational System in the German Democractic Republic.** Berlin: Volk und Wissen Volkseigener Verlag, 1979.

216. **Education and Training in the German Democratic Republic.** Berlin: Staatsverlag der Deutschen Demokratischen Republic, 1966.
The major portion of this volume is an English translation of the East German Law on the Integrated Socialist Educational System, passed on 25 Feb., 1965. The first part of the volume contains statements by various officials pertaining to the law and its intentions.

217. "The Educational System of the German Democratic Republic," in the series **Education Around the World,** published by the U.S. Department of Health, Education and Welfare, 1975.
This is a brief bulletin providing an abstracted overview of education in East Germany.

218. Guenther, Karl-Heinz and Christine Lost. **Development of Public Education in the German Democratic Republic.** Berlin: Ministry of Education, 1977.
A report presented to the 36th session of the International Conference on Education in Geneva. It looks at educational policy, preschooling, polytechnical schools, education for the handicapped, vocational education, and higher education. Some attention is also given to the role of educational research in East Germany.

219. Guenther, Karl-Heinz and Gottfried Uhlig. **History of the Schools in the German Democratic Republic: 1945-68.** Berlin: Volk und Wissen Volkseigener Verlag, 1973.
This is the most complete statement by those in East Germany of the developments of education in their country in the first two decades. It concentrates mainly on the party and government and their decisions, and it is written within the missionary spirit of the party leaders.

220. Hofmann, Erich. "The Changing School in East Germany." **Comparative Education Review,** 6 (June, 1965), 48-57.
Reviews how the school is being transformed from a Nazi school to a socialist school. The author touches also on youth organizations and the parent's role in education.

221. King, B. "Schools of Eastern Germany." **Times Educational Supplement**, 1963 (Feb. 12, 1949), 100; 1964 (Feb., 19, 1949), 116.

222. Klein, Helmut. **Education in a Socialist Country: Report on Educational Policy in the GDR.** Berlin: Panorama, 1974.

223. Klein, Helmut. **First Hand Information: Education in a Socialist Country** (2nd revised edition). Dresden: Verlag Zeit im Bild, 1976.

Klein stresses that while socialist education rests on a common foundation, the various socialist countries differ considerably in their practical make-up. This small publication attempts to provide a discussion of the foundation of socialist education and the way East Germany has implemented these principles. Valuable documentation materials are included.

224. Klein, Helmut and Ernst Behling. **German Democratic Republic Education.** Dresden: Verlag Zeit im Bild, 1972.

This small pamphlet provides a capsule account of various facets of education in East Germany.

225. Klein, Margrete S. **The Challenge of Communist Education: A Look at the German Democratic Republic.** New York: East European Monographs, 1980.

One of the recent good statements on East German Education, especially with regard to polytechnical education as it expresses communist ideology. The curriculum of various subjects is included in the appendix.

226. Moore-Rinvolucri, Mina J. **Education in East Germany.** Hamden Conn.: Archon Books, 1973.

The author charts several aspects of East German education including historical perspectives, the general system of education, polytechnical education, post-compulsory schooling, the disadvantaged child, youth clubs, parents, teachers and their training, tertiary education, education research, and book provisions. The book is mainly factual in substance with little interpretive data.

227. Senf, Hans. "Cooperation Between School and Family in the German Democratic Republic." **Prospects: Quarterly Review of Education**, 10 (1980), 340-45.

The author claims a successful program of cooperation between school and family has been developed in East Germany.

228. Shafer, Susanne M. "How Successful is Socialist Education?" **Comparative Education Review**, 22 (Feb., 1978), 99-114.
Shafer attempts to assess the success of the German Democratic Republic using eight specific criteria. After doing so, she claims that restrictions placed on freedom of thought and expression dim any image of success that has been determined.

229. Smart, Kenneth F. "Education in East Germany," **Educational Forum**, 25 (May, 1961), 463-71.
Smart discusses the structure of formal education in East Germany. He concludes that every attempt is made to ensure that the younger generation is conversant with the socialist transformation of the country.

230. UNESCO Commission of the German Democratic Republic. **Education for Today and Tomorrow**. Dresden: Verlag Zeit im Bild, 1973.
This booklet covers the full range of educational levels and schooling types in East Germany.

231. Ziemann, Michael J. "To Educate the Multi-Faceted and Harmoniously Developed Socialist Personality...:The Educational System of the German Democratic Republic." **Proceedings, Pacific Northwest Council on Foreign Languages**, 29 (April, 1978), 28-57.

WEST GERMANY

232. Beck, Earl R. "New Schools in Hamburg." **Peabody Journal of Education**, 40 (July, 1962), 44-48.
An account of a study trip where Beck, a historian, gives Hamburg schools an A-1 rating for fostering joyful learning.

233. Belding, Robert E. **European Classrooms: Schools of Four Nations**. Iowa City: Sernoll, 1966.
Chapter four is titled: "Germany's Reluctance to Change" (pp. 57-81).

234. Bodenman, Paul S. **The Educational System of the Federal Republic of Germany**. Washington: Office of Education (DHEW), 1976.
The pamphlet gives an overview of the entire system of formal education in West Germany.

235. Bodoh, Rachel. "European vs. American Education." **Educational Leadership**, (April, 1960).

236. Collier, K. "Comment on German Eduction." **Journal of Education**, (London), 87 (Jan., 1955), 18+.

237. Cramer, John F. and George S. Browne. **Contemporary Education: A Comparative Study of National Systems.** New York: Harcourt, Brace and Co., 1956.
Chapter 16 is titled: "Education in transition: The Schools of Germany." After a brief historical treatment, the general system and structure of education is outlined (pp. 432-73).

238. Dahrendorf, Ralf "The Crisis in German Education." **Contemporary History**, 2, 3(July, 1967), 139-147.
Dahrendorf attempts to highlight what he feels are basic deficiencies of German society by looking at its educational crisis. His major point is that the crisis is related to the proportion of each generation which went on to secondary schools and then on to universities.

239. "Education Around the World; Germany: How to Shed Eliteness with Grace." **Nations Schools**, 84(Aug.,1969), 34-35.

240. **Education in Europe: School Systems: A Guide.** Strasbourg: Council for Cultural Cooperation, Council of Europe, 1965.
West Germany is highlighted (pp. 81-96) with a description of the school system, diagrams, lists of terms and statistics.

241. **Education in Europe.** London: National Association of Schoolmasters, Apr., 1963.
A general discussion of West German education is included (pp. 57-69).

242. "Education in Scandinavian Countries and West Germany." **School and Society**, 96 (Jan. 20, 1968), 52+.

243. Forsbach, Marlene. "The School as a Democratic Institution." **Bildung und Wissenschaft**, No. 1-76(e), 1976, published by Inter Nationes.

244. Franzen, Carl G. F. "Educational Systems of Major Foreign Countries and their Cultural Functions and Outcomes." **North Central Association Quarterly**, 34 (Apr., 1960), 273-83.
Franzen looks at England, France, Germany and the USSR with concluding comments about educational change and social ferment.

245. Graff, Willard J. "Education in West Germany." **School and Community**. 54 (Dec., 1967), 10-11.
This is a brief sketch of 29 points about West German education.

246. Hausmann, Gerhard. "A Megalopolis: the Ruhr/Rhein Complex." **The World Year Book of Education**, (1970), 251-65.
The author discusses the industrial/economic setting and the structure of education in this setting.

247. Hearnden, Arthur. **Education, Culture, and Politics in West Germany**. Oxford: Pergamon Press, 1976.
The author attempts to show the difficulty of making general observations about education in West Germany. He is, however, able to make some generalizations, including a deep seated conservatism that has resisted the movement toward comprehensivism.

248. Hoy, J. D. **A Comparative Guide to the Educational Systems of England, Wales and Hamburg**. Hamburg: Die Brucke, 1956.

249. Huebener, Theodore. **The Schools of West Germany**. New York: New York University Press, 1962.
The author provides a brief historical overview of German education, a description of the various types of schools in the system, a brief account of those involved in schooling from teachers to parents, a comment on the curriculum and teaching, and concluding remarks about reform activities. The author relies heavily on actual visits to schools.

250. Hylla, Erich and Friedrich O. Kegel. **Education in Germany** (revised edition, 1958). Frankfurt a/M.: Hochschule fuer Internationale Paedagogische Forschung, 1954
This booklet serves as a first orientation of the foreign reader to German education. It deals with the structure of the school system, trends toward equality of educational opportunity, higher education, teacher education, aims and accomplishments of recent reforms, and progress in educational research.

251. Hylla, Erich. "Recent Developments in Education in the Federal Republic of Germany." **Comparative Education Review**, 2 (June, 1958), 12-16.
Hylla calls attention to recent interest in East German developments but focuses on a report by German industrialists to alleviate shortcomings in the educational system.

252. Jordon, Gilbert J. "German School System." **Texas Outlook**, 36(May, 1952), 12-15.
Jordon gives a general overview of the school system, including universities.

253. Knoll, Joachim Hans. **The German Educational System**. Bad Godesberg: Inter Nationes, 1967.
This is a general survey of education in West Germany.

254. Lauwerys, Joseph A. "General Education in a Changing World." **International Review of Education**, 11 (1965), 385-403.
A look at general education in many national contexts, including Germany (pp. 393-94).

255. Lee, William B. and Wayne Dumas. "Education in Western Germany: A Five Minute Update." **Contemporary Education**, 50(Fall, 1978), 50-51.
The authors ask ten questions and suggest brief answers to these.

256. Lindgren, Alina M. **Germany Revisited: Education in the Federal Republic**. Washington: U.S. Office of Education, 1957. Bulletin No. 12.
In contrast to her study in the late 1930's, where she was very descriptive, Lindgren deals with issues that have become important in the postwar period. She looks at control issues, equality of educational opportunity, social studies, bridging the gap between elementary and secondary teachers, and an array of higher education issues such as academic freedom and examinations.

257. Lingens, Hans G. and Barbara Lingens. **Education in West Germany: A Quest for Excellence**. Bloomington, Indiana: Phi Delta Kappa, 1980. Fastback No. 140.
Educational history, structure, curriculum, teacher education and education for the disadvantaged are discussed from the perspective of a ficticious Schmidt family in West Germany. An informal but informative format is used.

258. Littmann, Ulrich. **An Introduction to the Confusion of German Education**. Bonn-Bad Godesberg: DAAD, 1974.

259. McClain, Edwin W. "An American Looks at Schools in Three European Cities." **International Education**, 2 (Feb., 1972), 56-60.
The author describes schools in three European cities, including Munich.

260. Mallinson, Vernon. "Education in West Germany Today." **Journal of Education** (London), 86(Dec.,1954), 541-44.

261. Merritt, Richard L. and others. "Political Man in Postwar West German Education." **Comparative Education Review**, 15 (Oct.,1975), 346-61.
The authors trace the changes that were imposed on postwar Germany, including curricular and structural reforms. They then describe a more recent and less visible change, which they label "behaviorist" that threatens the classical humanist tradition of German education.

262. "Miss Millar Tours West Germany." **Montana Education**, 41 (Sept., 1964), 35-35.
The Montana State Superintendant describes her impressions of the German system of education and teacher training.

263. Mitter, Wolfgang. "Education in the Federal Republic of Germany: The Next Decade." **Comparative Education**, 16(Oct., 1980), 257-65.
Mitter argues that the immediate future seems to be characterized by a remarkable state of tranquility. He offers five examples to support his case.

264. Poignant, Raymond. **Education and Development in Western Europe, the United States and the USSR: A Comparative Study**. New York: Teachers College Press, 1969.
Poignant gives descriptive data, analytical and comparative treatment, including data on West Germany.

265. Prange, Gordon W. and Alina M. Lindgren. **Education in the German Federal Republic**. Washington: U.S. Office of Education, 1954.
This is a brief mimeographed report.

266. OECD. **Educational Statistics in OECD Countries**. Paris: OECD, 1981.

267. Randall, Earle S. "Things Are Happening in Bremen Schools." **German Quarterly**, 28 (May, 1955), 168-74.
Discloses his experience during a week long visit and he feels the Bremen schools are contributing to individual and national progress.

268. Ringer, Fritz K. **Education and Society in Modern Europe**. Bloomington: Indiana University Press, 1979.
Ringer pays special attention to the development of national systems, especially in Germany, France, England, and America to 1960. He finds social and political conflicts especially crucial in interpreting the history of education.

269. Ringkamp, Henry. "Impressions of the German School System." **Journal of Secondary Education**, 37(Apr., 1962), 209-15.
The author touches on many issues, many of which are related to private and religious education.

270. Ringwald, Siegfried C. "Some Observations on German Schools." **Phi Delta Kappan**, 36 (June, 1955), 377-380.
The author explains what is needed in the German schools, including democratic values, social studies, extra-curricular activities. He also touches on the vocational aims of secondary education.

271. Roth, Heinrich. "Educational Organization in Germany." **Journal of Teacher Education**, 1 (Dec., 1950), 274-78.
Roth reviews the general structure of education, describes its problems, compares it with American education, and outlines teacher education.

272. Schueler, Herbert. "Education in West Germany." **Education**, 76 (Feb., 1956), 384-89.
Schueler contrasts democratic and communistic education, then looks at the German educational tradition, teacher status, religious conventions in the school and administrative arrangements.

273. Schieser, Hans. "West German Education." In Edward Ignas and Raymond J. Corsini (eds.). **Comparative Education Systems**. Itasca, Illinois: F.E. Peacock, 1981.
Looks at the evolution of West German education before turning to a complicated set of labels to illustrate the theory and practice of education. He also discusses roles of administrators, faculty, parents and students, then concludes with an overview of the system.

274. Schueler, Herbert. "Education in West Germany." **Education**, 76 (Feb., 1956), 384-89.
Laments the backward nature of German education. He feels it is a fine example of nineteenth century education seeking to make do in the twentieth.

275. Schultze, Walter and Christoph Fuehr. **Schools in the Federal Republic of Germany** (trans. by Eunice Herfarth). Weinheim: Julius Beltz, 1967.
This is a revised and updated version of the two earlier versions by E. Hylla and W. Wrinkle.

276. Standing Conference of Ministers of Education of the States of the Federal Republic of Germany. **The Educational System in the Federal Republic of Germany.** New York: College Entrance Examination Board, 1979.
The manuscript discusses (1) legislation, administration and planning, (2) the school system, (3) vocational training, (4) qualifications for admission to institutions of higher learning, and (5) the system of higher education.

277. Standing Conference of Ministers of Education of the States of the Federal Republic of Germany. **Report on the Development of Education in the States of the Federal Republic of Germany.** Bonn, 1973/74 and 1974/75.

278. Standing Conference of Ministers of Education of the States of the Federal Republic of Germany. **Major Trends in Educational Development, 1974-76 in the Federal Republic of Germany.**
A report presented at the 36th International Conference on Education, Geneva, Aug. 30-Sept 8, 1977.

279. Stokes, William S. Jr. "Education in West Germany." **The Review of Politics**, 42, 2(April, 1980), 191-215.
Stokes examines whether German schools promote virtue,morality or the development of enlightened public opinion. His focus is on the concept of emancipation, which plays a central role in the discussion of educational aims.

280. UNESCO. **Statistical Yearbook**. published from 1963 to the current date.

281. von Recum, Hasso. "Education in the Affluent Society: Problems and Conflicts." **International Review of Education**, 27 (1981), 3-14.
The author claims that education in affluent societies take on the nature of a commodity for private consumption. He relates this notion to West Germany and problems related to egalitarian and meritocratic goals.

282. Warren, Richard L. **Education in Rebhausen.** New York: Holt, Rinehart and Winston, 1967.
This is an anthropological study of a village in transition as a result of industrialization. Warren concentrates on the school, especially as a transmitter of the community culture and as a potential mediator of cultural change.

283. Wenke, Hans. **Education in West Germany.** Washington: Library of Congress, European Affairs Division, 1953.
This report offers a survey of the educational situation during the different phases of the postwar period, of the various problems and how they have been handled in theory and practice. It also looks at the organization of the system today and the planning for tomorrow with regard to teaching and teacher training.

284. Wenke, Hans. "Education and Morals: Germany." **Year Book of Education**, (1951), 515-40.
Wenke looks at the moral crisis in Germany, giving a legal basis for the moral situation, especially in the family and the world of work.

285. Wenke, Hans. "Germany." **Year Book of Education**, (1952), 352-85.
This is a general statement as to the relation between the state and the school, and the structure of the educational system.

286. Wilhelmi, Hans-H. "The School System in the Federal Republic of Germany." **Bildung und Wissenschaft**, 12-79, 1979, published by Inter Nationes.
After discussing the fundamental aspects of the historical development and management of the school system, the author raises questions and problems surrounding the system of education.

287. Williamson, William. "Patterns of Educational Inequality in West Germany." **Comparative Education**, 13 (Mar., 1977), 29-44.
The author looks at various data to demonstrate that inequality persists in German education. He argues that "cultural federalism" may be a luxury that Germany can no longer afford.

288. Wood, Charles L. "Schools of West Germany." **Clearing House**, 42 (Nov., 1967), 179-83.
Describes personal impressions of German education.

EAST AND WEST GERMANY

289. Caldon, Michael. "Strangely Conservative." **Times Educational Supplement**, 3264 (Dec. 30, 1977), 8-9.
A West German School teacher describes his visit to East German schools and compares the two Germanies.

290. Davis, Kathleen. "Nationalism in German Schools." **Educational Forum**, 18 (May, 1954), 443-450.
Davis provides an overview of historical nationalist tendencies in German schools which are being carried over to the textbooks in both East and West German schools.

291. "East-West Education Contrasted." **Virginia Journal of Education**. 58 (May,1965), 24.
Contrasts East and West Berlin after a three week study tour.

292. Hearnden, Arthur. **Education in the Two Germanies**. Oxford: Basil Blackwell, 1974.
Traces the changes in the educational systems that have occurred since the establishment of the German Democratic Republic and the Federal Republic of Germany. Emphasis is on curricular developments and structural changes of the system that social, political, and economic forces have had.

POLICY AND PLANNING

PRE-WORLD WAR II

293. Swift, Fletcher H. **European Policies of Financing Public Educational Institutions**. Berkeley: University of California Press, 1933-1939|. vol. 8, No. 4, 345-694.
The German section of this study covers the years 1927-37, and goes into great detail about the organization and administration of Prussian educational systems at all levels.

EAST GERMANY

294. Brandt, Willy. "In Search of Uniform Standards for the Educational System." **Western European Education**, 5 (Spring, 1973), 80-82.
An abstract of Brandt's statement to the Bundestag, Jan. 18, 1973.

295. Klein, Helmut and Ulrich Zueckert. **First-Hand Information Learning for Living Education in the GDR.** Dresden: Verlag Zeit im Bild, 1979.

The authors attempt to give the reader insight into educational policy and practice in East Germany, especially as it relates to equality of educational opportunity. Some documentation is included at the end of this small bulletin.

WEST GERMANY

296. Crowson, Robert L. "Educational Planning and School Reform: A Report on West Germany." **Educational Planning**, 2 4 (March, 1976), 53-63.

Reviews educational planning in West Germany and concludes that even though little seems to have happened, the plans have been a powerful stimulant to a nationwide disucssion and critique of its schooling system.

297. Enderwitz, Herbert. "Two German Educational Reform Schemes: The Rahmanplan and the Bremerplan." **Comparative Education Review**, 7 (June, 1963), 47-50.

298. Friemond, Hans. "Educational Planning in the Federal Republic." **German Tribune Quarterly Review**, 15 (Aug., 1971), 8-12.

299. Huden, Daniel P. "Teacher's Organizations and Educational Policy: The Case of the Federal Republic of Germany." **Western European Education**, 10 (Spring, 1978), 22-32.

Huden discusses the role of teachers in policy making in West Germany, which he views as minimal.

300. Huebener, Theodore. "Proposed Reforms in the German Schools." **Comparative Education Review**, 6 (June, 1962), 44-47.

Briefly sketches the various schools and how they are being affected, mainly by the **Rahmenplan**.

301. Kirkpatrick, Ursula. "The **Rahmenplan** for West German School Reform." **Comparative Education Review**, 4 (June, 1960), 18-26.

Provides a basic outline of the masterplan for reform, then cites current shortcomings of the present school system and how the new plan will change and improve that system, how traditional features will be retained, and what weaknesses exist in the reform plan.

302. Kneller, George F. "A Response to Papers on Education and Changing Cultural Ideas in Europe." **Comparative Education Review**, 15 (Oct., 1971), 362-66.
A response to papers, including that cited here by Richard L. Merritt. The author is sympathetic with that paper.

303. Mallinson, Vernon. **An Introduction to the Study of Comparative Education**.
The purpose of this volume is to provide a conspectus of the contemporary scene in matters of educational policy and practice in several countries of Europe, including West Germany, and to try to trace how and why common problems are being tackled in different ways and with what results. He deals extensively with national character and its role in various facets of education.

304. Michalski, Catherine. **Responses of England, Germany and Switzerland to Declining School Enrollments**. Commission on Declining School Enrollments in Ontario, Canada, Aug., 1978.
By interviews the author found resistance to change in all three countries. She makes comparisons with Ontario as well as recommendations.

305. O'Connor, Roger D. "Curriculum Planning in a German State." **Michigan Education Journal**, 41 (Jan., 1964), 21-22+.
The author looks at Northrhine-Westphalia and its secondary and elementary curriculum planning.

306. OECD. **Educational Policy and Planning: Germany**. Paris: OECD, 1972.
Part I explains the basic federative structure of West Germany and the resulting competencies and responsibilities for the educational system. Part II describes the state regulations of the educational system. Part III gives some future perspectives, and Part IV presents a quantitative analysis.

307. OECD. **Reviews of National Policies for Education: Germany**. Paris: OECD, 1972.

308. "Report of the Federal Government on Education, 1970." Sonderdruck, **Bildung und Wissenschaft**, 2 Bonn, 1970.
This is an important document in that it outlines the educational system and then provides the basic form that the federal government hoped to put into practice, in cooperation with the various states. It signals the first general program for comprehensive educational reform to take place in West Germany since the war.

309. Ryan, Leo V. "Proposed German Educational Reforms." **Catholic Education Review**, 64 (May, 1966), 327-30.
Reports on information given by Hans Dichgans, a member of parliament, on proposed reforms.

310. "Statement by the Conference of Education Ministers on the Occasion of the 150th Plenary Session in Munich on December 3, 1971." **Western European Education**, 4 (Spring, Summer, 1972), 120-23.
The statement focuses on the development of the educational system to improve equality of opportunity and to raise the general level of performance.

311. Thomas, Helga. "Innovation in Education: Germany." Report Prepared for OECD/CERI, 1971.
Thomas looks at school reform in West Germany, the motives for change, examples of innovations, and the planning of innovative processes, trends and problems.

312. Weiler, Hans. **The Politics of Educational Innovation--Recent Developments in West German School Reform.** A Report to the National Academy of Education, Stanford University, 1973.
This report is designed to inform about the politics of educational innovation in a non-American setting, and he concludes that education lags far behind the economic, social and political realities in Germany.

313. Wilson, Ian C. "Education and Politics: The Education Policy of the German Social Democratic Policy." **Oxford Review of Education**, 3 (1977), 37-56.

314. Wulf, Christoph. "Decision-Sharing Plans under Fire." **Times Educational Supplement**, 3038 (Aug. 17, 1973), 9.
Discusses attacks on state plans to allow schools greater independence.

EAST AND WEST GERMANY

315. Hearnden, Arthur. "Inter-German Relations and Educational Policy." **Comparative Education**, 9 (March, 1973).
Looks at the evolution of both Germanies since World War II. There is little about the relations between the two, but he expresses hope that such will occur.

REFORM OF EDUCATION

EAST GERMANY

No references found.

WEST GERMANY

316. Bateman, Kenneth A. "Innovation in German Schools." **Educational Leadership**, 25 (Mar., 1968), 541-51.
Bateman is impressed with the unified trend toward reform in school programs, organization, community participation. He looks at village school reform and comprehensive school trends.

317. Chiout, Herbert. "Significant Experiments in the German Federal Republic." **Year Book of Education**. (1959), 515-527.
The author provides a brief overview of the education system of West Germany and then outlines the major reorganization tendencies at the upper level of the elementary school, and concludes by describing experiments with Jena-plan schools and differentiated intermediate classes.

318. Fuehr, Christoph. **Educational Reform in the Federal Republic of Germany** (trans. by W. D. Halls). Hamburg: UNESCO Institute for Education, 1970.
This volume represents a collection of papers delivered at a conference of leading German educators held at Hamburg in July, 1968. It attempts to throw light on the discussion of educational reform in the Federal Republic.

319. Fuehr, Christoph. "The Role of the Educational Sciences in Educational Reform." **Western European Education**, 8 (Winter, 2976/77), 5-29.
Raises serious questions about the effectiveness of school reform in West Germany and other industrialized societies. He especially questions the primacy of economics in educational planning.

320. Fuehr, Christoph. "Review of Ten Years of Educational Reform in the Federal Republic of Germany, or Was There an Educational Catastrophe?" **Western European Education**, 6 (Winter, 1974/75), 38-51.
This was originally a radio broadcast on June 9, 1974.

321. Heidenheimer, Arnold J. "The Politics of Educational Reform: Explaining Different Outcomes of School Comprehensivization Attempts in Sweden and West Germany." **Comparative Education Review**, (Oct., 1974), 388-410.

The author compares two countries and concludes that the Social Democratic Party, operating in less than optimal conditions, will be unable to compete with bureaucracies and interest groups in bring about fundamental reform.

322. Metzner, Helga and Gunther Probst. "Wezlar, Hesse, Federal Republic of Germany." In **Case Studies of Educational Innovation: II, At the Regional Level.** Paris: OECD, 1976. pp. 153-212.

The study describes the slow process of reform in one German state, Hesse, using two specific reforms as cases: the 'orientation stage,' and the comprehensive school.

323. Nixdorff, Peter. "The Pace of West German Educational Reform as Affected by Land Politics." Ph.D. Dissertation, Gainesville, University of Florida, 1969.

324. OECD. **Innovation in Education: Germany**. Paris: OECD, 1971.

325. Richter, Ingo. "Educational Innovation and the Constitution." **Education and Urban Society**, 6 (Nov., 1973), 5-21.

The paper focuses on the relations of the politics of educational innovation and the interpretation of the constitution, using West Germany as a case in point.

326. Robinsohn, Saul B. and J. Caspar Kuhlmann. "Two Decades of Non-Reform in West German Education." In Saul B. Robinsohn (ed.). **Erziehung als Wissenschaft.** Stuttgart, 1973.

327. Rommel, Hans Georg. "Instruments for the Promotion of Creativity in Schools in the Federal Republic of Germany." In **Creativity of the School**. Paris: OECD, 1974.

328. Scanlon, David. "Some Comparative Reflections on German and Italian School Reforms." **Comparative Education Review**, 4 (June, 1960), 31-34.

329. Schultze, Walter. "Recent Changes in the Secondary Schools: Federal Republic of Germany." **Phi Delta Kappan**, 43 (Nov., 1961), 64-8.

Focus on the second road to higher education, the middle school, and vocational guidance.

330. Schuppe, Erwin. "State, Problems and Trends in the Development of the West German School System." **Comparative Education**, 5 (June, 1969), 125-38.
The author deals with schools of general education rather vocational schools.

331. Springer, Ursula K. "West Germany's turn to **Bildungspolitik** in Educational Planning." **Comparative Education Review**, 9 (Feb., 1965).
Springer reviews the trend away from the tradition of keeping secondary education as an institution for the elite because it is finally being recognized that public education is a socio-economic institution of national importance.

332. Whiting, Charles H. "Report from Europe." **Educational Forum**, 35 (Jan., 1971), 247-52.
Reports on democratization activities in Europe, including West Germany. Describes them as something akin to birth pains.

ADMINISTRATION OF EDUCATION

PRE-WORLD WAR II

333. Stratemeyer, Clara G. **Supervision in German Elementary Education, 1918-1933**. New York: Teachers College, Columbia University, 1930.

OCCUPATION AND REEDUCATION

334. Cornell, F. "Administration and German School Reform." **School Executive**, 69 (Dec., 1949), 35-6.

335. **School Fiscal Policy Study**. Frankfurt: U.S. Office of the High Commissioner for Germany, Education and Cultural Relations Division, 1950.

EAST GERMANY

336. **World Survey of Education V: Educational Policy, Legislation, and** Administration|. Paris: UNESCO, 1971.
East Germany treated on pp. 515-523.

WEST GERMANY

337. Aviner, Saronet. "Community Participation in School Management: A Parent's Eye View." **International Review of Education**, 26 (1980), 390-93.
A parent discusses community participation at the International School in Hamburg.

338. Bayer, Manfred and Gerhard E. Ortner. "Professional Development of Educational Administration: Fundamentals and Applications." **Educational Administration**, 7 (Winter, 1978/79), 82-106.
The aims and work of the Institute for Applied Studies in Educational Administration and Management are described. It is located at the Northrhine-Westphalian Research Center for Applied Studies in Educational Science.

339. Beattie, Nicholas. "Formalized Parent Participation in Education: A Comparative Perspective (France, German Federal Republic, England and Wales)." **Comparative Education**, 14 (Mar., 1978), 41-48.
The paper attempts to establish a preliminary framework for the study of parent participation in three countries. The author finds school inadequate in explaining the phenomenon and leads his readers to the political arena as a more adequate explanation.

340. Bessoth, Richard. "Educational Administration in the Federal Republic of Germany." In David Friesen and Farine Avigdor. **Comparative Educational Administration.** Edmonton, University of Alberta, Department of Educational Administration, 1977.

341. Bergen, John J. "The Councils of Ministers of Education in Canada and West Germany." **Education Canada**, 14 3 (Sept., 1974), 20-28.
This is a comparison of the goals and objectives, organizational structure, powers and influence, and achievements of the councils of ministers in Canada and West Germany.

342. Bessoth, Richard. "First Steps in an Emerging Field: Educational Administration Preparation in West Germany." **UCEA Review**, 19 2 (Feb., 1978), 1-7.

343. Bierfelder, W. "Pool of Talent and Recruitment for Management in the German Federal Republic." **Year Book of Education**, (1962), 458-71.
Examines data on the distribution of talent generally and the distribution of managerial talent in Germany. He also discusses coming imperatives for management.

344. Edding, Friedrich. "Educational Planning in West Germany." In George Z. F. Bereday and others (eds.). **World Year Book of Education**, (1967), 100-17.
Edding provides the institutional framework for planning, the level of interest since 1960, the problems involved, as well as the techniques and results in West Germany.

345. Edding, Friedrich. **International Developments of Educational Expenditure, 1950-1965**. Paris: UNESCO, 1969.

346. Glowka, Detlef. "Models of Participation in the School System of the Federal Republic of Germany." **Western European Education**, 7 (Winter, 1975/76), 5-23.
Glowka looks at new legislation, concepts of democracy, decentralization, the role of the **Bildungsrat**, and school laws, and legislative tendencies related to participation.

347. Hopes, Clive. "Professional Development for Heads of Educational Institutions in the Federal Republic of Germany." **Educational Administration**, 7 (Winter, 1979), 1-14.

348. Landers, Thomas J. "Preparation, Selection of Principals in West Germany--Perspectives for Americans." **NASSP Bulletin**, 65 (Feb., 1981), 78-86.
Landers discusses the state of educational administrator training in West Germany.

349. Noah, Harold and Joel Sherman. **Educational Financing and Policy Goals for Primary Schools: General Report.** Paris: OECD/CERI, 1979.
Includes a brief two page summary of Germany, drawn from the country report of Volume I (see OECD below).

350. Siewert, Peter and Helmut Kohler. In OECD. **Educational Financing and Policy Goals for Primary Schools. Vol. 1. Australia, Canada, Germany.** Paris: OECD/CERI, 1979.

351. Smart, Kenneth F. "Educational Administration and the Curriculum in West Berlin." **Educational Administration**, 5 (Autumn, 1976), 60-66.
Explains that West German examinations are internal in nature and how control is exercised and standards are assured in the absence of external examining boards.

352. Strevell, Wallace H. "Centralized Control Handicaps German Schools." **Nations Schools**, 50 (Sept., 1952), 52-60.
Maintains that Germany is a good example of the dangers of centralized educational control.

353. Wernecke, Hahns B. "Interprovincial Cooperation in Education in West Germany and Canada, 1945-69: The West German Conference of Ministers of Education and the Council of Ministers of Education (Canada)." Unpublished Doctoral Dissertation, University of Pennsylvania, 1970.

354. **World Survey of Education V: Educational Policy, Legislation, and Administration.** Paris: UNESCO, 1971. West Germany discussed on pp. 495-515.

355. Wulf, Christoph. "Pupil Participation Spreads to Helping Choose Head." **Times Educational Supplement**, 3024 (May 11, 1973), 11.
Discusses Hamburg City Council decision giving parents and pupils extensive say in running schools.

CURRICULUM AND METHODS

GENERAL CURRICULUM

EAST GERMANY

No references found.

WEST GERMANY

356. Achtenhagen, Frank. "Curriculum Development in the Federal Republic of Germany." In P. A. Taylor and M. Johnson. **Curriculum Development: A Comparative Study**. Atlantic Highlands N.J.: Humanities Press, 1975. Chapter 6.

After tracing the recent historical context for curriculum development, the author discusses the meaning given to curriculum, the state of research activities, and proposals for future work in the Federal Republic of Germany.

357. Beattie, Nicholas. "Public Participation in Curriculum Change: A West German Example." **Compare**, 7 (1977), 17-29.

The Hessen Minister of Education declared in 1973 that curriculum guidelines should be broadly discussed. The author traces the various points of view and forces behind and against this move.

358. Beauchamp, George A. and Kathryn E. Beauchamp. **Comparative Analysis of Curriculum Systems**. Wilmetter, Ill.: Kagg Press, 1972.

West Germany is one of the seven countries discussed. The main focus is on curriculum planning, implementation, evaluation, and products.

359. Davis, Mary D. "Curriculum for German Schools." **School Life**, 30 (Oct., 1947), 19-20.

The focus is on curriculum development in Hesse, with specific attention to kindergarten and curriculum aids.

360. Haller, I. and H. Wolf. "School-Based Curriculum Development in Hesse, Germany." **School-Based Curriculum Development**. Paris: OECD/CERI, 1979. pp. 187-236.

361. Springer, Ursula K. **Recent Curriculum Developments in France, West Germany, and Italy**. New York: Institute of International Studies, Teachers College, Columbia University, 1969.

The author attempts to shed some light on official school programs in three European countries, including West Germany. Her focus is on what is being taught and how programs are being arranged, and she devotes most of her attention to middle level education, which would begin at grade five.

AUDIO-VISUAL AIDS

EAST GERMANY

No references found.

WEST GERMANY

A. General

362. Bohlen, Adolf. "The History and Theory of Mass Media in Germany." **Year Book of Education**, (1960), 377-393.
Bohlen looks at the historical use of audio-visual aids in education and in general in Germany.

363. Bussman, H. "Programmed Learning in West Germany." **Times Educational Supplement**, 2869 (May 15, 1970), 51.

364. Rebenklauber, Arno. "Working with the Radio Recorder." **Educational Media International**, 2 (June, 1974), 6-10.
A teacher explains how he uses a radio-recorder.

365. Reman, Seigried. "Equipment and Systems for Still Photography in Schools." **Educational Media International**, 1 (March, 1975), 23-26.
General discussion of still photography equipment and systems in West Germany.

B. Computer Assisted Instruction

366. Allendorf, Otmar. "BAKKALAUREUS: The German Teaching System." **Visual Education**, (June, 1971), 25-26.
By 1970, the audio-visual feedback classroom, in conjunction with the computer BAKKALAUREUS, had been installed in several schools. Allendorf describes the structure of the system.

367. Hallworth, H. J. and others. "Computer-Aided Learning in the Federal Republic of Germany." A report prepared for the National Research Council of Canada, October, 1974.
A report of a visit by Canadian educational experts to West Germany to examine programs in Computer-Aided Learning, which is somewhat equivalent to the American notion of Computer Assisted Instruction (CAI).

368. Keil, Karl-August. "Cooperation in the use of Computers in Bavarian Schools." **Computers and Education**, 3 (1979), 17-22.
The author claims that the distribution of computers in German schools has reached a point where coordination of the activities and support of the teacher are indispensable. A method of the use of computers in Bavarian schools is described.

C. Films

369. Greetfeld, Hans. "Evolution of Educational and Teaching Films in the Federal Republic of Germany." **Educational Media International**, 3 (1979), 2-6.
The author reviews the historical development of teaching films in West Germany including the impact of media such n, as sound, television and videotape. He also explores the impact of the media on curriculum development and research.

D. Games and Simulation

370. Schran, Henning. "Urban Systems Gaming: Developments in Germany." **Simulation and Games**, 3 (Sept., 1972), 309-28.
The authors describe the evolution of the use of gaming and simulation techniques in West Germany. They pay particular attention to the use of games in studying urban environments (urban systems gaming). They suggest that there will be extensive use of these techniques for learning about urban environments.

TEXTBOOK DEVELOPMENT

EAST GERMANY

No references found.

WEST GERMANY

371. Becker, Joerg J. R. "Textbooks and the Political System in the Federal Republic of Germany: 1945-1975." **School Review**, 86 (Feb., 1978), 251-70.
Becker looks at the important role of the textbooks and their relationship to the teacher, the state and the administration. He traces the textbook, as a product and a factor of social processes, through three major phases of German history after World War II.

ART EDUCATION

EAST GERMANY

372. Halsall, Tom. "Towards a More Effective Art Education Curriculum: Comparing American Art Education Theory with Marxist/Leninist Art Education Theory in the German Democratic Republic." **Art Education**, 27 (Sept., 1974), 2-6.
The author claims art education that encourages people to participate in the shared objective reality is more beneficial than that which stresses social detachment and individuality.

WEST GERMANY

373. Boettcher, R. "Teaching Art to Children." **School Arts**, 50 (Jan., 1951), 150-53.
The role of art in the German school curriculum with its focus on artistic development and contact with the world of art is discussed.

374. Franz, Peter. **Cultural Policy in the Federal Republic of Germany: Studies and Documents on Cultural Policies**. Paris: UNESCO, 1974.
Surveys how various state agencies promote cultural life, with some attention given to the training of artists and art teachers and to art education.

375. Giffhorn, Hans. "Ideologies of Art Education." **Studies in Art Education**, 19 (1978), 50-60.
The author uses West Germany's educational practice and philosophy to illustrate the social and political consequences of ideologies and justifications of art education.

376. Krahmar, Catherine. "The Promotion of Artistic Creativity in West Germany." **Education and Culture**, 30 (Spring/Summer, 1976), 14-21.
Describes efforts by the West German government to stimulate and make art available to the widest possible public.

377. Soika, J. A. "German Art Education." **Studies in Art Education**, 5 (Spring, 1964), 67-74.
An overview of art education at every level. The author maintains its purpose is the development of the inner person. A description of how this is accomplished is also given.

378. Zimmerschied, Dieter. "Art and Education: Instruction in the Liberal Arts at Schools in the Federal Republic of Germany." **Bildung und Wissenschaft**, No. 4-76(e), 1976, Published by Inter Nationes.
The pamphlet looks at visual and music education at all levels.

CAREER EDUCATION

EAST GERMANY

No references found.

WEST GERMANY

379. "Career Education, German Style." **Phi Delta Kappan**, 55 (Sept., 1973), 37.
A summary of an address to the West German Chapter of Phi Delta Kappa by William B. Lee, who contrasts German and U.S. career education programs.

GERMAN LANGUAGE

EAST GERMANY

No references found.

WEST GERMANY

380. "Oral Methods Emphasized: German Comparisons." **Times Educational Supplement**, 2444 (Mar. 30, 1962), 572.
Report of a symposium on language teaching (German), which reported that oral methods are emphasized, written exams fairer, and teacher status is higher than in England.

HOME ECONOMICS

EAST GERMANY

No references found.

WEST GERMANY

381. Holtzclaw, Katherine. "Germany Plans Home Economics Education." **Journal of Home Economics**, 40 (May, 1948), 559-61.
She outlines the meagre offerings in home economics in Germany but explains the work in the reeducation efforts that is being done to expand the program.

MATHEMATICS EDUCATION

EAST GERMANY

382. "Educational Experimentation Concerning Mathematics." **International Bureau of Education Bulletin**, 37, 2 (1963), 79.

383. Homagk, Fritz. "Concerning Plane Geometry in the Textbooks of Classes 7 and 8." **Mathematics Teacher**, 60 (Feb., 1967), 165-72.
A translation of a publication in German about plane geometry in grades 7 and 8 in East Germany.

WEST GERMANY

384. Athen, Herman "Teaching of Vectors in the German Gymnasium." **Mathematics Teacher**, 59 (Apr., 1966), 382-93; (May, 1959), 485-95.
Because vector study has not been a part of American mathematics instruction, the editors invited Athen to describe the work being done in the German Gymnasium. this field was instituted shortly after World War II and plays a great role in combining geometry and algebra.

385. Bodenman, Paul S. "Secondary School Mathematics in the Federal Republic of Germany." **Mathematics Teacher**, 52 (Oct., 1959), 465-70.
Describes the educational system and the mathematics program in Baden-Wuerttemberg, including a brief account of subject matter in grades 5-13, textbooks, and examination procedures. A rejoinder by F. Malsch is found in 53 (Apr., 1960), 260+, where he explains how other states differ in their programs.

386. Kulm, Gerald. "Multiplication and Division Algorithms in German Schools" **Arithmetic Teacher**, 72 (May, 1980), 26-7.
Kulm gives examples of multiplication and division in a fourth grade arithmetic textbook.

MODERN FOREIGN LANGUAGE EDUCATION

PRE-WORLD WAR II

387. McMurry, Ruth Emily and others. **Modern Foreign Languages in France and Germany; The Training of Teachers and the Methods of Instruction**. New York: Teachers College, Columbia University, 1930.

EAST GERMANY

388. Moore-Rinvolucri, Mina. J. "Foreign Languages in the German Democratic Republic." **Modern Languages**, (June, 1966), 66-69.
Observes that foreign language learning in East Germany is serious business. Discusses foreign language programs, textbooks, language laboratories, diversity of methods of instruction, etc.

WEST GERMANY

389. McAndrew, Alex. "Seeing Once is Better than Hearing a Thousand Times." **NALLD Journal**, 10 (Autumn, 1975), 11-18.
This is a report of a study done of language centers in Germany and Japan using language laboratories and audio-visual approaches.

390. Black, Colin and Wolfgang Butzkamm. "Classroom Language: Materials for Communicative Language Teaching." **English Language Teaching Journal**, 32 (July, 1978), 270-74.
The authors have prepared materials with an 11th grade class where practice dialogues are developed originating in classroom situations. These materials are described in some detail.

391. "English Literature for Young German's Political Bias in Choice." **Times Educational Supplement**, 2041 (June 11, 1954), 577.
Describes what the correspondent feels is a sorry tradition set in the Kaiser period where the literature is intended to sow contempt for English manners and customs. Further discussion of this issue is found in 2042 (June 18, 1954), 605 and 2044 (July 2, 1954), 655.

392. Hoy, P. H. "The Early Teaching of Modern Languages." Committee for General and Technical Education, Council of Europe, April, 1977.
This is a summary of papers presented at a symposium from 20-25 Sept., 1976 in Denmark. Programs for language instruction in the lower grades are outlined.

393. Huebener, Theodore. "Teaching Foreign Languages in the Schools of West Germany." **Modern Language Journal**, 46 (Feb., 1962), 69-70.

394. Jung, Udo O. H. "The Language Laboratory and Foreign Language Teaching in Germany." **NALLD Journal**, 12 ((Spring/Summer, 1978), 21-32.
This is an unfavorable report of recent studies on the effectiveness of language laboratories. He recommends that language learning research is urgently needed.

395. Kahrs, Helga. "Teaching English as a Foreign Language." **Educational Forum**, 31 (Mar., 1967), 303-6.
Describes experiences in the upper level of the **Volksschule**, where she teaches English. She explains the English program generally and appeals for such undertakings with foreign languages in the U.S.

396. Koelle, Willi. "Teaching of English in German High Schools." **PMLA**, 71 (Apr., 1965), 21-30.
Discusses curricular patterns, objectives of English language teaching, methods of instruction, the syllabus, examinations, and the training of teachers.

397. Schloss, Brigitte. **The Uneasy Status of Literature in Second Language Teaching at the School Level: An Historical Perspective**. Quebec: International Center for Research on Bilingualism, 1981.
Schloss reviews secondary level second language programs in Germany, Great Britain, Canada, and the U.S.A, concluding that literature is virtually absent.

398. Seif, N. S. "The Teaching of Modern Languages in Belgium, England, Holland, and Germany." **Comparative Education Review**, 9 (June, 1965), 163-69.
A comparative study of four countries.

399. Verderber, Heide-Rose "English Language Series in School Broadcasting, W.D.R. Cologne." **Programmed Learning and Educational Technology**, 11 (Sept., 1974), 258-64.
W.D.R. Cologne now broadcasts 35 series of radio programs to schools; of these 31 have teacher's work books and sheets for pupils. The main focus here is on the English series.

EAST AND WEST GERMANY

400. Borsdorf, Hans Joachim. "A Comparison of the Image of the U.S.A. as portrayed in selected English language textbooks in East and West Germany." A Doctoral Dissertation, University of Sarasota, 1978.

MORAL EDUCATION

EAST GERMANY

No references found.

WEST GERMANY

Beattie, Nicholas. "Moral Education in the Real World: A Bavarian Case Study." **Journal of Moral Education**, 6 (May, 1977), 191-97.

Gives an account of the way moral education was added to the curriculum in 1977. Attention is drawn to certain inconsistencies and it is suggested that these reflect the ambiguous position of the school in a country whose commitment to pluralism remains partial.

MUSIC EDUCATION

PRE-WORLD WAR II

401. Livingstone, Ernest. "Place of Music in German Education from the Beginnings through the 16th Century." **Journal of Research in Music Education**, 15 (Winter, 1967), 243-77.

Actually begins with Charlemagne and takes the reader through the 16th century, indicating the place of music in the educational program at various periods. He draws heavily from Frederich Paulsen in the study.

EAST GERMANY

No references found.

WEST GERMANY

402. Cykler, Edmund A. "A Study of Comparative Music Education: An Evaluation of Techniques Employed in Elementary and Secondary Schools in Selected Foreign Countries." A research report to the U.S. Office of Education, December 31, 1971.
Includes West Germany in the report.

403. Eicke, K. "Duesseldorf School Music Program: Jugendmusikschule." **Music Educators Journal**, 50 (April, 1964), 73-4+.

404. Kraus, Egon. "School Music Education in Germany." **Music Educators Journal**, 42 (Apr., 1956), 25, 66-70.
Discusses the relative importance of music education in Germany, putting it in some historical context. He then discusses music teaching at the Volksschule, in the secondary schools, the teacher training institutes, and inservice training.

405. "Music in German Schools: Comparison with England." **Times Educational Supplement**, 1832 (June, 1950), 451.
Describes compulsory music requirements, contemporary attitudes toward music, and music teacher training.

406. Sands, L. B. "Audio-Visual Resources for Music." **Grade Teacher**, 77 (June, 1960), 28+.

PHYSICAL EDUCATION, RECREATION AND SPORTS

PRE-WORLD WAR II

407. Bolz, Wolfgang and Veronika Taping. "Pedagogic Reform and Sport--The Historical and Intellectual Development of Mutual Influences." **International Journal of Physical Education**, 17 (Fall, 1981), 15-23.
The authors trace the reform movement in education in all its various forms and makes some connection to sport.

EAST GERMANY

408. Bennett, B. L. "Visit to the German Democratic Republic." **Physical Education**, 23 (May, 1976), 98-101.
Account of a visit to the German College of Physical Culture in Leipzig, which trains physical education teachers and coaches.

409. Erback, Gunter and Edelfried Buggel. "Sociological Problems in the Presentation of Development Tendencies of Socialist Physical Culture in the German Democratic Republic." **International Review of Sport Sociology**, 7 (1972), 103-10.
The authors describe the role of sport in the socialist system of East Germany and explain how sport sociology interfaces with socialist physical culture.

410. Marschner, Paul. "Sports Education in the German Democratic Republic." **Prospects**, 6 (1976), 132-34.
A brief description.

411. Sabirov, I. A. "Gymnastics Lessons in the German Democractic Republic and Japan." **Soviet Education**, 16 (Feb., 1974), 108-114.
This Russian author describes personal impressions of new curricula for children in East Germany and Japan.

WEST GERMANY

412. Brock, N. "Mary Wigman Studio." **Journal of Health, Physical Education and Recreation**, 27 (Nov., 1956), 44-45+.
A descriptive account.

413. Goering, Oswald H. "Fifty Years of Outdoor Education in the Frankfurt, Germany Schools." **Journal of Outdoor Education**, 5 (Spring, 1971), 6-9.

414. Hammerman, Donald R. "Outdoor Education in Germany, Australia and Switzerland." Occasional Paper No. 11, Department of Outdoor Teacher Education, Northern Illinois University, Oregon, Illinois, 1979.
A series of brief papers highlight the programs at the Schullandheim in West Germany.

415. Howell, M. L. and M. L. van Vliet. 'Physical Education and Recreation in Europe." Department of National Health and Welfare, Ottawa, no date.
The authors look at six countries, including West Germany, in seeking to make recommendations for Canadian programs. The Cologne Sport High School and the Max Planck Institute in Dortmund (Arbeitsphysiologie) are highlighted.

416. Lotz, Franz. "German Sport Federation." **International Journal of Physical Education**, 16 (Summer, 1979), 26-28.

417. Richter, Lina and Gustav Richter. "Outward Bound in Germany." **Times Educational Supplement**, 2405 (June 23, 1961), 1304.
Describe the program at Wiessenhaus, where entire eighth and ninth grade classes spend a short term in an outward bound program.

418. Rust, Val D. and Terry Schofield. "The West German Sports Club System: A Model for Lifelong Learning." **Phi Delta Kappan**, 59 (April, 1978), 543-46.
A model for lifelong learning is presented, using the German Sports Club system as a case study. The role of sports in the schools is also outlined.

419. Schneider, Karl. "Problems and Practices of Health Education in the Federal Republic of Germany." **Journal of School Health**, 33 (Nov., 1963), 407-13.
In spite of the lack of professional health educators, some work is being done in health education. Prejudice against health education is great, but claims are made that this prejudice can be overcome.

420. Trent, John K. "Square Dancing in West Germany." **Journal of Health, Physical Education and Recreation**, 29 (Dec., 1958), 43.
Account of progress and how square dancing differs from German folk dancing.

READING AND READERS

EAST GERMANY

421. Grund-Slepack, Donna. "What Children are Reading in GDR Schools." **Interracial Books for Children Bulletin**, 8, 3 (1977), 10-13.
Analysis of children's readers in grades 1-6 in East Germany, focusing on sex roles.

WEST GERMANY

422. Tabbert, Reinbert. "The Impact of Children's Books: Cases and Concepts." **Children's Literature in Education**, 10 (Fall, 1979), Parts 1 and 2, 92-102, 144-50.
Part I concentrates on the possible impact of children's books using three basic concepts of reception theory. Part 2 looks at some results of empirical research related to readings and attitudes.

423. Jantzen, Marc J. "Teaching Reading in West Germany." **Elementary English**, 41 (Oct., 1964), 640-42.
Brief report based on a study tour. The author discusses the global and the synthetic methods of reading.

424. Orlow, Maria. "Literacy Training in West Germany and the United States." **Reading Teacher**, 29 (Feb., 1976), 460-67.
Outlines the reading problems in West German elementary schools and how German officials deal with them. She notes that programs are modeled to a considerable extent after American theory and practice.

425. Preston, Ralph C. "Reversals in Reading and Writing among German and among American Children." **Elementary School Journal**, 57 (Mar., 1957), 330-34.
This is a part of the study of Philadelphia-Munich kindergarten children.

426. Schwartz, Roswitha and Richard L. Allington. "A Comparison of American and West German Basal Texts." **Reading Teacher**, 3l (Dec., 1977), 280-82.
The authors conclude that basal readers in the two countries seem more often similar than dissimilar, suggesting that there maybe some inherent qualities in basal readers.

SCIENCE EDUCATION

EAST GERMANY

427. Falk, Doris F. "Some Problems in East German Science Education." **Science Education**, 48 (Oct., 1964), 330-33.
Provides a general overview of education, then outlines the science curriculum, training of teachers, and teacher salaries.

428. Klein, Margrete S. "Science Instruction in East Germany: Where Education Meets Ideology." **The Science Teacher**, 43, 9(Dec., 1978), 24-28.
Brief review of general and polytechnical education, showing the amount of science and technology required of students. Emphasizes compulsory nature of socialist education.

WEST GERMANY

429. Bach, Klaus-Dieter. "Some Remarks on Science Education in West Germany." **Science Education**, 60 (Apr.-June, 1976), 269-75.
The author responds to an article by H. Munson on science education in West Germany.

430. Baurmann, Erwin A. "Science Teaching in German Secondary Schools." **Science Education**, 43 (Apr., 1959), 268-70.
General overview of aims of German education and the purposes of science education in this context. He discusses some organizational factors involved.

431. Dumpert, Klaus. "An Inquiry into the Use of Living Organisms in Biological Education in West German Schools." **European Journal of Science Education**, 1 (July-Sept., 1979), 339-46.
Discussed is a study on the use of living organisms in biological instruction.

432. Haller, Hans-Dieter. "The Curriculum 'Children and Their Natural Environment' of the Working Group for Educational Research at Goettingen." **European Journal of Science Education**, 2 (Oct.-Dec., 1980), 457-59.
Described is an elementary science curriculum. Objectives are listed and attempts are made to integrate particular teaching concepts with the scientific way of looking at problems.

433. Haussler, Peter and June Pittman. **A Curricular Material Analysis System for Science**. Kiel: Institut fuer die Paedagogik der Naturwissenschaften, 1973.
The volume contains a German and an English version of the system which analyses five aspects of curriculum use: content, instructional methods, adaptiveness, effectiveness, and administration.

434. Millar, R. H. "Science Curriculum and Social Control: A Comparison of Some Recent Science Curriculum Proposals in the United Kingdom and the Federal Republic of Germany." **Comparative Education**, 17 (Mar., 1981), 23-46.
The author compares the work at IPN (Institute for Science Education) with English language curriculum efforts. He contrasts the social location of U.K. teachers and the German academics, and advances a "social control" model to explain the divergent trends in science education.

435. Munson, Howard. "An American's Observations on Science Education in the Federal Republic of Germany." **Science Education**, 60 (Apr.-June, 1976), 263-68.
The author was a Fulbright scholar in West Germany where he observed the practices and consulted with teachers and publishers associated with the new science curriculums. He also looked at teacher education practices related to science.

436. "News and Comment: Physics Teaching in Germany." **Physics Education**, 12 (Nov., 1977), 398.
This is a brief report of a survey taken of secondary physics teachers in West Germany.

437. Schaefer, Gerhard. "Frame Syllabus for Biology Teaching at Schools." **European Journal of Science Eduction**, 3 (Jan.-Mar., 1981), 47-61.
This is a frame syllabus for biology teaching covering the age range from six to 18 years. The topics listed can be used to prepare state-level biology syllabi and engage in curriculum reform.

438. Schaefer, G. and U. Kaffmann. "IPN Unit Bank Biology--A New Type of Biology Curriculum." **Journal of Biological Education**, 10 (Oct., 1976), 242-48.
IPN (Institute for Science Education) in Kiel, has developed single curriculum units since 1969 for biology teaching in the schools. These units are available as a flexible "unit bank." This article describes these units, their themes, etc.

439. Schlichting, Hans Joachim. "Energy and Energy Waste: A Topic for Science Education." **European Journal of Science Education**, 1 (Apr.-June, 1979), 157-68.
This is a criticism of current physics textbooks in West Germany. The author claims they fail to deal adequately with energy and energy waste. Suggestions are made as to how the physics teacher can contribute to the development of an appropriate attitude toward the energy crisis.

440. Weltner, Klaus. "The Development of Study Techniques by Integrated Master Programmes." **British Journal of Educational Technology**, 8 (Jan., 1977), 34-44.
Describes a series of independent study guides which accompany a mathematics textbook. Two experiments are discussed. The first to test the effectiveness of personal tuition vs. independent study, and the second is to show the effect of independent study on student teachers. They were shown to be more effective than the lecture course.

441. Westphal, Walter. "Physics Curriculum Work at IPN, Kiel." **Physics Education**, 12 (Jan., 1977), 32-37.
Discusses physics programs being developed at IPN (Institute for Science Education) at Kiel, West Germany.

SOCIAL STUDIES

PRE-WORLD WAR II

442. Bason, Cecilia. **Study of the Homeland and Civilization in the Elementary Schools of Germany**. New York: Teachers College, Columbia University, 1937.

OCCUPATION AND REEDUCATION

443. Anderson, Howard R. "A Program of Social Studies for German Schools." **School Life**, 30 (Oct., 1947), 14-15.
Anderson, a member of the U.S. Education Mission to Germany, outlines his thinking of social studies guidelines in the re-education program.

444. **International Workshop of Social Studies: Proceedings and Suggestions for the Formation of Social Studies in the Public Schools of Germany**. Frankfurt: U. S. Office of the High Commissioner for Germany, Office of Public Affairs, 1951.

445. Kelty, Mary G. "Specific Advances in Germany's New Task of Social Education." **Social Education**, 13 (Jan., 1949), 15-21.
Argues for the need to develop democratic living and worldmindedness in Germany, then traces the writing of new school history texts in Berlin.

446. Singer, Kurt. "American Evolution in German Textbooks." **Catholic School Journal**, 51 (Apr., 1951), 42+.
Reports that German textbooks are being humanized and internationalized.

EAST GERMANY

447. **Contribution made by Curricula and Textbooks, Particularly for History and Social Studies, Towards Implementing the Recommendations Concerning Education for International Understanding, Cooperation and Peace and Education Relating to Human Rights and Fundamental Freedoms, Adopted by the 18th Session of the General Conference of UNESCO, 1974) in the German Democratic Republic**. Berlin: Volk und Wissen, 1981.

448. Huebener, Theodore. "History as Taught Through East German Textbooks." **School and Society**, 99 (Jan., 1971), 56-9.
The author focuses on the history texts published by the state in pointing out how communism strives toward peace and how Western democracies are corrupt, war-minded and monopolistic autocracies.

WEST GERMANY

449. Arndt, Christian O. "Teaching the Nazi Period in the German Gymnasium." **School and Society**, 88 (Nov. 19,1960), 442-44.
Report of a four week visit to history classes in several West German cities. He looks at the students in general, and the teachers and their teaching. He concludes that the Nazi period is treated lightly in most classes.

450. Bunn, Ronald F. "Treatment of Hitler's Rise to Power in West German School Textbooks." **Comparative Education Review**, 6 (June, 1962), 34-43.
The author looks at eight modern history textbooks individually, then makes generalizations about their treatment of Hitler's rise to power.

451. Dumas, Wayne and William B. Lee. **Social Studies in West German Schools: First Hand Perspectives for Educators**. Columbia, Mo.; University of Missouri Press, 1978.
The authors look at **politische Bildung** as it takes place in German schools. They do so by putting it in the context of the school system and the Social Democratic Party curricular plans. They have chapters on curriculum, instructional goals, methods and education of teachers. They conclude by reflecting on implications for American social studies teachers.

452. Dumas, Wayne and Willaim B. Lee. "Politische Bildung: The Social Studies in West Germany." **History Teacher**, 9 (Feb., 1976), 228-43.
After providing some contextual information, the authors look at the sequence and content, instructional goals, methods of instruction, materials used, and classroom tone of West German social studies courses.

453. Forsbach, Marlene. "The School as a Democratic Institution: The Problems of Teaching Social Studies in the Federal Republic of Germany." **Inter Nationes**, (1974), 1-11.
Describes attempts of various states to develop guidelines for teachers in which social studies becomes more than imparting knowledge.

454. Foster, Charles R. "Civic Education in the United States and the Federal Republic of Germany." **Western European Education**, 8 (Fall, 1976), 5-29.
The author points out certain areas of contention within the field of civic education in both the U.S. and West Germany. He notes factors that influence civic education and compares the status and perceived future in the two countries.

455. Fries, Gunter. "Methods of History Teaching in the Ninth School Year." **Western European Education**, 3 (Summer-Fall, 1971), 145-53.
A **Hauptschule** teacher writes about his experiences teaching history. He gives some detail on instructional activities using textbooks, documents, reports, and student projects.

456. Glum, Friedrich. "Political Education: A Survey of France, U.S.A., Great Britain, and West Germany." **International Review of Education**, 1 (1955), 166-69.

457. Hagener, Caesar. "On the Project 'Party Democracy.'" German Studies Notes published by the Institute of German Studies, Indiana University, 1976.
Describes a curriculum project on political party democracy in West Germany developed mainly for grades 9-10.

458. History Teaching in Germany: The Brunswick Group." **Times Educational Supplement**, 1815 (Feb. 10, 1950), 97.
Describes the work of Georg Eckert in producing "Aids to the Teaching of History."

459. Holtzmann, Antonius. "Some Remarks on the Theory of Political Education." Bloomington, Indiana: Institute of German Studies, Indiana University, 1976. pp. 1-49.
The author explores pedagogical assumptions of political education in West Germany. He discusses the normative ontological, empirical analytical, and dialectical-historical orientations.

460. Huebener, Theodore. "What is German Youth Taught about the Nazis?" **German Quarterly**, 35 (Mar., 1962), 171-78.
Provides examples, written and observed, of direct confrontation with the Nazi period by students. The paper is anecdotal in nature.

461. Kuhn, Annette. "Social Studies in the Federal Republic of Germany." In Howard D. Mehlinger and Jan L. Tucker (eds.). **Teaching Social Studies in Other Nations**, Bulletin No. 60. Washington D.C.: National Council for Social Studies, 1979. pp. 15-28.

462. Kuhn, Annette. "Leading Positions in Political Education in the Federal Republic of Germany Today." **International Journal of Political Education**, 1 (1977), 33-43.
Looks at neoconservatives, liberals, and socialists in terms of political education.

463. LaFollette, Robert. "History Textbooks and International Understanding." **Social Education**, 17 (May, 1953), 201-6.
Discusses the American-German Historian and History Teacher Workshop Conference in Brunswick, Germany from May 12-23, 1952, to resolve issues in history interpretation.

464. Marchant, E. C. **Education in Europe: The Teaching of Geography at School Level**. London: George Harrap, 1971 (for the Council of Europe).
Includes a brief overview of geography courses at every level in West Germany.

465. Marsden, W. E. "The German Geography Project." **Teaching Geography**, (Jan., 1979), 128-30.
The author describes a West German curriculum research project for spatial sciences, its chronology, organization, content, evaluation, and dissemination.

466. Merritt, Richard L. and others. "Democratizing West German Education." **Comparative Education**, 7 (Dec., 1971), 121-36.
Focuses on curricular changes, especially social studies but also deals with the role of the family and structural changes. He finds democratization is taking place on an accelerated level.

467. Minssen, Friedrich. "Political Education in the Schools of the Federal Republic of Germany." Bloomington, Indiana: Institute of German Studies, Indiana University, 1976. pp. 1-33.
Looks at social studies K-12, including its purpose, empirical studies dealing with the results of political education and the problems related to political education.

468. Morrissett, Irving and Ann M. Williams. **Social/Political Education in Three Countries**. Boulder, Colo.: Social Science Education Consortium, Eric Clearinghouse for Social Studies/Social Science Education, 1981.

469. Neumeister, Hermann. "Education for International Understanding in the Federal Republic of Germany." **Phi Delta Kappan**, (Jan., 1970).
Describes efforts to impart international understanding in social studies, languages, teacher and student exchanges and school correspondence.

470. Pillsbury, Kent. "International Cooperation in Textbook Evaluation: The Braunschweig Institute." **Comparative Education Review**, 10 (Feb., 1966), 48-52.
Focus here is on the work being done on history textbook revision.

471. Rebel, Karlheinz. "Social Studies: A Multimedia Study Project in the Education Section of West Germany's South-West Broadcasting Company." German Studies Notes published by the Institute of German Studies, Indiana Universtiy, 1977.

472. Renken, Gerd. "The Stony Path Toward Responsible Citizenship, Forms of Political Education in the Federal Republic of Germany." **Western European Education**, 6 (Winter, 1974/75), 52-68.
Traces the history of civic education but maintains much needs to be done. He looks at experiments with political newspapers, and the integration of vocational and political education.

473. Shafer, Susanne M. "American Social Studies in West German Schools." **Comparative Education Review**, 8 (Oct., 1964), 146-52.
An account of attempts to impose American social studies in the American zone, and some measure of their successes and failures.

474. Sussmuth, Hans. "Curriculum Development in Political Education: A Report on the Federal Republic of Germany." **Teaching Political Science**, 8(Apr., 1981), 363-84.
Discusses guidelines for political education in two West German states. These curriculum development projects also deal with the advantages and disadvantages of integrating social science disciplines.

475. Ulsofer, Robert. "Political Education in German Instruction: Three Models of a Politically Oriented Pedagogy." **Deutschunterricht**, 24 (1972), 5-18.

476. Wirth, Fremont P. "Broadening the Bavarian Curriculum." **Educational Leadership**, 6 (Oct., 1948), 12-14.
Provides a glance at the scope of courses offered in Bavarian schools and how the need for social studies in the curriculum is being met.

477. Young, Anne P. "Germany, History, and the Nazi Past." **Social Education**, 45 (Feb., 1981), 86-98.
The author looks at the history of the Nazi period as it is treated in the West German secondary schools. She looks at scholarly work on the period, how it influences secondary teachers, the impact of reforms on history, and the effects of actions by the government. She concludes that students learn enough to determine to avoid any recurrence.

EAST AND WEST GERMANY

478. Krug, Mark M. "Teaching of History at the Center of the Cold War: History Textbooks in East and West Germany." **School Review**, 69 (Winter, 1961), 461-87.

SPEECH

EAST GERMANY

No references found.

WEST GERMANY

479. Hadwiger, K. E. and others. "West German Speech Education and the SCA: Toward a Truly International Association." **Speech Teacher**, 21 (Jan., 1972), 15-21.

TEACHERS AND TEACHER ORGANIZATIONS

PRE-WORLD WAR II

480. Learned, William S. **The Oberlehrer: A Study of the Social and Professional Evolution of the German Schoolmaster**. Cambridge: Harvard University, 1914.

Assesses the schoolmaster through various historical periods in Germany and concludes with observations of the solidarity of schoolmaster and its professional significance. He ends the manuscript by reflecting on possible American applications. He draws heavily from F. Paulsen in the study.

481. Lynch, James. "The Birth of a Profession: German Grammar School Teachers and New Humanism." **Comparative Education Review**, 16 (Feb., 1972), 89-97.

Attempts to show how and with what instruments the elite grammar school profession was established during the nineteenth century.

482. Olson, James M. "The Social Views of Prussian Primary School Teachers during the Wilhelmian Era." **Paedagogica Historica**, 15 (1975), 73-89.

OCCUPATION AND REEDUCATION

483. Lederer, J. "Teacher Organizations in Germany." **Minnesota Journal of Education**, 29 (Dec., 1948), 15.

EAST GERMANY

484. Hahn, Walter. "Teachers under Communism - The Case of East Germany." **Educational Leadership**, 30 (Jan., 1973), 331-35.

Hahn describes the East German system of teacher education, teaching positions and salaries, and expresses hope that East Germany will break away from its isolation.

WEST GERMANY

485. Blaettner, Fritz. "West Germany." **Year Book of Education**, (1953), 324-42.
Discusses teachers, financial elements, status in the various groups and teacher unions.

486. **The Changing Role of Teachers Required by Educational Innovations**. Berlin: Max-Planck Institute, 1965.

487. Dunham, Jack. "An Exploratory Comparative Study of Staff Stress in English and German Comprehensive Schools." **Educational Review**, 32 (Feb., 1980), 11-20.
The author compares staff stress in two West German and two English comprehensive schools. From questionnaires and interviews, the author found greater reported stress in England with Germans more certain of role responsibilities and ability to participate in decision-making.

488. Fine, Benjamin. "New German Teacher and Student." **Educational Forum**, 26 (Mar., 1962), 261-72.
Finds both teachers and students to reflect alert democratic tendencies.

489. Fuhrig, Wolf D. "West Germany." In Albert Blum (ed.). **Teacher Unions and Associations**. Urbana: University of Illinois Press, 1969.
Fuhrig traces, historically, the development of the teaching professions in Germany. He breaks the periods down to (1) beginnings to 1849, (2) 1849 to 1933, (3) after 1945. He distinguishes between the academic secondary teachers and those teaching in the common schools.

490. Gouault, J. M. **Synthesis Study of Educational Leave in the European Community**. Social Policy Studies No. 26. Brussels: Commission of European Communities, 1975. pp. 121-68.
The study is concerned with leaves of absence in EEC countries and gives an account of worker leaves in West Germany.

491. Jonas, B. "Committee of German Physical Education Teachers." **International Journal of Physical Education**, 16 (1979), 28-30.
Describes the Ausschuss Deutscher Leibeserzieher.

492. Kisiel, Chester A. "Some Perspectives on the Role of the German Teacher." **School Review**, 74 (Autumn, 1966), 292-318.
Traces the origins of the elementary and secondary teacher and his current status. Assumes that social class values and their historical roots predominate in recruiting to the professions.

493. Kob, Janpeter. "Teacher in Industrial Society." **Year Book of Education**, (1963), 390-98.
Looks at the teaching profession in the context of industrialization, the teacher's social status, and the teacher's specialized social role.

494. Luttringer, Jean-Marie and Bernard Pasquier. "Paid Educational Leave in Five European Countries." **International Labor Review**, 119 (July-August, 1980), 407-23.
Looks at educational leave provisions in legislation in Belgium, France, West Germany, Italy, and Sweden, then compares aims, ways of organizing leaves, and financing leaves.

495. OECD, **Training, Recruitment, and Utilization of Teachers: Germany, Belgique, United Kingdom**. Paris: OECD, 1969.

496. OECD. **Training, Recruitment, and Utilization of Teachers**. Paris: OECD, 1969.
Discusses the issue in all OECD countries.

EAST AND WEST GERMANY

497. International Labour Office. **Teacher's Pay**. Geneva: ILO, 1978.
Considers teachers' pay in 27 countries, including East and West Germany.

498. International Labour Office. **Employment and Conditions of Work of Teachers**. Geneva: ILO, 1981.
Considers world-wide employment trends, teacher surplus and shortages, class size and pupil/teacher ratios, health and safety, and teachers in rural and isolated areas. A number of references to the two Germanies are made.

PUPILS

GENERAL

EAST GERMANY

499. Belding, Robert E. "School Impressions from Gudron." **Education**, 81 (Mar., 1961), 440-43.
Report of an interview with a refugee in West Berlin about her experience in coming to Berlin and the schooling she underwent.

500. Erickson, Harold B. "East German Youth Decide for Themselves." **California Journal of Secondary Education**, 31 (Feb., 1956), 75-78.
Report on secondary education with an emphasis on the resistance of youth to communist indoctrination.

501. Leonhard, Wolfgang. **Child of the Revolution** (trans. by C. M. Woodhouse). Chicago: H. Regnery, 1958.
This is a story of a young German who was reared in Russia but finds his way to East Germany and eventually comes West, while remaining committed to Marxism. He details his life as a Soviet student as well as experiences in East Germany. An important personal life story.

Youth Organizations in East Germany

502. Lottich, Kenneth V. "Extracurricular Indoctrination in East Germany." **Comparative Education Review**, 6 (Feb., 1963), 209-11.
Describes the various youth organizations in East Germany.

503. "Youth in East Germany." **Survey**, 87 (Oct., 1951), 417.
A report published anonymously by a former school teacher in East Germany giving an account of the FDJ (Free German Youth), an organization set up by the Communists for young people.

WEST GERMANY

504. Kischke, Martina I. "Adults of Tomorrow." **Inter Nationes**, SR 1-79, (1979), 1-16.
A collection of brief articles which were written in West Germany and compiled for the International Year of the Child. Many of these touch on education.

505. Shafer, Susanne M. "Germany's European Children." **Teachers College Record**, 65 (Jan., 1964), 361-71.
Assesses the dramatic differences that exist between youth and the older generation in Germany, and the problems this creates as well as the opportunities it offers.

ACHIEVEMENT OF PUPILS

EAST GERMANY

No references found.

WEST GERMANY

A. General

506. Foshay, Arthur W. and Robert L. Thorndike. **Educational Achievements of Thirteen Year Olds in Twelve Countries**. Hamburg: UNESCO Institue for Education, 1962.
This is to be considered a pilot study of short answer testing of children in many countries to discover the possibilities and difficulties attending large scale international studies. The study formed the basic framework for the International Achievement Studies during the next two decades. Germany was one of the countries in this pilot study.

507. Husen, Torsten. "Policy Implications of Individual Differences in Learning Ability: A Comparative Perspective." **Scandinavian Journal of Educational Research**, 22 (Dec., 1978), 173-91.
Husen uses Germany as one example of how the diversity-unity problem is dealt with in education, especially regarding learning ability differences.

508. Schwarzweller, Harry K. "Scholastic Performance, Sex Differences, and the Structuring of Educational Ambition among Rural Youth in Three Societies." **Rural Sociology**, 41 (Summer, 1976), 194-216.
The paper looks at youth in Germany, Norway, and America and the author finds that the effect of scholastic ability on educational ambition is reinforced by the influence of social origins in all three countries.

509. Walker, D. **The IEA Six Subject Survey: An Empirical Study of Education in Twenty-One countries.** Stockholm: Almquist and Wiksell International; New York: Wiley-Halsted Press, 1976.

B. Achievement Related to Special Subjects

1. Literature

510. Purves, Alan C. **Literature Education in Ten Countries.** New York: John Wiley, 1974.
This is one of the International Association for the Evaluation of Educational Achievement (IEA) studies, which includes West Germany.

2. Mathematics

511. "How the U.S. Compares with Other Countries." **Educational Leadership**, 38 (Feb., 1981), 368-70.
This is an account of a NSF claim that the U.S. lags behind the Soviet Union, Japan, and West Germany in science and mathematics education.

512. Husen, Torsten (ed.). **International Study of Achievement in Mathematics: A Comparison of Twelve countries.** Stockholm: Almquist and Wiksell International; New York: John Wiley, 1967. 2 vols.
This study of 12 countries, including West Germany, assesses the mathematics achievement of young people in various systems. The major focus is on the relationship between input variables and mathematics outcomes and comparisons are made between both input and output.

3. Reading

513. Biglmaier, F. "Germany." In John Downing (ed.). **Comparative Reading: Cross National Studies of Behavior and Processes in Reading and Writing**. New York: Macmillan, 1973.

514. Klein, Howard A. "A Closer look at Cross-Cultural Sex Differences in Reading." **Reading Teacher**, 32 (Mar., 1979), 660-64.
Here is a reassessment of Ralph Preston's study of American and German children. Klein argues that the study of Preston may have been overgeneralized by others.

515. Preston, Ralph C. "Reading Achievement of German and American Children." **School and Society**, 90 (Oct. 20, 1962), 350-54.
Results of a study done in collaboration with Walter Schultze to assess reading ability of school children in Philadelphia and Wiesbaden.

516. Preston, Ralph C. "Issues Raised by the Philadelphia-Wiesbaden Reading Study." **Comparative Education Review**, 7 (June, 1963), 61-65.
Responds to criticisms and interpretations of a reading study conducted by himself and Walter Schultze in 1959. (See **School and Society**, xc (Oct. 20, 1962), for data on the original study.

517. Preston, Ralph C. "Comparisons of Knowledge and Directions in German and American Children." **Elementary School Journal**, 57 (Dec., 1956), 158-60.
A part of the Philadelphia-Wiesbaden study, where American children scored well in comparison with the Germans.

518. Preston, Ralph C. "Reading Achievement of German Boys and Girls Related to Sex of Teacher." **Reading Teacher**, 32 (Feb., 1979), 521-26.
A study of Hamburg School children found that the sex of the teacher had no effect on either the boy's or girl's reading achievement, casting doubt on the claim that elementary school children are being feminized.

519. Preston, Ralph C. "Comparison of Word Recognition skill in German and American Children." **Elementary School Journal**, 53 (Apr., 1953), 443-46.
A study of Munich and Hamburg elementary pupils.

520. Preston, Ralph C. "A Comparative Study of the Achievement of German and American Children." In **Changing Concepts of Reading Instruction, Proceedings of the Sixth International Reading Association**. New York: Scholastic Magazine, 1969.

521. Thorndike, Robert L. **Reading Comprehension Education in Fifteen Countries**. New York: John Wiley, 1973.
This is one of the International Association for the Evaluation of Educational Achievement (IEA) studies, which includes West Germany.

4. Science

522. Comber, L. C. and John P. Keeves. **Science Education in Nineteen Countries**. New York: John Wiley, 1973.
This is one of the International Association for the Evaluation of Educational Achievement (IEA) studies, which includes West Germany.

C. Social Sciences and Attitudes of Pupils

523. Baker, Kendall L. "Political Participation, Political Efficacy, and Socialization in Germany." **Comparative Politics**, 6 (Oct., 1973).
An analysis of a survey taken of German youth. The findings indicate a high sense of political efficacy, but a low expectation of actual political participation. The author also believes the socialization process is important in the development of some political attitudes, whereas in the growth of others it is the socialization agent.

524. Dennis, Jack and others. "Political Socialization to Democratic Orientations in Four Western Systems." **Comparative Political Studies**, 1 (Apr., 1968), 71-100.
The authors studied samples of children of three age ranges in the U.S., U.K., West Germany, and Italy and found Germany to exhibit anti-democratic feeling in more areas than do the youth of the other three countries.

525. Kattmann, Ulrich. "The Attitudes of 11-Year-Old Pupils Toward People of Other Races." **Studies in Educational Evaluation**, 5 (1979), 243-52.
Kattmann uses a semantic differential scale to assess the racial prejudices of fifth graders to determine what effect teaching about race has on these prejudices. He found that prejudice, at least in Germany, can be reduced.

526. Lawson, Robert F. "Comparison of Political Attitudes Among a Sample of Urban Youth in West Germany and Canada." **International Review of Education**, 19 (1973), 460-78.

527. Lawson, Robert F. "Developing Democratic Attitudes in German Schools." **Journal of Education**, 13 (May, 1967), 71-77.

528. Oppenheim, Abraham. **Civic Education and Participation in Democracy: The German Case**. London: Sage, 1977.

529. Oppenheim, A. N. and Judith Torney. **The Measurement of Children's Civic Attitudes in Different Nations.** New York: John Wiley, 1974.
This is one of the International Association for the Evaluation of Education Achievement (IEA) studies, which includes West Germany.

530. Spada, Hans and others. "Student Attitudes toward Nuclear Power Plants: A Classroom Experiment in the Field of Environmental Psychology." **Studies in Educational Evaluation**, 3 (Summer, 1977), 109-28.
This is a discussion of a project on nuclear power plants and problems of energy supply were analysed. Some positive outcomes were measured although others were disappointing.

EDUCATION AND EMPLOYMENT

531. Schwarzweller, Harry K. "Educational Aspirations and Life Chances of German Young People." **Comparative Education**, 4 (Nov., 1967), 35-49.
Reports a study of aspirations and the factors that affect life chances at different levels of schooling.

532. Schwarzweller, Harry K. "Community of Residence and Career Choices of German Rural Youth." **Rural Sociology**, 33 (March, 1968), 46-63.
The paper explores whether or not the degree of rurality affects career choices of young West Germans. The author finds this is the case, even when controling for social class.

533. Suda, Zdenek. "Universal Growth of Educational Aspirations and the 'Overequalization' Problem: Conclusions from a Comparative Data Analysis." **European Journal of Education**, 14 (June, 1979), 113-64.
The author looks at educational aspirations and overqualification in Finland, France, West Germany, Poland, and the United States. He provides a theoretical background before looking at data on aspirations and overqualification.

534. von Dohnanyi, Klaus. **Education and Youth Employment in the Federal Republic of Germany**. Berkeley: Carnegie Foundation for the Advancement of Teaching, 1978.

535. von Dohnanyi, Klaus. "Federal Republic of Germany." In Margaret S. Gordon (ed.). **Youth Education and Unemployment Problems: International Perspectives**. Berkeley: Carnegie Foundation for the Advancement of Teaching, 1979.
Brief overview of the unemployment situation in West Germany, including observations about changes in apprenticeship, educational issues and policies and juvenile delinquency.

Chapter 6

SPECIAL GROUPS IN SCHOOL

EDUCATION OF GIRLS

PRE-WORLD WAR II

536. Bernstein, George and Lottelore Bernstein. "The Curriculum for German Girls' Schools, 1870-1914." **Paedagogica Historica**, 18 (1978), 275-95.

537. Green, Lowell. "The Education of Women in the Reformation." **History of Education Quarterly**, 19 (Spring, 1979), 93-116.

The investigation has shown that Reformation leaders not only advocated an education for everyone, including women, but that they also carried out these aspirations in a notable manner.

EAST GERMANY

538. Grund-Slepack, Donna and Marvin J. Berlowitz. "Sex Role Stereotyping in East German versus U.S. Textbooks." **Reading Teacher**, 31 (Dec., 1977), 275-79.

In a study of elementary school textbooks the authors found that the image of women in East Germany is generally more positive than in the United States. Females appear more often in career roles and males are less dominant.

WEST GERMANY

539. Byrne, Eileen M. **Equality of Education and Training for Girls (10-18 years)**. Brussels: Commission of the European Communities, 1980.
Looks at equality issues in nine countries including West Germany.

EDUCATION OF MINORITIES

PRE-WORLD WAR II

540. Levine, Herbert S. "Educating Jewish Children in Weimar and Nazi Germany." **Integrated Education**, 13 (Sept.-Oct., 1975), 33-36.

EAST GERMANY

No references found.

WEST GERMANY

541. Altschull, J. Herbert. "Germany's Guest Workers." **Phi Delta Kappan**, 62 (June, 1981), 708-09.
Like the U. S., Germany is finding it difficult to integrate ethnic minorities into its society. The resulting "social erosion" is most apparent in German schools.

542. "Bibliography: Education of Minorities." **World Year Book of Education**, (1960), 361-91.

543. Castles, Stephen. "The Social Time-Bomb: Education of an Underclass in West Germany." **Race and Class**, 21 (Spring, 1980), 369-89.
Reviews with situation of the migrant workers and their children's education, which he feels contributes to the formation of an explosive new underclass in the country.

544. Council of Europe. **Country Reports: Federal Republic of Germany**. Strasbourg: Council of Europe, 1975.
Deals with the measures adopted to deal with the education of the children of migrant workers.

545. Council of Europe. **Ad Hoc Conference on the Education of Migrants**. Strasbourg: Council of Europe, 1974.

546. Council of Europe. **The Integration of Migrant Children into Preschool Education**. Strasbourg: Council of Europe, 1976.
A working paper presented at a symposium from Dec. 6-11, 1976 in Berlin. It was intended as a stimulus for discussion of problems during the symposim rather than a report of the discussion itself.

547. Gutfleisch, Ingeborg and Bert-Olaf Rieck. "Immigrant Workers (Gastarbeiter) in West Germany: Teaching Programmes for Adults and Children." **World Year Book of Education**, (1980), 341-58.

548. Kirkman, S. "Separate Classes Prompt Allegations of Introducing Apartheid." **Times Educational Supplement**, 3370 (Jan. 23, 1981), 12.

549. Kirkman, S. "Positive Policies Needed to Defuse Social Time Bomb." **Times Educational Supplement**, 3367 (Jan. 2, 1981), 6.

550. Mark, Gordon R. "Out of the Ghetto: German Jews and American Blacks." **Integrated Education**, 12 (May-June, 1974), 46-48.
A set of personal impressions regarding anti-semitism in Germany with some comments about its relevance to Blacks in America.

551. Meisel, Jergen M. "Research Report on Second Language Acquisition by Immigrant Workers in West Germany." **Second Language Acquisition Notes and Topics**, 9 (June, 1979), 1-20.
Various research activities of second language learning of immigrant workers are listed.

552. Pienemann, Manfred. "The Second Language Acquisition of Immigrant Children." In S. W. Felix (ed.). **Recent Trends in Second Language Acquisition**. Tuebingen: TLB Verlag, 1979.

553. Rabura, Horst M. "How the Federal Republic of Germany tries to Solve Problems in Bilingual and Bicultural Education." In Howard Lee Nostrand (ed.). **American Civic Issues in the Light of European Experience**. Seattle: Department of Romance Languages and Literature, University of Washington, 1977. pp. 51-58.

Brief outline of general undertakings especially for immigrant children.

554. Rist, Ray C. "Migration and Marginality: Guestworkers in Germany and France." **Daedalus**, 108 (Spring, 1979), 95-108.

Rist examines the migration of workers from South to North in Europe, especially to France and West Germany. The discussion does not address educational issues directly, but their implications are profound.

555. Rist, Ray C. "The Education of Guestworker Children: Federal Republic of Germany." **Integrated Education**, 16 (May-June, 1978), 6-9.

Rist reviews the education tradition in Germany of transmitting the values, beliefs, and skills thought important to preserve that society and describes the problems guestworker children are creating within this perspective.

556. Rist, Ray C. "On the Education of the Guest-Worker Children in Germany: Public Policies and Equal Educational Opportunity." **Comparative Education Review**, 23 (Oct., 1979), 355-69.

Rist describes three phases in West German policies regarding the education of chlidren of guestworkers. His major focus is on the issue of equality of educational opportunity, which he feels is not a part of West German policy.

557. Schrader, Achim. "Vulnerable Age: Findings on Foreign Children in Germany." **Sociology of Education**, 51 (July, 1978), 227-30.

Study of foreign children in German schools shows that adaptation is more complete, the younger the child.

558. Schwarzweller, Harry K. "Regional Variations in the Educational Plans of Rural Youth: Norway, Germany and the United States." **Rural Sociology**, 38 (Summer, 1973), 139-58.

The paper explores the influence of regional socioeconomic circumstances on the educational plans of youth in three societies. Variations exist and in Europe an equalizing pressure on the stratification system seems to be at work more than in America.

559. Willke, Ingeborg. "Schooling of Immigrant Children in West Germany, Sweden, England." **International Review of Education**, 21 (1975), 357-82.
The analysis is based on the concept that children of immigrants belong to the disadvantaged people in our societies. Language is a special issue that underlines the urgency of action.

RELIGION AND EDUCATION

PRE-WORLD WAR II

560. Helmreich, Ernst C. "Religious Education in Germany." **Current History**, 19 (Sept., 1950), 154-62.
This is a study of religious education during the Weimar Republic and Hitler periods. He finds that Hitler moved from coordination, to exclusion, to oppression.

561. Hunt, Chester L. "Religious Instruction versus Secularization: German Experience." **Journal of Educational Sociology**, 22 (Dec., 1948), 304-10.
Looks at religious education, its supervision, changing content and results, especially during the period of National Socialism.

EAST GERMANY

562. "Forget not Their Distress." **Religious Education**, 57 (Jan., 1962), 37-8.
Report on religious education in East Germany.

563. Jordheim, A. "Religious Education in East Germany." **Journal of Religious Education**, 43 (June, 1967), 16-17.

WEST GERMANY

564. Bolewski, H. "Evangelical Academies and Religious Education." **Religious Education**, 55 (Nov., 1960), 430-36.

Describes academies that have arisen since World War II, where people come for several days to discuss topics of public importance.

565. Driscoll, Justin A. "Education in West Germany." **Catholic Education Review**, 59 (Feb., 1961), 108-12.

Provides a brief overview of education and the role of religion in the school.

566. Froer, Kurt. "Influence of Contemporary Theology on Christian Education in Germany," (trans. by J. S. Damm). **Religious Education**, 55 (Nov., 1960), 445-51.

Focus on the significance of Barth and Gogarten for religious education thinking.

567. Helmreich, Ernst C. **Religious Education in German Schools**. Cambridge: Harvard University Press, 1959.

Traces the place of religious education in the German school curriculum from the Middle Ages to the present.

568. Hilker, Franz. "Religion and the Control of Teachers: The Case of Germany." **World Year Book of Education**, (1966), 293-314.

569. Jacob, W. "Education and the Jew: A German View." **Religious Education**, 58 (May, 1963), 269-71+.

A study of education in relation to the Jews in post-Nazi West German religious education and history texts.

570. Lynch, James. **Religion and Politics in German Education, 1945-1973**. Ph.D. Thesis, University of Durham, England, 1973.

571. "School Prayers Are Illegal? Hessen's Dilemma." **Times Educational Supplement**, 2634 (Nov. 12, 1965), 1025.

Discusses a court ruling exempting a pupil from school prayer.

572. Stallman, M. and J. D. Smart. "Bible and Education in Germany: Review of **Die biblische Geschichte im Unterricht, katechetische Beitraege**." **Religious Education**, 60 (Mar., 1965), 131-35.

573. Whiting, Charles H. "Religion and Politics in German Schools." **Educational Forum**, 32 (Nov., 1967), 93-96.

SPECIAL EDUCATION

OCCUPATION AND REEDUCATION

574. Franke, Karl. "Deaf in Post-War Germany." **Volta Review**, 50 (June, 1948), 268+.
Reviews deaf education programs prior to Hitler and explains how little was done until the end of the war. Things are beginning to move again, expecially since the publication of **Neue Blaetter fuer Taubstummenbildung** began.

EAST GERMANY

575. Mannschutz, Eberhard. "Special Education in the German Democratic Republic." **Prospects**, 6 (1976), 637-40.
An overview of how East Germany attempts to develop the personality of each child to the full, including those with handicaps.

576. Segal, S. S. "Special Schools Beyond the Wall." **Times Educational Supplement**, 2508 (June 14, 1963), 1303.
Describes the 25 boarding schools for handicapped children in East Germany.

WEST GERMANY

577. Barkey, Peter. "Behavior Modification in Special Education in the Federal Republic of Germany." **Exceptional Child**, 24 (Mar., 1977), 44-49.
Discusses the literature and the empirical studies done on behavior modification in special education in West Germany.

578. "Fresh Therapeutical Paths; Work in Progress at Wittekindshof." **Times Educational Supplement**, 2682 (Oct. 14, 1966), 855.
Describes work done in drama therapy for young people with severe handicaps.

579. Kischke, Martina I. "Opportunities for Children in the Shade: Handicapped Persons in the Federal Republic of Germany: New Paths Towards Education and Integration from Pre-School Age Onwards." **Bildung und Wissenschaft**, No. 3 76(e), 1976. Published by Inter Nationes.

580. Kuder, K. "Hard of Hearing in Post-War Germany." **Volta Review**, 50 (June, 1948), 270.
Discusses a particular school for the hard of hearing in Neurtingen, West Germany.

581. Lowe, Armin. "Mainstream Education for Deaf Pupils." **Special Education: Forward Trends**, 5 (Dec., 1978), 19.
Discussion of mainstreaming, regular and reverse, for deaf pupils in West Germany.

582. Lundmark, Susan. "Deaf Education in West Germany: Some Traditions and Transitions." **American Annals of the Deaf**, 123 (June, 1978), 500-02.
The article is based on a visit to the school for the deaf and hard of hearing at Stegen, West Germany, where oral communication is used totally in the school setting. Other details of the program are also outlined.

583. Redkey, Henry. "A Way of Looking at Sheltered Workshops for the 1970's." Interface No. 3, Research and Training Center, Stout Vocational Rehabilitation Institute, University of Wisconsin, Menomonie, 1977.
Describes sheltered work programs for handicapped in five European countries, including West Germany.

584. von Bracken, H. "Situation of Handicapped Children in the German Federal Republic." **Training School Bulletin**, 63 (Nov., 1966), 113-23.

Chapter 7

PRESCHOOLS AND KINDERGARTENS

EAST GERMANY

585. Luszki, Margaret B. "Cold War in the Kindergarten." **National Education Association Journal**, 45 (Nov., 1956), 492-93.
Describes the indoctrination process in East German kindergartens.

586. Ministry of Education. **Performance of the Educational and Child-rearing Plan in the Kindergarten**. Berlin: Volk und Wissen Volkseigener Verlag, 1975.

587. Oschmann, Isolde. **Kindergartens in the German Democratic Republic**. Berlin: Ministry of Education and UNESCO Commission of the GDR, 1974.

588. Sailor, Dorothy Holin. "The Nurturing of Young Children in Child Care Centers (in Czechoslovakia and East Germany)." **Childhood Education**, 56 (Apr.-May, 1980), 281-84.
Discusses the child care offered at minimal cost for the six month to six year-old children. Describes the degree of participation, the focus of research projects, and parent involvements.

589. "They all Love Walter." **High Points**, 46 (May, 1964), 54-56.
Report of an East German kindergarten teacher in connection with a picture of Walter Ulbricht. The article was drawn from an East German periodical.

WEST GERMANY

590. Austin, G. R. **Early Childhood Education in Germany**. Paris: OECD, 1973.

591. Brudny, Wolfgang. "Audiovisual Media in the Kindergarten." **Educational Media International**, 4 (Dec., 1974), 23-27.
How media are used in West German kindergartens.

592. Goebel, Helmut. "The First Steps Towards Independence: Preschool Education in the Federal Republic of Germany." **Inter Nationes**, 7(e) (1980), 61-76.

593. Kischke, Martina I. "Learning About Life the Playful Way: From Kindergarten to Play Group. Situation Report." **Inter Nationes**, SR 10-77(e), (Oct. 1977), 1-15.

594. Kischke, Martina I. "The First Steps Towards Independence: Preschool in the Federal Republic of Germany." **Bildung und Wissenschaft**, 7(e), (1980), published by Inter Nationes.

595. Kuhmerker, Lisa. "When Sesame Street Becomes Sesamestrasse: Social Education for Preschoolers Comes to Television." **Social Education**, 40 (Jan., 1976), 34-7.
The paper reviews the parent and teacher guides to the West German Sesame Street program segment. The author finds the reorientation refreshing and insightful to Americans.

596. Moore, Dennis R. and others. "Lessons from Europe: A Report on European Pre-Schools and Child Care." **Childhood Education**, 53 (Nov./Dec., 1976), 66-70.
Authors look at several countries, including West Germany, where the stress remains on children remaining at home.

597. "Reform of Preschool Education in West Germany." **School and Society**, 99 (Summer, 1971), 289-90.
A conference report.

598. Ritter, Annelies J. "New Paths for Preschool Education: Preliminary Guidelines and Experiments in the Federal Republic of Germany." **Western European Education**, 1 (Summer/Fall, 1969), 157-64.
Review of the current West German preschool movement and sketches of experimental projects in two states.

599. Rodney, Clare. "Commentary: More About Child Care in Europe." **Childhood Education**, 53 (Nov./Dec., 1976), 71-76.
General discussion with an occasional reference to preschools in West Germany.

600. Schmalohr, E. "Evaluation of Pre-School Education: Research in the Federal Republic of Germany." In **Problems in the Evaluation of Pre-School Education**. Strasbourg: Council of Europe, 1975.

The volume looks at evaluation of preschool education in seven countries of Europe. Discussion centers on different evaluation purposes and procedures.

601. Zimmer, Juergen. "A Curriculum Based on Life Experiences." **International Understanding at School**, 32 (1977), 21-23,

The author gives an account of an interview with the developer of a kindergarten curriculum in West Germany based on life experiences common to the children.

Chapter 8

PRIMARY AND SECONDARY SCHOOLS

GENERAL EDUCATION

EAST GERMANY

A. Polytechnical Schools

602. Kohn, Erwin and Fred Postler. **Polytechnical Education in the GDR**. Dresden: Verlag Zeit im Bild, 1973.
This is an update on a previous pamphlet by W. Rosenkranz and others.

603. Ministry of Education. **Act on the Integrated Socialist Educational System of the German Democratic Republic.** Berlin: Staatsverlag der Deutschen Demokratischen Republik, 1972.

604. Rosenkranz, W. and others. **Polytechnical Education for All**. Dresden: Verlag Zeit im Bild, 1965.

605. Smart, Kenneth F. "The Polytechnical Principle." In Edmund J. King (ed.). **Communist Education**. London: Methuen and Co., 1965.
Provides a conceptual framework for polytechnical education and how it is implemented in countries such as East Germany.

606. **World Survey of Education II: Primary Education**. Paris: UNESCO, 1958.
East Germany treated on pp. 472-78.

607. **World Survey of Education III: Secondary Education.** Paris: UNESCO, 1961.
East Germany treated on pp. 526-34.

B. Extended Secondary and Abitur Classes

608. "East German Examination Papers." **Times Educational Supplement**, 2063 (Nov. 12, 1954), 1058.
Reprints of four oral papers in English set for the **Abitur** examination in East German Schools.

609. Moehle, Horst. "German Democratic Republic: Organization of Examinations System." **World Year Book of Education**, (1969), 146-51.

WEST GERMANY

A. Primary Schools

610. Lee, William B. "Fresh Perspectives from Western Europe." **Phi Delta Kappan**, 57 (Jan., 1976), 306-09.
Lee describes a number of elementary education concepts in Europe, including the German Country Home School, which may be of interest to Americans.

611. **World Survey of Education II: Primary Education**. Paris: UNESCO, 1958.
West Germany treated on pp. 454-472.

B. Secondary Schools

1. General

612. Belding, Robert E. "Junior High Years Take Over in Europe." **Journal of Secondary Education**, 39 (Nov., 1964), 304-10.
Reviews the reform movements in Sweden and Germany which make special provisions for the lower secondary schools.

613. Combs, Stanley. "German Gymnasium." **California Journal of Secondary Education**, 33 (Oct., 1958), 328-34.
Compares the **Gymnasium** to the American high school, giving descriptive data about instruction, attendance ratios, buildings, subjects of study, grading, and teacher preparation.

614. Fischer, Curt. "Americanization and the German Secondary School." **Journal of Secondary Education**, 40 (Nov., 1965), 325-30.
Suggests the secondary school has taken on many American attributes, it has become a mass institution.

615. Flitner, Wilhelm. "Problems of German Secondary Education" (trans. by J. R. Wilkie). **University Quarterly**, 8 (May, 1954), 230-43.

616. Goldschmidt, Dieter. "General Education; German Gymnasium Today." **Times Educational Supplement**, 2031 (Nov. 27, 1953), 1005.

617. Hahn, Walter. "Changing School Patterns in West Germany." **Clearing House**, 45 (Jan., 1971), 300-04.
Discusses the origin of innovations in West German school policies and the major trends. He engages in some comparisons between German and American secondary education.

618. Hahn, Walter. "High School in Divided Germany." **California Journal of Secondary Education**, 26 (Jan., 1951), 42-46.
Hahn looks at the varying concepts of school administration, the many versions of secondary schools, and trends in instruction and teacher training of secondary teachers.

619. Lee, William B. and Wayne Dumas. "German Secondary Schools: Perspectives and Questions for Americans." In James J. Jelinek (ed.). **Philosophy of Education, 1977/78**, Proceedings of the Far Western Philosophy of Education Society Conference. pp. 96-105.

620. Loffler, E. "The Gymnasium in the German Federal Republic." **Higher Education Journal**, (Spring, 1958), Supplement.

621. Schroeder, Max. "Secondary Education in France and Western Germany." **California Journal of Secondary Education**, 31 (Nov., 1956), 428-31.
Brief statement of aims and purposes of secondary education in two countries.

622. Whiting, Charles H. "Evening Grammars; 46 Years on." **Times Educational Supplement**, 2982 (July 14, 1972), 13.
Report of the 46th birthday of the evening **Gymnasium**.

623. **World Survey of Education III: Secondary Education**. Paris: UNESCO, 1961.
West Germany treated on pp. 502-526.

2. Access to the Gymnasium

624. Koelle, Willi. "Selection Procedures in the Schools of the Federal Republic of Germany." **Year Book of Education**, (1962), 259-70.
Koelle highlights selection procedures in the city state of Hamburg, giving critical remarks and comparisons with other states in Germany.

625. "Nine Plus in Germany: Six Days of Competition." **Times Educational Supplement**, 2143 (June 15, 1956), 825.
Describes the selection process for secondary schools at the end of the four year primary schooling process in West Germany.

626. Segel, David. "Evaluation and Guidance in German Schools." **School Life**, 30 (Oct., 1947), 15+.
Looks at the selection process of students for secondary schools.

3. The Abitur

627. DeWitt, Charles M. "The German Abiturial System." **Phi Delta Kappan**, 36 (June, 1955), 353-56.
Here is a brief outline of the history of the **Abitur** with a description of the written, oral, and physical fitness sections.

628. Henderson, James L. "The Abitur Examination in Germany." **Educational Forum**, 28 (Jan., 1964), 179-86.
Discusses the German secondary school leaving examination.

629. Ingenkamp, K. "West Germany: Organization of Examinations Systems." **World Year Book of Education**, (1969), 140-45.

630. Spalding, J. "G.C.E. and the German Abitur: Comparison of Two Examination Systems." **Journal of Education** (London), 87 (Mar., 1955), 112+.

631. van de Graff, John H. "West Germany's Abitur Quota and School Reform." **Comparative Education Review, 11** (Feb., 1967), 75-86.
The author describes the raising of the quota system to improve equality of educational opportunity, but he questions if true equality can be attained within the existing track system.

632. "German Abitur Examination: Comparison with G.C.E." **Times Educational Supplement**, 2021 (Jan. 22, 1954), 65.
Describes the written and oral sections and the final marking system of the **Abitur**.

4. The Comprehensive School

633. Korner, Annegret. "Comprehensive Schooling: An Evaluation--West Germany." **Comparative Education**, 17 (Mar., 1981), 15-22.
The author looks at comprehensive schools in West Germany--how they differ from the English schools, research results, and training teachers for these schools.

634. Scheerer, Hans Jorg. "Choice Schemes and the Q.S.L. in West German Comprehensive Schools." In Joyce Levy Epstein (ed.). **The Quality of School Life**. Lexington, Mass.: Lexington Books, D.C. Heath Co., 1981. 117-135.
This study is an adaption of a Quality of School Life questionnaire that has been used in innovative school programs. The results of the study are summarized.

635. Winter, Stephen S. "Programming for the 'Free Time' in West German Comprehensive Schools: Social Pedagogics." In Thomas Bernard and George Urch (eds.). **International Perspectives on Nonformal Education**. Proceedings of the New England Regional Conference of the Comparative and International Education Society, May, 1979.

VOCATIONAL SCHOOLS AND VOCATIONAL EDUCATION

EAST GERMANY

636. Berndt, Siegfried. "Training in the Karl Liebknecht Transformer Works--East Germany." **World Year Book of Education**, (1969), 286-93.

637. Wilke, Alfred. "Industrial Training in the German Democratic Republic." **World Year Book of Education**, (1968), 129-35.
This is a descriptive statement.

638. Zelenskii, G. "Vocational-Technical Training in the German Democratic Republic." **Soviet Education**, 14 (May, 1972), 34-40.
Describes the three types of vocational school which students may enter after they leave the ten year general school.

WEST GERMANY

639. Abraham, Karl. "The System of German Technical Schools." **Year Book of Education**, (1958), 191-97.

640. Bawden, W. "Vocational Schools in Germany." **Industrial Arts and Vocational Education**, 41 (Apr., 1952), 119-22.

641. Belding, Robert E. "Perennial Model Revisited." **Journal of Secondary Education**, 40 (Mar., 1965), 120-25.
Describes the German compulsory continuation school as a well worn model of vocational education.

642. Eddy, W. P. **Vocational Education in West Germany.** Edmonton, Alberta: Department of Education, Planning and Research Branch, Feb., 1981.
This report looks at vocational education in West Germany. It covers all levels and assesses history, training places and personnel, trainee placement, examinations and qualifications.

643. Edenhofner, Siegfried A. "Training in the Retail Trades in the German Federal Republic." **World Year Book of Education**, (1968), 256-57.

644. Fahle, Walter. "Vocational Education in the Federal Republic of Germany." **Western European Education**, 5 (Spring, 1973), 6-22.
Fahle provides background data, describes the present situation, and move to developing trends in vocational education in West Germany.

645. Freeman, D. H. "Training in Scandinavian and German Shipyards." **Training Officer**, 49 (Feb., 1973), 44-50.
The training and recruitment of shipbuilders in Norway, Sweden, and Germany is described.

646. Hagopain, Laura. "Review of Approaches to Providing Vocational Training and Development in Six Advanced Nations and Comparisons with the United States." Washington D. C.: U.S. Office of Education, Bureau of Occupational and Adult Education, Dec., 1978.

647. Henderson, Marrietta and others. "To Aid Home Economics Teachers in Germany." **Journal of Home Economics**, 39 (Dec., 1947), 625-28.

Three people spent a brief time in Germany to see how home economics teaching could aid in the reeducation of the Germans. This is an outline of their report to the U.S. Office of Education.

648. Howard, A. "Apprentices to Culture: Hiberniaschule in the Ruhr." **Times Educational Supplement**, 2626 (Sept. 17, 1965), 480.

649. Hylla, Erich and A. Schwarzlose. "Vocational Guidance in Germany." **Personnel and Guidance Journal**, 33 (Mar., 1954), 416-17.

Reactions to articles in this journal in Apr., 1953 (Froelich and Davis) on vocational education.

650. Jochimsen, Reimut. "Aims and Objectives of German Vocational and Professional Education in the Present European Context." **Comparative Education**, 14 (Oct., 1978), 199-209.

The author stresses the importance of providing for opportunities to move ahead in the world of work regardless of formal educational qualifications, and of taking the equivalence of vocational and general education more seriously.

651. Johnson, Verner B. "Vocational Education in Scandinavia and Germany." **Illinois Career Education Journal**, 34 (Spring, 1978), 37-41.

The vocational education programs of Denmark, West Germany, Norway, and Sweden are described and compared with the United States.

652. Keller, Franklin J. "Vocational Guidance in Germany." **Occupations**, 26 (Apr., 1958), 403-409.

Points out that planned guidance does not exist, but it is carried out in some form which he describes in certain states. He appeals for the institution of vocational guidance programs.

653. Kiesewalter, Dietrich P. "Vocational Training and Skill Development: A Comparison Between Canada and West Germany." **Canadian Vocational Journal**, 14 (May, 1978), 15-7,29, 31-5.

After explaining vocational training in Canada, the author discusses how it compares with programs in West Germany. He also compares the relationship between wages and achievement.

654. Lutz, Burkart. "Education and Employment: Contrasting Evidence from France and the Federal Republic of Germany." **European Journal of Education**, 16 (1981), 73-86.

Looks at France and Germany, drawing relationships between employment structures and educational training systems. He argues each affects the other in important ways. He discusses these implications in terms of educational policy.

655. Meyn, Hermann. "Journalist Training in the Federal Republic of Germany." **Bildung und Wissenschaft**, No. 9, 78(e), 1978, Published by Inter Nationes.

The author discusses activities for learning by doing, then he turns to formal centers at higher education institutions, academies, and other centers. Further training is outlined, what journalists earn, their prestige and privileges as well as the labor market for journalists.

656. "New Outlook at Krupps; Change in Training Methods." **Times Educational Supplement**, 2622 (Aug., 1965), 295.

Describes apprenticeship training at Krupps in West Germany.

657. Niens, Walter. "The Historical and Social Background to Education within Industry in West Germany." **World Year Book of Education**, (1968), 108-19.

658. Norton, Robert E. and Roy L. Butler. "West German Productivity: Every Other Youth an Apprentice." **Voced**, 56 (May, 1981), 31-34.

Describes the West German apprentice system and suggests that the U.S. could benefit from the model it provides.

659. Peterson, Norbert. "Vocational Training in the Federal Republic of Germany." **Bildung und Wissenschaft**, N. 9/10(e), 1981, Published by Inter Nationes.

660. Renken, Gerd. "Vocational Training and Promotion in the Federal Republic of Germany." **Bildung und Wissenschaft**. No. 7-76(e), 1976, Published by Inter Nationes.

661. Reubens, Beatrice. "Apprenticeship in Foreign Countries." Washington D.C.: U.S. Department of Labor, Employment and Training Administration, 1980.

This report is based on visits to Australia, Austria, Belgium, Canada, Denmark, France, Finland, West Germany, Great Britain, Ireland, the Netherlands, New Zealand, Norway, Sweden, and Switzerland.

662. Reubens, Beatrice. "The Transition from School to Work--The European Experience: Implications for Vocational Education, Research and Development." Occasional Paper No. 49. Columbus, Ohio: The National Center for Research in Vocational Education, the Ohio State University, Feb., 1979.

Reubens makes reference to West Germany throughout this brief study.

663. Richert, Henry G. "Business Education in Germany." **National Business Education Quarterly**, 28 (Mar., 1960), 45-48+.

Richert puts business education in the context of the general system of education.

664. Rust, Lucile. "Home Economics in Germany." **American Vocational Journal**, 25 (Apr., 1950), 20-1.

Explains that home economics is on housekeeping skills and it has no place in higher education; rather, it takes place in vocational schools for girls, at least in Germany.

665. Schaefer, Carl J. "Educational Reform--Not Change: A Role for Epsilon Pi Tau Leadership." **Journal of Epsilon Pi Tau**, 2 (1975), 33-4.

The author served as a Fullbright Fellow in West Germany and reflects here on the reform of vocational education. This reform is intended to reduce community involvement by formalizing vocational education and integrating it with formal schooling.

666. Schaefer, Hans-Peter. "Current Problems of Vocational Education in the Federal Republic of Germany." Occasional Paper No. 54. Columbus, Ohio: The National Center for Research in Vocational Education, Ohio State University, Aug., 1979.

667. Schmidbauer, Michael. "Tele-Beruf: A Training Course for Apprentices." **Educational Media International**, 1 (Mar., 1974), 26-27.

Describes a course in Munich, Germany.

668. Smart, Kenneth F. "Vocational Education in the Federal Republic of Germany: Current Trends and Problems." **Comparative Education**, 11 (June, 1975), 153-63.

Outlines what he feels is a growing cooperation between the Federal government and the various states in research about vocational education.

669. Spelberg, Karl. "West Germany." In Carl J. Schaefer (ed.). **Comparative Education for Occupations: An International Conference Report.** Prepared by the University Council for Vocational Education. pp. 45-60.
Describes vocational education in West Germany, pointing out its many problems.

670. Thomas, Betti Luise. "Business Education in Frankfurt." **American Business Education**, 11 (Mar., 1955), 181-1+.
Describes the two types of business education found in Germany: training following apprenticeship and training preparing for apprenticeship.

671. Toews, Emil D. "Vocational Education in the Making of a Nation." **American Vocational Journal**, 47 (Dec., 1972), 44-46.
Gives a glowing historical account of the role of vocational education in the technological advancement of Germany.

672. Turner, Solveig M. (ed.). "Berufsakademie Baden-Wuerttemberg, Federal Republic of Germany." In "Cooperative or Work Experience Education: An International Overview." **CIHED Newsletter**, 4, 2 (April, 1981), 18-21.
Brief description of an adult vocational education center in West Germany.

673. Ware, George W. "Vocational Education in Germany." **American Vocational Journal**, 24 (Oct., 1949), 13-14.
Discusses extent of vocational training, the staffing limitations during reeducation, the value orientation of vocational educators and the aims of the military government in vocational education.

674. Yates, A. H. "Compulsory Part Time Education in West Germany." In **The Development of FEII (Further Education)**. Coombe Lodge Report. Study Conference 75/11 and Study Conference 75/14, 1975. 299-302.
Brief statement of the legal requirement that young people, who are not in full time education from the ages of 15-18, must attend a part-time vocational school in West Germany.

675. "The Attitude of the German Worker: Shaping by Vocational Training." **Times Educational Supplement**, 2039 (May 28, 1954), 525.
Discusses the influence of the vocational school on the attitudes of the German workers.

Chapter 9

HIGHER EDUCATION

GENERAL

PRE-WORLD WAR II

676. Bureau of Education. "German and Other Foreign Universities." Circular of Information. Washington: Government Printing Office, 1872.

677. Bird, Charles. **Higher Education in Germany and England**. London, 1884.

678. Craig, J. "A Mission for German Learning: The University of Strasbourg and Alsation Society, 1870-1918." Ph.D. dissertation, Stanford University, 1973.

679. Flexner, Abraham. **Universities: American, English, German**. Oxford: Oxford University Press, 1930.

Flexner outlines the idea of a modern university, then deals with that institution in three separate national contexts. In the German chapter he tries to deal with the individual national characteristics and how they have made themselves a part of the modern world in the university setting.

680. Hart, James Morgan. **German Universities: A Narrative of Personal Experience Together with Recent Statistical Information, Practical Suggestions, and a Comparison of the German, English, and American Systems of Higher Education**. New York: G. P. Putnam's Sons, 1874.

681. Hartshorne, Edward Y. **The German Universities and National Socialism.** Cambridge: Harvard University Press, 1937.

The author spent the year 1935/36 in Germany and attempts to give a balanced study of his findings of the reorganization of the universities under National Socialism. He finds much to laud in the reforms, such as clear life ideals and stress on physical fitness, but there have also been losses, especially regarding science and detached academic study. This is an important study of early developments under National Socialism by a sociologist from Harvard University.

682. Lilge, Frederic. **The Abuse of Learning: The Failure of the German University.** New York: Macmillan, 1948.

Lilge seeks to explain the catastrophe of German intellectual culture during the period of National Socialism. He finds sophistry and glibness of German science and philosophy to be especially distressing.

683. McClelland, Charles E. **State, Society, and University in Germany: 1700-1914.** Cambridge: Cambridge University Press, 1980.

The premise of the book is that the university is not as autonomous and independent as many professors hold up as their ideal, and that the university is integrally connected with the events that take place in the broader culture.

684. Paulson, Friedrich. **The German Universities and University Study** (trans. by F. Thilly and W. W. Elwang). New York: Longmans Green and Co., 1906.

The study is divided into five books: (1) An Outline of the Historical Development, (2) The Modern Organization of the Universities and their Place in Public Life, (3) University Teachers and University Instruction, (4) Students and Academic Study, (5) Particular Faculties. It all adds up to a systematic account of the nature, function, organization and historical development of the German university. One of the important documents on higher education.

685. Ringer, Fritz K. "Higher Education in Germany in the Nineteenth Century." **Journal of Contemporary History,** 2, 3(July, 1967), 123-38.

Ringer focuses mainly on the academic or "cultivated" group that emerged as a unique social group that developed its own characteristic set of values.

686. Scott, D. F. S. **Wilhelm von Humboldt and the Idea of a University.** Durham: University of Durham Inaugural Lecture, 1960.

687. Thwing, Charles F. **The American and the German University: One Hundred Years of History**. New York: Macmillan, 1928.
After giving attention to student and professor exchanges, Thwing describes the German university as an institution and pays special attention to the medical, theological, and law faculties.

688. von Gizycki, Rainald. "Centre and Periphery in the International Scientific Community: Germany, France, and Great Britain in the 19th Century." **Minerva**, 11 (Oct., 1973), 474-494.
After reviewing the concept of center and periphery as it relates to the scientific community, the author assesses the centers and their displacement in Europe during the nineteenth century.

689. Yarnall, Edward. **The German Universities and National Socialism**. London: Allen and Unwin, 1937.

690. Wooton, Edwin. **A Guide to Degrees in Arts, Science, Literature, Law, Music and Divinity, in the United Kingdom, the Colonies, the Continent, and the United States**. London: L.U. Gill, 1883.

OCCUPATION AND REEDUCATION

691. Bretton, Henry L. "Reforming a German University." **Journal of Education**, 129 (Sept., 1946), 198-200.
Focuses on the university town of Marburg and what has been going on with regard to getting the University back on its feet.

692. Cottrell, Donald P. "Higher Education and the Problem of Germany Today." **Educational Forum**, 12 (Mar., 1948), 267-75.
Points out the difficult general problems in Germany and he lays out a brief reeducation program that the military government should initiate, which would help it modify German culture generally.

693. Cottrell, Donald P. "University in Germany Today." **School and Society**, 66 (Dec., 1947), 481-84.
Commencement address where the author recounts his experiences in Germany working with the occupational forces. He casts the university in the broader social framework.

694. Cumming, W. "What Is Happening in the German Universities?" **South Atlantic Quarterly**, 46 (Apr., 1947), 167-81.

695. Donovan, H. L. "Observations of German Universities in the American Zone." **Peabody Journal of Education**, 26 (Sept., 1948), 70-75.
Report of visits to universities in the American zone to prepare an outline or blueprint for a survey of institutions of higher learning.

696. Havighurst, Robert J. "Higher Education in Germany." **Journal of Higher Education**, 19 (Jan., 1948), 13-20.
A look at higher education immediately following World War II.

697. Jaspers, Karl. **The Idea of a University** (trans. by H.A.T. Reiche and H.F. Vanderschmidt). Boston: Beacon Press, 1959.
Written toward the end of the Nazi period and he attempts to explain the deepest roots of universities in Western tradition. In doing so he illuminates the German philosophic and academic tradition.

698. Jaspers, Karl. "Reeducation of German Scholarship," (trans. by M. Zuckerkandl). **American Scholar**, 15 (April, 1946), 180-88.
A translation of a speech at the University of Heidelberg as the School of Medicine was reopened on August 15, 1945. He calls for a regeneration of the University based on its origins--seeking after truth and humaneness.

699. Lilge, Frederic. "German University Re-Opens." **Harvard Education Review**, 16 (Mar., 1946), 79-84.
Provides the gist of an address given by Julius Ebbinghaus on the occasion of the re-opening of the University of Marburg.

700. Lindsay, A. "Commission on German Universities." **University Quarterly**, 4 (Nov., 1949), 82-88.

701. May, A. "Austrian and German Universities in 1948." **Journal of Central European Affairs**, 9 (Oct., 1949), 315-20.

702. Phillips, David. "Lindsay and the German Universities: An Oxford Contribution to the Post-War Reform Debate." **Oxford Review of Education**, 6 (1980), 91-105.
Discussion of the university reform debates in the British zone after World War II.

703. Read, James M. "German Universities." **Yale Review**, 42 (Sept., 1952) 83-94.
Claims the universities were reopened too soon after the war and that needed reforms are therefore more difficult to institute. He gives some account of changes that have been made, especially regarding student organizations, general education, and student-professor relationships.

704. Read, James M. "Present Status of German Universities." **Higher Education**, 8 (Dec. 1, 1951), 81-83.

705. Schuetz, W. W. "German Universities." **New Statesman and the Nation**, 30 (Dec. 8, 1945), 386.
Describes the difficulties, even of food and clothing, in maintaining any semblance of university life immediately following the war. Democracy is only a word to this point.

706. Stirk, Samuel Dickinson. **German Universities Through English Eyes**. London: V. Gollancz, 1946.
A brief sketch of German universities by a British observer.

707. "The Universities in the British Zone of Germany." **The Universities Review**, 19 (May, 1947).

708. Zucker, F. "Present Intellectual Situation and the Tasks of Education in Germany." **Association of American Colleges Bulletin**, 31 (Oct., 1945), 377-83.
Calls for a reestablishment of humanism once National Socialism has been destroyed.

EAST GERMANY

709. Brickman, William W. "Academic Adventures in East Germany." **Educational Forum**, 35 (May, 1971), 461-69.
The author describes the experiences from an invitation to attend and lecture at the 550th anniversary of Rostock.

710. Giles, Geoffrey J. "The Structure of Higher Education in the German Democratic Republic." **Higher Education,** 7 (May, 1978), 131-56.

This article describes the three university reforms in East Germany which have taken place and examines the implications of policy decisions. He claims that the ability to produce large cohorts of highly skilled graduates has contributed to East Germany's high status in the industrialized world.

WEST GERMANY

711. Ben-David, Joseph. **Centers of Learning: Britain, France, Germany, United States.** New York: McGraw Hill, 1977.

This report, prepared for the Carnegie Commission on Higher Education, attempts to compare the effectiveness of different national systems of higher education. His treatment is historical rather than quantitative, and the university is considered in the broader social, economic and political context.

712. Breitenbucher, "Climate of Higher Education in West Germany." **Institute of International Education News Bulletin**, 35 (May, 1960), 10-15.

713. Fallon, Daniel. **The German University: A Heroic Ideal in conflict with the Modern World**. Boulder: Colorado Associated University Press, 1980.

The author traces the history of higher education from the university of Berlin, founded in 1808 until the 1970's. His post World War II discussion deals with West Germany.

714. German Universities Commission. **Report on German Universities**. New York: International Council on the Future of the University, 1977.
This report is one of a number of investigations undertaken to assess the condition of higher education in Western societies. It does not deal with specifics so much as upon certain overriding themes in German higher education.

715. German Universities Commission. "Report on the German Universities." **Minerva**, 16 (Spring, 1978), 103-148.
This is a copy of a report submitted to the International Council on the Future of the University in 1977. Comments by John Passmore and Charles Frankel follow the report.

716. Goldschmidt, Dietrich and Ingrid N. Sommerkorn. "Some University Problems Today: Transmission from School to University in the Federal Republic of Germany." In **The University Within the Education System**, Proceedings of the Comparative Education Society of Europe, Ghent, 1967. (1968), 59-75.

717. **Higher Education in the Federal Republic of Germany, Problems and Trends**. Bonn-Bad Godesberg: DAAD, 1965.

718. Kerr, Anthony. **Universities of Europe**. Court Place: Canterbury Press, 1962.
Deals with Germany on pp. 64-68.

719. King, Edmund J. **Education and Development in Western Europe**. London: Addison-Wesley, 1969.
Gives particular attention to higher education (chapter 6) in West Germany.

720. McKay, Llewelyn R. "Higher Education in Germany." **School and Society**, 83 (Mar. 31, 1956), 113-15.
A report of West German universities based on visits in 1955.

721. Peisert, Hansgert and Gerhild Framhein. **Systems of Higher Education: Federal Republic of Germany**. New York: ICED, 1978 .
One of 12 ICED studies on higher education and it is divided into three main sections: (1) Description of the System, (2) Management of the System, including coordinating and planning bodies, and (3) Effectiveness of Higher Education, including innovation and flexibility, higher education in the social context, and efficiency.

722. Potter, G. "German Universities Today." **University Quarterly**, 13 (Feb., 1959), 145-51.
Reply by H. T. Betteridge 13 (May, 1959), 300-02.

723. **Report on the German Universities.** New York: International Council on the Future of the University, 1977.

724. Sandberger, Johann-Ulrich and Georg Lind. "The Outcomes of University Education: Some Empirical Findings on Aims and Expectations in the Federal Republic of Germany." **Higher Education,** 8 (Mar., 1979), 179-203.
The authors look at the aims and expectations of the population in general, university graduates, and legislators and find divergent views in these groups.

725. Whiting, Charles H. "Crisis in Higher German Education." **Educational Forum,** 31 (Jan., 1967), 189-94.
Whiting highlights the popular literature that claims education at every level is inadequate to the task.

726. Wilder, Amos N. "Opening and Closing Doors in Germany." **Christian Century,** 70 (June 24, 1953), 738-40.
After teaching for two semesters in Germany, Wilder recounts the difficulties of maintaining Christian perspectives but he finds the students to be eager, responsive and friendly

727. **World Survey of Education IV: Higher Education.** Paris: UNESCO, 1966.

POLICIES AND PLANNING

EAST GERMANY

728. Lehmann, H. and H. J. Schulz. "Planning the Teaching Work at Humboldt University, Berlin." In Onuschkin, V. G. (ed.). **Planning the Development of Universities IV: Five Case Studies.** Paris: UNESCO, 1975.
Covers a wide range of topics including courses of study, curricula, teaching staff activities, student assignments, instructional techniques, methods of evaluating instruction.

729. Nast, Manfred. "The Planning of Higher Education in the German Democratic Republic." **Higher Education,** 3 (1974), 201-12.

In East Germany, as in other socialist countries, all planning goals are subordinate to the development of the socialist state. Planning takes place centrally and is designed to accommodate a high percentage of the population.

730. Sachse, E. **Higher Education and Manpower Planning in the German Democratic Republic.** Geneva: ILO, 1977.

731. Schulz, H. J. "The Development of Higher Education in the GDR in the Eighties." **Higher Education in Europe,** 6 (April-June, 1981), 50-54.

WEST GERMANY

732. Cole, R. Taylor. "Federalism and Universities in West Germany: Recent Trends." **The American Journal of Comparative Law,** 21 (Winter, 1973), 45-68.

Cole observes that increasing involvement between the states in cultural affairs has led to formal contraction of the reserved constitutional competencies of the individual states with increasing central control even though certain institutional restraints remain.

733. Dungworth, D. "Compromise Law Heralds Modest University Shakeup." **Times Educational Supplement,** 3163 (Jan. 16, 1976), 17.

734. Fulton, Oliver and Others. "Higher Education and Manpower Planning: A Comparison of Planned Market Economies." **Education Policy Bulletin,** 8 (Spring, 1980), 83-113.

Reports evidence from four European countries which suggests some convergence in the application of manpower and social demand criteria in higher education planning.

735. Goldschmidt, Dietrich. "Autonomy and Accountabilty of Higher Education in the Federal Republic of Germany." In Philip G. Altbach (ed.). **The University's Response to Social Demands.** New York: ICED, 1975. pp. 151-172.

736. "Higher Education Framework Law: An Analysis." **Western European Education**, 8 (Fall, 1976), 116-26.
An analysis of the Higher Education Framework Law of Jan., 1976, which appeared in **Bildung und Wissenschaft**, 1976.

737. "Higher Education Framework Law of January 26, 1976." **Western European Education**, 8 (Fall, 1976), 60-115.
This is a translation text of the **Hochsculrahmengesetz** from January 26, 1976, translated by Halsey Westphal.

738. Huden, Daniel P. "Higher Education Policy Formation in the Federal Republic of Germany, A Closer Look at Neglected Aspects." **Western European Education**, 10 (Winter, 1978/79), 26-75.
Huden looks at higher educational policy formation, using the University of Duisberg as a case in point. He stresses that legal documents, legislative debates and official pronouncements are of little help until one understands the rules of the game.

739. Kewinig, W. A. "The German Advisory Council for Higher Education and Research (**Wissenschaftsrat**)." In **Reform and Development of Higher Education: A European Symposium**. Atlantic Highlands, N.J.: Humanities Press, Inc., 1979.

740. Pfeiffer, Heinrich. "The Support of the Sciences and Humanities in the Federal Republic of Germany." In **The Support of the Sciences and Humanities in West Germany and the United States**. Bloomington: Institute of German Studies, 1977.
Discusses science and humanities in higher education.

741. Schuster, H. J. and G. Elstermann. "The Institutionalization of Planning and Data Processing in University Administration." Bulletin No. 9 of the OECD Centre for Educational Research and Innovation.

742. Science Council. "Recommendations of the Science Council for the Development of Scientific Institutions in Western Germany." **Minerva**, 1 (Autumn, 1962), 87-105.

743. Science Council. **Recommendations by the Science Council for the Structure and Expansion of Higher Education after 1970: Summary.** Tuebingen: J.C.B. Mohr, 1970.

744. Science Council. "Recommendations of the Science Council for the Development of Scientific Institutions in Western Germany. Part III: Non-University Research Institutes, Academies of Science, Museums and Scientific Collections." **Minerva,** 5 (Spring, 1967), 413-28.
A summary of the **Wissenschaftsrates** recommendations, 1965.

745. van de Graff, John H. "Legislating German University Structure: The Politics of Tradition in Hesse, 1960-1966." Yale Higher Education Program Working Paper, Institution for Social and Policy Studies, Yale University, Jan., 1975.
The author traces the process by which Hesse's University Law of 1966 was enacted. In spite of its forward focus, it still did not enable the university to deal with the pressures placed on it.

UNIVERSITY REFORM

EAST GERMANY

746. **How does the GDR Solve the Problems of Higher Education?** Zeit im Bild, undated, but published about 1970.
After the establishment of East Germany the universities underwent three basic reforms prior to 1970. This pamphlet describes the political process involved in the third reform, especially the outcomes and the various inputs into the reform.

747. "Recent Developments in East German Universities." **Universities Quarterly,** 13 (Feb., 1959), 152-56.

748. Wirzberger, Karl-Heinz. "The Third Reform of Higher Education in the German Democratic Republic." **Prospects,** 3 (Winter, 1973), 497-503.
The author explains that three higher education reforms have taken place in East Germany. The third is an attempt to embark on a full fledged socialist society.

WEST GERMANY

749. Altbach, Philip G. **University Reform: An International Perspective.** Washington: American Association for Higher Education/ERIC Higher Education Research Report No. 10, 1980.

Altbach takes a general look at university reform then concentrates on seven national settings including West Germany (pp. 29-34).

750. Bodenman, Paul S. "Academic Reforms in Selected Universities of the Federal Republic of Germany." Unpublished Ph.D. Dissertation, University of Maryland, 1973.

751. Brezinka, Wolfgang. "German Universities: Crisis and Reform." **Educational Record**, 49 (Fall, 1969), 419-28.

The author assesses the tradition of higher education and turns to various reforms, including division of labor among universities, cooperation within the university, reorganization of study courses, and the participation of students in decision making.

752. Carpenter, Marjorie. "American Investment in German Universities." **Journal of Higher Education**, 24 (Feb., 1953), 70-76.

Recounts that higher education was initially neglected during the occupation period, but that some collaborative work is now going on regarding higher education.

753. Council of Europe. **Reform and Expansion of Higher Education in Europe: National Reports.** Strasbourg: Council for Cultural Cooperation, Council of Europe, 1967.

754. Crausaz, Roselyne. **Diversification of Tertiary Education**. Strasbourg, Council of Europe, 1974.

A working party of representatives visited five capitals, including Bonn, to hear accounts of noteworthy innovations or experiments in post-secondary education. The document summarizes their observations.

755. Froese, Leonard. "University Reform: A comparative Analysis of the American, Russian and German Universities." In Brian Holmes and David Scanlon (eds.). **Higher Education in a Changing World**. New York: Harcourt Brace Jovanovich, 1971. pp. 135-46.

756. Geiger, Roger L. "European Universities--The Unfinished Revolution." Yale Higher Education program Working Paper. Institution for Social Policy Studies, Yale University, Sept., 1976.

The thesis of this paper is that the traditional university is extinct and that the present institutions are unstable and transitory; its replacement is dimly perceptible.

757. Goldschmidt, Dietrich and S. Huebner. "Changing Concepts of the University in Society: The West German Case." In Brian Holmes and David Scanlon (eds.). **Higher Education in a Changing World**. New York: Harcourt Brace Jovanovich, 1971.

758. Hahn, Walter. "Higher Education in West Germany: Reform Movements and Trends." **Comparative Education Review**, 7 (June, 1963), 51-60.

759. Kloss, Guenther. "University Reform in West Germany: The Burden of Tradition." **Minerva**, 7 (Spring, 1968), 323-353.

Kloss traces the evolution of the West German university from the end of World War II until 1968.

760. Kraushaar, Otto F. T. "New Stirrings in German Universities." **Scientific Monthly**, 78 (Apr., 1954), 201-07.

After ten years Kraushaar finds the universities are again providing a high level of training. There are, however, few signs that the world of scholars exists who will lead the way to a moral and spiritual regeneration.

761. Krueger, Marlis and Baerbel Wallisch-Prinz. "University Reform in Progress: The Current Debate in West Germany." **Comparative Education Review**, 16 (June, 1972), 340-51.

The authors look at the historical context of German universities and society, then they turn to recent higher education reform activities.

762. Luebbe, Hermann. "The University Yesterday and Today." **Western European Education**, 11 (Fall-Winter, 1979/80), 1-20.

Looks at the post war university evolution and points out many of the stresses and strains involved in the reforms.

763. Nipperday, Thomas. "The German University in Crisis." In Paul Seabury (ed.). **Universities in the Western World.** New York: Free Press, 1975.
Accounts of the crisis sustained when the university shifted from an elite to a mass institution in terms of students, but has not adjusted its research and teaching to the altered conditions.

764. Teichler, Ulrich. "Problems of West German Universities on the Way to Mass Higher Education." **Western European Education**, 8 (1976), 81-120.
Outlines the attempts to make the university a mass institution while retaining characteristics of elite higher education.

765. Teichler, Ulrich. "University Reform and Skeleton Legislation on Higher Education in the Federal Republic of Germany." **Western European Education**, 4 (Feb., 1972), 224-38.
Teichler surveys the key points and problems in reform efforts of higher education in West Germany.

766. **University Reform in Germany--Report by a German Commission**. London: HMSO, 1949.
Translation of **Gutachten zur Hochschulreform**, printed in full in Rolf Neuhaus (ed.). **Dokumente zur Hochschulreform, 1945-1959**. Wiesbaden, 1961.

767. van de Graff, John H. "Can Department Structures Replace a Chair System? Comparative Perspectives." Yale Higher Education Research Group Working paper. New Haven: Higher Education Research Group, Yale University, 1980.
Gives particular attention to reform tendencies in West Germany, where the chair system is giving way to the department system. He gives an extensive list of problems in such undertakings.

768. West German Rectors' Conference. **Documentation Regarding University Reform, 1968-69.** Bonn-Bad Godesberg: The West German Rectors' Conference, 1969.

769. West German Rectors' Conference. **Documentation Regarding University Reform, 1969-70.** Bonn-Bad Godesberg: The West German Rectors' conference, 1970.

770. Wilk, Helmut O. "German Universities Revisited." **Journal of Higher Education**, 34 (Oct., 1963), 390-92.
Describes briefly Germany's attempt to overcome its traditional institutions of higher learning.

MANAGEMENT IN HIGHER EDUCATION

PRE-WORLD WAR II

771. Giles, Geoffrey J. "University Government in Nazi Germany: Hamburg." **Minerva**, 16 (Summer, 1978), 196-221.
Giles points out how Hamburg University was atypical of other universities in Germany at the beginning of the National Socialist reign. He then discusses how a new university government was set up, the distribution of power, and the quality of academic life at Hamburg.

772. Schroeder-Gudehus, Brigitte. "The Argument for the Self Government and Public Support of Science in Weimar Germany." **Minerva**, 10 (Oct., 1972), 537-570.
A detailed account of the tensions existing between the states and the federal government over financial support of science research during the Weimar period.

EAST GERMANY

773. Ebbutt, Keith. "The Administration of Higher Education in the German Democratic Republic." **Journal of Educational Administration**, 18 (July, 1980), 132-39.
The author attempts to show how power is distributed through the system of higher education in East Germany, both nationally and institutionally.

WEST GERMANY

774. Bender, I. and W. Henning. **Survey of the State-of-the-Art and likely Future Trends of University Management in Europe: Austria, Germany, the Netherlands**. Paris: OECD/CERI, 1980.

775. Fitzpatrick, Edward A. "His Magnificence: The Rector of the German University." **School and Society**, 75 (Mar. 15, 1952), 161-64.
The author gives an overview of the rector at the university, his duties, election, the Rectors Conference, and the reorganization being considered.

776. Goldschmidt, Dietrich. "Participatory Democracy in Schools and Higher Education: Emerging Problems in the Federal Republic of Germany and Sweden." **Higher Education**, (May, 1976), 113-33.

This is a personal interpretation of the findings of a cooperative inquiry by commissions set up by West Germany and Sweden to investigate the problem of democratization and participation in the educational and research systems of the two countries.

777. Hahn, Walter. "Patterns and Trends in West German Universities: Academic Self-Government versus State Control." **Journal of Higher Education**, 36 (May, 1965), 245-53.

778. Hennis, Wilhelm. "The Legislator and the German University." **Minerva**, 15 (Autumn-Winter, 1977), 286-315.

The author discusses the various forces that have contributed to change in the laws governing higher education in West Germany. He reviews the recent crisis in higher education, the legislative responses of the various states, and their consequences and repercussions.

779. Jochimsen, Reimut. "Managing Universities in the Eighties--Introductory Remarks." **International Journal of Institutional Management in Higher Education**, 3 (May, 1979), 5-19.

Introductory remarks at the IMHE Programme in Paris. He uses West Germany for illustrative purposes about what should be done in the next decade regarding training, research, finance, and other functions of the university.

780. Kaltefleiter, Werner. "The Inherent Dynamics of the Group University." **International Journal of Institutional Management in Higher Education**, 3 (Oct., 1979), 303-14.

The author argues that the democratization process of the late 1960's and early 1970's did not lead to a 'group university,' but to a 'corporate state' model. This has broken the conventional communication channels and set up competing power groups.

781. Kloss, Guenther. "The Growth of Federal Power in the West German University System." **Minerva**, 9 (Oct., 1974), 510-527.

Kloss traces university governance in West Germany, highlighting the emergence of Federal university involvement and policy, even though higher education is the responsibility of the individual states.

782. Mason, Henry L. "Reflections on the Politicized University: 1. The Academic Crisis in the Federal Republic of Germany." **AAUP Bulletin**, 60 (Sept., 1974), 299-312.

Assesses the judgment of the Federal Constitutional Court in May, 1973 regarding admissions and also requiring so-called priorities in the decision making power among the components of the university. He speculates that the leftist groups could easily take over the university.

783. Merten, Peter. "Comparative Indicators for German Universities." **International Journal of Institutional Management in Higher Education**, 3 (May, 1979), 155-68.

A description of an experiment carried out under the IMHE Programme for ascertaining whether comparative indicators for enterprises could be applied to universities. Data presented indicate there may be scope for rationalization.

784. Rueegg, Walter H. "The Intellectual Situation in German Higher Education." **Minerva**, 13 (Spring, 1975), 103-120.

Professor Rueegg claims that the universities in West Germany have lost their social significance and that little can be done internally to change the situation. He calls on external economic, political and other nonacademic spheres to counteract the ideological swamp in which the university is engulfed.

785. Science Council. "The Reform of Courses of Study in West German Universities." **Minerva**, 8 (April, 1970), 250-267.

A translation of "The Recommendations for the Reorganization of Courses of Study in Higher Educational Institutions," presented to the plenary session of the Science Council **(Wissenschaftsrat)**, 14 May, 1966.

786. van de Graff, John H. "Academic Power, Excellence and Equality: Evolving Patterns in Seven National Systems." **Higher Education Bulletin**, 4 (Summer, 1976), 139-57.

787. van de Graff, John H., Burton Clark, and Others. **Academic Power: Patterns of Authority.** New York: Praeger, 1978.

The authors look at patterns of authority in seven national systems of higher education. Five of these, including West Germany, are in Europe. Van de Graff writes the German chapter (No. 2) and focuses on the traditional structure, then legislative reforms of the university in the 1960's and 1970's.

788. Zuber, Ortrun. "Advisory Centres for Tertiary Education in West Germany." C.A.T. Education Monograph No. 11. Macquarie University Centre for Advancement of Teaching, Sydney, 1974.
Gives locations, addresses, objectives, tasks, and some projects of centers for tertiary education (**Hochschuldidaktisches Zentrum**) in West Germany.

FINANCES

EAST GERMANY

No references found.

WEST GERMANY

789. Blaug, Mark and Maureen Woodhall. "Patterns of Subsidies to Higher Education in Europe." **Higher Education**, 7 (Aug., 1978), 331-61.
The authors look at higher education subsidies in France, West Germany, the Netherlands, Sweden, and the U.K. The study concludes that the ideal package from the stantpoint of efficiency and equity is (1) a grants system in the last few years of secondary education, (2) a system of fees to about 30-50% of institutional incomes, and (3) an income contingent loan scheme.

790. Bockstael, Eric and Otto Feinstein. **Higher Education in the European Community: Reform and Economics.** Lexington, Mass.: Heath Lexington, 1970.
Although the authors look at higher education in several countries, they do give specific attention to German higher education planning and finances.

791. Hussain, K. M. **Institutional Resource Allocation Models in Higher Education**. Paris: OECD, 1976.
Includes a description of resource allocation models from the U.S., West Germany, Portugal, and the Netherlands.

792. Whiting, Charles H. "Widespread Foreboding over Financial Cuts." **Times Educational Supplement**, 2923 (May 28, 1971), 15.

RESEARCH ORGANIZATION

PRE-WORLD WAR II

793. Humboldt, Wilhelm von "On the Spirit and the Organizational Framework of Intellectual Institutions in Berlin." **Minerva**, 8 (April, 1970), 242-250.
A translation taken from Humboldt's **Gesammelte Schriften**. Berlin: B. Behr's Verlag, 1903. pp. 250-260.

794. Turner, R. Steven. "The Growth of Professional Research in Prussia, 1818 to 1848-- Causes and Context." **Historical Studies in the Physical Sciences**, 3 (1971), 137-82.
Turner traces the remarkable shift from medievalism to increasing reliance on specialization and empirical research methods in Germany, especially at the University of Berlin.

EAST GERMANY

No references found.

WEST GERMANY

795. Cathy, G., G. Drilhon, and Others. **The Research System.** Vol. I. Paris: OECD, 1972.
A comparative survey of the organization and financing of fundamental research in France, Germany and the United Kingdom.

796. Deich, Ingrid. "The Redistribution of Authority in National Laboratories in Western Germany." **Minerva,** 17 (Autumn, 1979), 413-444.
Deich traces the redistribution of authority in institutions similar to R&D centers in America and she traces the consequences of this action.

797. Flamig, Christian. "Organisation of Research--A Basic Condition for Efficient Research at Universities." **International Journal of Institutional Management in Higher Education.** (Nov., 1980), 271-90.
The author discusses the types of organizational measures that might be taken to make university research more efficient in West Germany.

798. Geimer, Reinhold and Hildegard Geimer. "Science in the Federal Republic of Germany--Organization and Promotion." Bonn-Bad Gotesberg: DAAD, 1971.

799. Huber, L. "Developments in Higher Education in Europe: Background Report, German Speaking Countries." In Noel Entwistle (ed.). **Strategies for Research and Development in Higher Education.** Council of Europe publication. Amsterdam: Swets and Zeitlinger, 1976.

800. Massow, Valentin. "Organization and Promotion of Research (in particular University Research) in the Federal Republic of Germany." **Higher Eduction in Europe,** 6 (Apr.-June, 1981), 14-16.

801. OECD. **The Research System: France, Germany, United Kingdom.** Vol. I. Paris: OECD, 1972.

802. Pfetsch, Frank. "Scientific Organization and Science Policy in Imperial Germany, 1871-1914: The Foundation of the Imperial Institute of Physics and Technology." **Minerva,** 8 (Oct., 1970).

803. Walsh, John. "OECD Report sees Closer Links between Research, Social Objectives." **Science,** 176 (Apr., 1972), 150-53.
Reports on an OECD study of the organization and financing of fundamental research in France, Germany, and the U.K.

RESEARCH LIBRARIES AT UNIVERSITIES

EAST GERMANY

No references listed

WEST GERMANY

804. Andrews, John S. "Learned Libraries in West Germany." **Journal of Librarianship**, 1 (1969), 20-40.
The focus of this article is on university libraries. After some remarks on the three-tier staff structure and its implications, some account is given of education for librarianship and the part played by library schools. Andrews describes the relative prosperity of libraries in regard to their stocks. He also deals with the debate on the relationship of the library to the institutes, which have their own collections, and he closes with some remarks on the role of the computer in librarianship.

805. Breitenbach, Edgar. "Free University Library." **Library Journal**, 79 (Dec. 15, 1954), 2355-59.
Describes the physical layout of the library funded by Ford Foundation and the volumes in the facility.

806. Bunett, A. D. "Impressions of West German University Libraries." **Libri**, 20 (1970), 35-58.

807. Guttsman, W. L. "Learned Libraries in Germany; More Prosperous than Britain." **Times Educational Supplement**, 2601 (Mar. 26, 1965), 928.
Describes the state of academic research libraries in West Germany.

808. Jones, Harold D. "Postwar University Library Buildings in West Germany." **College and Research Libraries**, 36 (July, 1975), 283-94. Discusses the recent construction of a number of West German university libraries.

809. Koettelwesch, Clemens. "Optimum Procedures for the Publication of Results in Library Research." IFLA Council, Division of Education and Research, 1979.

810. Lehmann, Klaus-Dieter. "Interlibrary Loan in the Federal Republic of Germany, and the responsibility for International Loan." **LIBER Bulletin**, 12 (1978), 23.

811. Oertel, Dieter. "Coordinating the Acquisitions of Research Libraries in the Federal Republic of Germany." **UNESCO Bulletin Library**, 19 (1963), 285-89.

812. Ostrem, W. M. "Daring Design for a German Library." **Wilson Library Bulletin**, 38 (Jan., 1964), 406-07.
Description ofthe University of Giessen Library.

813. Ostrem, W. M. "Ruhr University Bochum Library." **Wilson Library Bulletin**, 41 (Dec., 1966), 418-20.
Account of a computerized library facility in West Germany, with open-shelf offerings.

814. Rovelstad, Mathilde V. "Open Shelves/Closed Shelves in Research Libraries." **College and Research Libraries**, 37 (Sept., 1976), 457-67.
Describes the tradition of making books accessible through open stacks and outlines why the method was abandoned in German research libraries.

815. von Busse, Gisela. **West German Library Developments since 1945, with Special Emphasis on the Rebuilding of Research Libraries.** Washington D. C.: Library of Congress, 1962.
This study attempts to describe the recovery of West German research libraries from the Nazi oppression and war devastation. It gives an account of modernization efforts and pays special attention to the resional union catalogue system, the cooperative acquisitions program, interlibrary loan procedures, and exchange arrangements.

816. Wehmer, Carl. "The Organization and Origins of German University Libraries." **Library Trends**, 12 (1964), 491-512.
The author's main concern is with the politics of central libraries in relationship with university institutes and with other libraries throughout the country.

SPECIFIC INSTITUTIONS OF HIGHER LEARNING

SPECIFIC UNIVERSITIES

EAST GERMANY

817. "Dresden Technical University." **International Bureau of Education Bulletin** 36, 1 (1962), 11.

818. Silveston, Peter. "Visit to the University of Leipzig." **Institute of International Education News Bulletin**, 31 (Oct., 1955), 25-9.
Account of a brief visit to Leipzig University and his impressions of the institution. He discusses changes that have occured including admissions policies, state scholarships, and assignment of careers.

WEST GERMANY

A. Free University of Berlin

819. Anthon, Carl G. "Free University of Berlin." **Survey**, 87 (Oct., 1951), 413-16.
Account of the events surrounding the opening of the Free University. Anthon expresses hope that it can be a light to progressive, democratic education throughout both Germanies.

820. Anthon, Carl G. "Birth of the Free University." **American Scholar**, 24 (1954), 49-64.
Describes what has happened in the past six years of the Free University, during which time it has become a full fledged university. It has some traditional characteristics, but remains a "fighting university," and outpost of the free world.

821. Catudal, Honore M. "University Reform in the Federal Republic: The Experiment in Democratization at the Free University of Berlin." **Comparative Education**, 12 (Oct., 1976), 231-41.
Traces the inception of the Free University, the period of the student revolt, university reform legislation, the election of a new president, the intervention of the constitutional court, and the establishment of a new law governing elections.

822. Domes, Jurgen and Armin Paul Frank. "The Tribulations of the Free University of Berlin." **Minerva**, 13 (Sum., 1975), 183-99.

The authors describe the base on which the Free University is built and they trace the elements that have prevented it from being a genuine institution of education and higher learning. They conclude that the restoration of the Free University as a university in which honest scholarship is conducted is only a remote possibility.

823. Duggar, Margaret. "Impressions of the Free University of Berlin and Mary Wigmans Dance Studio." **Journal of Health, Physical Education and Recreation**, 31 (Mar., 1960), 71.

Describes impressions of physical education programs at Free University and Wigmans Dance Studio.

824. "Free University of Berlin in Open." **Institute for International Education News Bulletin**, 24 (Jan., 1949), 33-4.

Brief outline of events leading to the establishment of the Free University.

825. Gruener, Karl. "Recent Developments at the Free University of Berlin." **Institute of International Education News Bulletin**, 28 (May, 1953), 34-36.

Discussion of the introduction of general studies, the revival of student unions, and the adoption of student advisors.

826. Huebner, Wolfgang O. L. "Education in the Shadow of the Iron Curtain." **Science**, 118 (July 31, 1953), 121-24.

Describes the events that led to the establishment of the Free University.

827. Joy, Charles R. "A Fighting University." **American Association of University Professors Bulletin**, 38 (June, 1952), 266-71.

Provides some contextual background for the Free University of Berlin, established mainly from a gift from the Ford Foundation and located deep in communist territory.

828. Schoenbaum, David. "The Free University of Berlin, or How Free Can a University Be?" **AAUP Bulletin**, 59 (1973), 5.
The author gives an account of the clashes between students and university as well as city officials. He outlines what historical decisions lay behind these troubles and the law outlining a new model of governance, worked out in 1968 and passed in 1969 which led to the election of an assistant professor from East Germany as its first president.

829. Sommerkorn, Ingrid N. "The Free University of Berlin: Case Study of an Experimental Seminar." In W. Neblett and R. I. Butts (eds.). **Universities Face the Future**. San Francisco: Jossey Bass, 1972. pp. 336-46.

830. Whiting, Charles H. "Young Radical Gets Top Job." **Times Educational Supplement**, 2849 (Dec. 26, 1969), 8.
Reports appointment of the new head of the Free University of Berlin.

B. Other Universities

831. Angelloz, Joseph A. "University of the Saar." **Institute of International Education News Bulletin**, 28 (Apr., 1953), 14-16.
Descriptive account of the beginning of the University of the Saar in 1946, with its several faculties and institutes.

832. Boening, E. and K. Roeloffs. **Three German Universities: Aachen, Bochum, Konstance: Case Studies on Innovation in Higher Education**. Paris: OECD, 1970.
This is a survey of three new German Universities to determine in what way they had adopted the reforms being promoted in higher education circles. It was found that substantial innovations in administration and organization had taken place, although they apparently had not become a part of the wider university reform discussion.

833. Dale, A. J. "Two European Universities: A Report on Visits to Study the Administration of the University of Dijon and the University of Muenster." An Occasional Paper Published by the Conference of University Administrators, No. 2, July, 1978.

834. Gimbel, John. "Origins of the **Institut fuer Zeitgeschichte**: Scholarship, Politics, and the American Occupation." **American Historical Review**, 70 (1964/4), 714-51.

Gimbel describes the origins of this institute as revealing aspects of the German response to the American occupation.

835. Gray, J. Glenn. "Munich University: Class of '50; Case Study in German Re-education." **Commentary**, 5 (May, 1948), 440-48.

Offers a good case study of life at the University of Munich in 1946/47, based on interviews with students, because he was the control officer.

836. Haag, Herbert and Bodo Schmidt. "'Institute of Sport and Sport Sciences' of the Christian-Albrechts-University, Kiel--Structure and Function." **International Journal of Physical Education**, 16 (1979), 21-23.

837. Huebener, Theodore. "**Germersheim**: A Unique Language Institute." **Modern Language Journal**, 37 (Feb., 1953), 80-1.

Describes an institute of higher learning established by the French for language training.

838. Markmann, Charles M. "Heidelberg in the Twentieth Century." **Change**, (Feb., 1975), 20-23.

Discusses the contrasts between the old and the new Heidelberg, mentioning growth, admissions, trends, language focus, and faculty status.

839. "New Universities for West Germany: Bochum, Bremen, Konstanz." **Times Educational Supplement**, 2599 (Nov. 8, 1963), 659.

RESEARCH INSTITUTES

EAST GERMANY

No references listed

WEST GERMANY

840. Henaman, John F. "West German Science: Trends Mirrored in a Max Planck Institute." **Science**, 194 (Oct., 1976), 410-12.
The author describes the conceptualization of the Max Planck Institute for Biophysical Chemistry in Goettingen, then its establishment, programs and relationship with the university.

841. Weinert, F. E. and Herbert Simons. "The Bavarian State Institute for Educational Research and Planning, Germany." In **Case Studies of Educational Innovation: I. At the Central Level**. Paris: OECD, 1973.

TECHNICAL INSTITUTES

EAST GERMANY

842. Goettner, Reinhard. "**Ingenieurhochschulen** in the GDR--Engineering Institutes with Close Interrelationships between Education, Research and Production." **Higher Education in Europe**, 4 (July-Sept., 1979), 23-24.

WEST GERMANY

843. Conference of Engineering Societies of Western Europe and the United States of America. **Report on Education and Training of Professional Engineers**.

844. Gieseke, Ludwig. "The '**Fachhochschulen**' in the Federal Republic of Germany." **Higher Education in Europe**, 6 (Apr.-June, 1981), 42-45.

845. Kendall, James T. "Science and Technical Education in Germany." **Nature**, 160 (Nov. 22, 1947), 721-23.
Report of an international congress for technical education at Darmstadt, giving insight about science and technical education in West Germany.

846. Lawrence, Peter. "Engineering Education and Meritocracy." **Higher Education Review**, 111 (Summer, 1979), 27-35.

Lawrence looks at the status, function and education of engineers in West Germany and makes some comparisons with Britain.

847. Leussink, Hans. "Engineering Sciences in Today's World." Occasional Paper No. 16 prepared by the International Council for Educational Development, New York, 1975.

The discussion is in the context of Germany, but it transcends one country and explores the current dilemmas of science and engineering in higher education.

848. Ulbricht, Kurtand and Peter Zimmermann. "Problems Relating to Examinations in Three Year Technical/Natural Science Courses of Study at the Federal Armed Services University, Munich." **Higher Education**. 10 (Jan. 1981), 1-23.

849. Vogtmann, L. **New Trends in Higher and Technical Education (with Particular Reference to Advanced Technical Colleges and Polytechnics) in the Federal Republic of Germany**. Strasbourg: Council of Europe, 1972.

COMPREHENSIVE UNIVERSITIES

EAST GERMANY

No references listed

WEST GERMANY

850. Draheim, Hans. "The **Gesamthochschule**: A Model of Mobility." **Prospects**, 3 (Winter, 1973), 504-14.

After laying down the deficiencies of the classical and technical universities, the author describes how the **Gesamthochschule** will provide greater opportunities for mass education and integrated higher education.

851. Drescher, Bernd. "**Gesamthochschulen** (Comprehensive Universities) in the Federal Republic of Germany." **Bildung und Wissenschaft**, No. 1/2(e), 1981, a Publication of Inter Nationes.
Here is a full discussion of the issues surrounding the establishment of comprehensive universities.

852. Gieseke, Ludwig and Rupert Eilsberger. "The Development of the Comprehensive University in the Federal Republic of Germany." Working Paper for a meeting on 1-3 March, 1978. Strasbourg: Council for Cultural Cooperation, Council of Europe, 1977.
Describe the emergence of an institution that combines the aims of a number of traditional types of institutions of higher learning. Problems are discussed and future developments assessed.

853. Hamm-Bruecher, Hildegard. "Towards the Comprehensive University in Germany." **The World Year Book of Education**, (1972/73), 325-35.
Historical outline of higher education in Germany.

ART ACADEMIES

EAST GERMANY

No references are cited.

WEST GERMANY

854. Longyear, R. M. "Music at the **Hohe-Karlsschule**." **Journal of Research in Music Education**, 12 (Summer, 1964), 123-33.
Discusses the school founded by Duke Karl Engen in 1770 and dissolved shortly after his death in 1794. The focus here is on the music department of the school.

855. Phelan, Andrew. "The **Bauhaus** and Studio Art Education." **Art Education**, 34 (Sept., 1981), 6-13.
The history, theory, and methods of the German **Bauhaus** are described. Its influence on American studio art education is also discussed.

856. Thomas, Sarah. "Taking it Seriously." **Times Educational Supplement**, 2699 (Feb., 1967), 462.
Praises the professional preparation of German musicians in music academies.

OTHER INSTITUTIONS

EAST GERMANY

857. Kunze, Horst. "The Training of Librarians and Documentalists in the German Democratic Republic." **Journal of Librarianship**, 2 (Jan., 1970), 44-45.
Account of the situation in 1968.

858. Burrington, G. A. "Outline of Education and Training in the German Democratic Republic." **Research in Librarianship**, 3 (Jan., 1971), 114-15.
Discusses the training necessary to become a librarian in East Germany.

WEST GERMANY

859. Dixon, J. "German Physical Education: Cologne Sporthochschule." **Times Educational Supplement**, 2014 (Dec. 4, 1953), 1021.

860. Lane, M. R. and F. W. Seibel. "A Binary Divide in West Germany." **Higher Education Review**, 11 (Sum., 1979), 70-74.
Discusses the problem of including or excluding the professions from academic study at the university. Draws comparisons between the U.K. and one state in West Germany.

861. Matley, Bruce. "West Germany's Systematic Approach to Actor Training." **Theatre Journal**, 32 (Oct., 1980), 329-35.
Discusses the nature of theaters in general and focuses on public acting schools. The author feels the system of actor training in the U.S. is inferior.

862. UNESCO. **World Guide to Library Schools and Training Courses in Documentation**. London: Clive Bingley, 1972. pp. 70-79.

863. Verner, Mathilda "Librarianship in Western Germany." **Journal of Library History, Philosophy, and Comparative Librarianship**, 2 (1967), 144-51.
Outlines the educational requirements of librarians in West Germany. She points out that three levels exist: academic, community college level, and clerical workers.

EAST AND WEST GERMANY

864. Neenan, Peter. "Development of Library Education Programs in the two Germanies since 1945." In William Williamson. **A Search for New Insights in Librarianship: A Day of Comparative Studies**. Madison: Library School, University of Wisconsin, 1976.

DISTANCE STUDY

EAST GERMANY

No references found.

WEST GERMANY

865. Grunwald, Klaus-Dieter. "Distance Study in the Federal Republic of Germany: **Fernuniversitaet-Gesamthochschule** in Hagen." **Higher Education in Europe**, 5 (Oct.-Dec., 1980), 46-49.

866. Heidt, Erhard C. "Higher Education at a Distance: Developments and Projects in Germany." **Teaching at a Distance**, 2 (Feb., 1975), 49-60.
Heidt describes three main projects of academic distance studies in Germany, then moves to a discussion of the debate on distance studies in intellectual and political terms in Germany since the mid-1960's.

867. Hetzel, Michaele and others. "Women in Distance Study--Women Students at the **Fernuniversitaet** in Hagen (Federal Republic of Germany)." **Higher Education in Europe**, 6 (July-Sept., 1981), 18-21.

868. Hilligen, Wolfgang. "Report on the Distance Studies Course 'Social Studies.'" Bloomington, Indiana: Institute of German Studies, Indiana University, 1976.
Describes an innovative social studies teacher education program at the University of Tuebingen, including problems, aims, and structure of the course of studies.

869. Ortmeier, Anno. "Developing External Studies in West Germany: An Idealized Model." **Journal of Educational Administration**, 17 (Oct., 1979), 255-58.
Discusses distance study in Germany including the prospective student, the autonomy of the distance university, the department of external studies, the nation-wide service center, and study centers.

870. Tauber, Michael. "A Computer-Aided Management System in Distance Education." **European Journal of Education**, 15 (1980), 285-97.
The article describes a project known as CAVA, which is a computer assisted management system for distance training in West Germany.

871. "TV College, Germany's First." **Times Educational Supplement**, 2679 (Sept., 23, 1966), 617.
A television series is described which is developed to prepare anyone to pass the **mittlere Reife** examinations.

FIELDS OF STUDY

GENERAL EDUCATION STUDIES

EAST GERMANY

No reference cited.

WEST GERMANY

872. Anderson, Eugene N. **The Humanities in the German and Austrian Universities**. Washington D.C.: American Council of Learned Societies, 1950.

The small booklet deals with **Dozenten**, the curriculum, libraries and equipment, university administration and policy, and the Free University of Berlin. In the spirit of reeducation, the author feels the Germans must revive the practice of their predecessors, keeping their studies close to contemporary needs.

873. Rueegg, Walter H. "Humanism and **Studium Generale** in German Higher Education." **Journal of General Education**, 8 (Apr., 1955), 137.

Rueegg looks at the concept of **Studium Generale** in historical perspective and what has happened at the university since World War II. This is a comprehensive study.

NATURAL SCIENCE FACULTY

PRE-WORLD WAR II

874. Freudenberg, Karl. "Beginnings of Chemical Instruction at Heidelberg" (trans. by R. E. Oesper). **Journal of Chemical Education**, 34 (Apr., 1957), 181.

The first signs of chemistry teaching at Heidelberg are traced. This came into existence in the 1770's, with other work evolving in the nineteenth century.

EAST GERMANY

No references found.

WEST GERMANY

875. Audrieth, L. F. and R. J. A. Otto. "Inorganic Chemistry at German Universities." **Journal of Chemical Education**, 36 (Sept., 1959), 441-44.
After describing the German system of education, the authors discuss instruction in inorganic chemistry at German universities.

876. Ben-David, Joseph. "The Universities and the Growth of Science in Germany and the United States." **Minerva,** 7 (Autumn-Winter, 1968/69), 1-35.
After discussing the structure of the German university and the U.S. graduate school, the author comparatively discusses issues and problems particularly related to internal structures and traditions and external forces imposing themselves on the systems.

877. Bunnett, Joseph F. "German and American Professors of Chemistry: A Contrast." **Journal of Chemical Education**, 39 (May, 1962), 225-29.
Bunnett traces the university and postdoctoral experience of the chemistry professor. He also outlines the different levels of the professor with their differing responsibilities. He discusses the consequences of their training and compares their work.

878. "Physics in Germany." **Nature**, 163 (Feb. 19, 1949), 299.
The deliberations to make technical physics a subject in its own right are discussed.

879. Schoen, Herbert M. "Chemistry and the West German Education System." **Journal of Chemical Education**, 35 (August, 1958), 399-400.
After discribing the system of education, the author outlines the course of study in chemistry at the Braunschweig Technical High School.

880. von Laue, M. "Report on the State of Physics in Germany." **American Journal of Physics**, 17 (Mar., 1949), 137-41.
Physics apparently suffered greatly after 1933. The author mentions several names of people who were lost during National Socialism. He lists the contemporary names and institutions of the better known physicists in Germany. He also describes the life of a physics student as well as the reasons physicists are leaving Germany.

MEDICAL FACULTY

PRE-WORLD WAR II

881. Flexner, Abraham. **Medical Education in Europe.** A Report to the Carnegie Foundation for the Advancement of Teaching. New York, 1912.

Deals with many facets of German medical training, including medical sciences, clinical instruction, curriculum, and examinations.

EAST GERMANY

No references found.

WEST GERMANY

882. Dahmer, J. and Others. "Evaluation of an Integrated Multi-Media Learning System." **Medical Education,** 10 (Nov., 1976), 491-95.

German educators describe two teaching methods at the medical school in Hanover, West Germany, the traditional method and an integrated multi-media system. They give results of a comparative study of the two systems with the new system showing significantly more gain.

883. Parry, K. M. "Medical Education in France, Germany, Italy and the United Kingdom." **Medical Education**, 10 (Jan., 1976), 59-66.

This report by a Scotish scholar assesses the nature of "postgraduate" medical education programs in various countries. He then engages in a comparison of the programs. Postgraduate programs refer to the 15 month post M.D. training experience, specialist careers and public health experience.

884. von Bexkuell, Thure. "Federal Republic of Germany." In **Reforms and New Trends in Undergraduate Medical Education**. Strasbourg: Council of Europe, 1973.

Medical undergraduate education is discussed in relation to the health needs of society and to premedical, postgraduate and paramedical training. Legal and administrative aspects are also considered.

LAW FACULTY

PRE-WORLD WAR II

885. Rabel, Ernst. "The System of Legal Education in Germany." **Journal of the Society of Public Teachers of Law**, 22 (1930).

886. Schweinburg, Eric F. **Law Training in Continental Europe**. New York: Russell Sage Foundation, 1945.

After a brief overview, the author discusses law education in Austria, France, Germany, and the Soviet Union. His focus is on the tradition in Germany although he devotes some space to National Socialist peculiarities.

EAST GERMANY

No references found.

WEST GERMANY

887. Rothman, Mitchell L. "Classroom Law: Early Development of University Legal Education in England, the United States, and Germany." Yale Higher Education Research Group Working Paper. New Haven: Higher Education Research Group, 1980.

888. Shartel, Burke. "Report on German Legal Education." **Journal of Legal Education**, 14 (1962), 425-483.

An extensive report of the German system of legal education, claimed to be the most complete program of training in the world. The report follows six headings: (1) general features of legal education, (2) admission to law study--policies and standards, (3) Academic phase--university study, (4) proposed practical study semester, (5) practical service phase, and (6) examinations.

PHILOSOPHICAL FACULTY

PRE-WORLD WAR II

889. Hartshorne, Richard. "The Nature of Geography, a Critical Survey of Current Thought in the Light of the Past." **Annals of the Association of American Geographers**, 29 (1939).

890. van Valckenburg, Samuel. "The German School of Geography." In Griffith Taylor (ed.). **Geography in the XX Century**. New York: Methuen, 1951.

This essay is divided into several historical sections after the turn of this century. The author, who is Dutch, indicts the German geographers for advocating aggression and being passive when they should have defended human rights.

891. Wassermann, Felix M. "Haushofer and the German Geopolitics: A Tragic Experiment in Power Politics and Education." **Education**, 72 (Feb., 1952), 360-70.

Discusses the contribution of Haushofer, who organized a particular brand of German geography-politics, and how this was coopted by the Nazis.

EAST GERMANY

No references found.

WEST GERMANY

892. Anweiler, Oskar. "Study of Soviet and East European Education in West Germany." **Comparative Education Review,** 9 (Oct., 1965), 341-45.
Descriptive account of the work in West Germany on Eastern European education. He details the various institutes and publications as well as what he feels are the future tasks of the field.

893. Cerf, Walter. "Existentialist Mannerism and Education." **Journal of Philosophy**, 54 (Mar. 17, 1955), 141-52.
After two months listening to German philosophy lectures and seminars, Cerf concludes that the prevailing mode is a sort of existential mannerism, which he finds to be destructive and unwholesome.

894. Cerf, Walter. "Field Trip to German Universities." **Journal of Higher Education**, 26 (Mar., 1955), 134-40+.
After visiting several campuses and attending lectures, Cerf concludes that the authoritarian German tradition still holds, at least in philosophy lectures and seminars.

895. Galinsky, Hans. "American Studies in Germany: Their Growth, Variety, and Prospects." In Robert H. Walker (ed.). **American Studies Abroad**. Westport, Conn.: Greenwood Press, 1975, pp. 82-88.

896. Hausmann, Gerhard. "A Century of Comparative Education: 1785-1885." **Comparative Education Review,** 11 (Feb., 1977), 1-21.
Comparative education as a field of study, mainly in Germany, is looked at.

897. Iggers, George C. "The Dissolution of German Historicism." In R. Herr and H. T. Parker (eds.). **Ideas in History: Presented to Louis Gottschalk by his Former Students**. Durham: Duke University Press, 1965. pp. 288-329.
Explains that Germans have maintained a conscious philosophy of history for two centuries, but with the advent of Marxism-Leninism this philosophy has been disrupted to the point that there is no longer a "German" philosophy of history.

898. Iggers, George C. **The German Conception of History.** Middletown, Conn.: Wesleyan University Press, 1968.
Claims that after World War II German historians followed older, pre-National Socialist patterns of historiography. He feels a younger generation of historians is emerging, who are still heavily influenced by their mentors, but who are making a clear and conscious attempt to move away from the idealistic tradition. He does not deal with Nazi or East German historiography.

899. Mommsen, Hans. "Historical Scholarship in Transition: The Situation in the Federal Republic of Germany." **Daedalus**, 100 (Spring, 1971).
Reviews the changes taking place in German historiography--changes toward a critical dissociation from traditional historiography and an openness to new methods and a conscious orientation toward comparative sociohistorical analysis.

900. Snell, John L. "Recent German History in German Universities, 1945-53." **Journal of Central European Affairs**, 14 (July, 1954), 174-80.
Indicates recent professor interest in writing about twentieth century affairs. He includes a selected list of dissertations that have been completed between 1945 and 1953 in Germany which focus on this period.

901. Lacey, James F. "American Studies at German Universities: Failure of the Interdisciplinary Approach." **International Education and Cultural Exchange**, 6 (Summer, 1970), 27-33.
Catalogues programs at various institutions of higher learning.

902. Pfaffenberger, Hans G. "On the Training of Psychologists in Germany." **American Psychologist**, 7 (Mar., 1952), 98-9.

903. **Report on American Studies at German Universities: 1958-1965**. Bonn: Office of the Cultural Attache, American Embassy, 1965.

904. Skard, Sigmund. **American Studies in Europe: Their History and Present Organization**. Philadelphia: University of Pennsylvania Press, 1958.
Skard looks at a large number of countries, but he devotes one entire chapter to American Studies in Germany. He takes the reader through five historical periods and concludes by discussing work at individual institutions.

905. Streitz, Norbert A. "A Graduate Programme in Science Education: Experiences and Suggestions." **European Journal of Science Education**, 1 (July-Sept., 1979), 307-13.

The author participated in a science education program at UC Berkeley and makes some suggestions for the adaptation of such a program in West Germany.

906. Vater, Heinz. "Linguistics in West Germany." **Language Sciences**, 6 (Aug., 1971), 6-24.

The article discusses West German linguistic publications in at attempt to inform the American linguists about what is going on in the field in that country.

907. Wode, Henning. "Research Activities in Germany." **Second Language Acquisition Notes and Topics**, 8 (May, 1978), 22-39.

SOCIAL SCIENCES

EAST GERMANY

No references found.

WEST GERMANY

908. Flohr, G. "Business and Economics Education at Western German Universities." **American Business Education**, 15 (Dec., 1958), 91-2+.

909. George, Siegfried. "Society and Social Justice: Problems of Political Education in West Germany." **Teaching Political Science**, 8 (April, 1981), 281-96.

910. Schweigler, Gebhard L. "Federal Republic of Germany." **International Studies in Six European Countries--United Kingdom, France, Federal Republic of Germany, Sweden, Netherlands, Italy**. New York: Ford Foundation, June, 1976.

The study deals with political science, current history, sociology, and economics at institutions of higher learning in West Germany and their engagement with international studies.

THEOLOGY FACULTY

EAST GERMANY

No references found.

WEST GERMANY

911. Cully, Kendig B. "German Works in Religious Education." **Religious Education**, 52 (May, 1957), 209-11.
An account of the books currently being used in the fields of religious education and practical theology.

912. Littell, Franklin H. **The German Phoenix**. Garden City, New York: Doubleday, 1960.
This book, though lacking a tight structure, lays out some dimensions of the religious movement in Germany and especially the role of religion in higher education.

913. Schaff, Philip. **Germany: Its Universities, Theology and Religion**. Philadelphia: Lindsay and Blakiston, 1857.
Sketches of German theologians in the context of university life.

OTHER FIELDS

PRE-WORLD WAR II

914. Rust, Val D. "Negro Schools: A Model for Nazi Colonial Education." **Journal of Negro Education**, 40 (Spring, 1971), 103-107.
Describes the work of the Hamburg Colonial Institute between the world wars.

915. Spidle, Jake W. Jr. "Colonial Studies in Imperial Germany." **History of Education Quarterly**, 13 (Feb., 1973), 231-48.
The author claims that the Germans engaged in extensive efforts to prepare themselves for their colonial responsibilities, and by 1914 they had established themselves as one of the most progressive and energetic of all colonial powers.

916. Weber, Max. "Towards a Sociology of the Press." **Journal of Communication**, 26 (Summer, 1976), 96-101.
This is a reprint of a speech delived by Weber in 1910 giving the first comprehensive proposal for an institutional approach to research on modern media.

EAST GERMANY

917. McGuire, Michael and Lothar Berger. "Speech in the Marxist State." **Communication Education**, 28 (July, 1979), 169-78

WEST GERMANY

No references found.

STUDENTS

GENERAL

PRE-WORLD WAR II

918. Brown, Cynthia Stokes. "The American Discovery of the German University: Four Students at Goettingen, 1815-1822." Unpublished Ph.D. Dissertation. Johns Hopkins University, 1964.

919. Diehl, Carl. "Innocents Abroad: American Students in German Universities, 1810-1870." **History of Education Quarterly**, 16 (Feb., 1976), 321-41.
Diehl looks at a large sample of American students in Germany prior to 1870 and assesses their influence on the development of American higher education. He finds they focused more on the humanities than natural sciences.

EAST GERMANY

Fricke, Karl Wilhelm. "Soviet Germany's Skeptical Youth." **The Sudeten Bulletin**, 10 (April, 1962), 93-96.
It is claimed that the young people are far from being convinced of the communist way of life, even though little is heard of active and outspoken protest.

920. Waeltage, H. **Student in the GDR**. Dresden: Zeit im Bild, 1968.

WEST GERMANY

921. Newell, Peter. "Bavaria Clambers on Ladder of Discipline." **Times Educational Supplement**, 2806 (Feb. 28, 1969), 656.
Measures toward discipline of Bavarian University students by the state are outlined.

STUDENT ACCESS AND DEMAND

EAST GERMANY

922. Nast, Manfred. "Right to Education and the Tasks of Higher Education in GDR." **Higher Education in Europe**, 2 (Mar.-Apr., 1977), 25-27.

923. Peck, Reginald. "Universities Behind the Iron Curtain." **Spectator**, 188 (May 23, 1952), 666-67.
The "Sovietisation' of East German universities is described. Peck suggests that the claim that present universities are being populated by peasants, minors, and factory workers is a sham.

WEST GERMANY

924. Becker, Willi. **Barriers to Higher Education in the Federal Republic of Germany**. New York: International Council for Educational Development, 1979.
The study focuses on access and admission to higher education in West Germany. The history and administration of admission to higher education are described, and changes in current laws governing access and admission are examined.

925. Beckerhoff, Dirk. "Germany." In **Individual Demand for Education**. Paris: OECD, 1980.
A look at attendance rates at all levels with a conclusion that demand for education is increasing while the labor market for so many highly educated people remains uncertain.

926. Burn, Barbara B. "Access to Higher Education in the Federal Republic of Germany and the United States." **International Review of Education**, 22 (1976), 193-201.
Compares access in West Germany and the United States. She raises questions about the balance between meritocratic and equalitarian policies, and also stresses that access policies must be determined in relationship to other factors as well.

927. Burn, Barbara B. **Higher Education in Nine Countries**. New York: McGraw Hill, 1971.
Burn did a study for the Carnegie Commission on Higher Education in order to assess higher education within national contexts. She found some trends, including rapid enrollment growth, expenditures, increasing public support, and greater involvement in society on the part of the academic community.

928. Edding, Friedrich. "The University Enrollment in West Germany." **Comparative Education Review**, 9 (Feb., 1965), 5-10.
The author addresses the issue of the number of university students needed in West Germany. He considers a number of variables that must be considered in making such a determination.

929. Hahn, Walter. "Extending Equal Opportunity in West German Higher Education." **Educational Record**, 58 (Feb., 1977), 403-17.

The author examines changes in the West German higher education system since World War II, and he details efforts to promote equal access to institutions of higher learning. Political and educational rationales behind enrollment restrictions and economic uncertainties surrounding educational mobility are outlined.

930. Hecquet, I. and others. **Recent Flows in Higher Education.** New York: International Council for Educational Development, 1976.

Part one gives comprehensive statistical data on student flows in higher education in eleven countries, including West Germany. Part two is analytical, posing and answering questions.

931. Karpen, Ulrich. "Constitutional Problems Concerning Admission to Institutitons of Higher Education--Questions Relevant to a German-American Comparison." **International Review of Education**, 24 (1978), 3-20.

Karpen gives an overview of the university, especially its admissions system, in the United States and West Germany and analyses how the constitutions of these countries are applied to key problems of access to higher education.

932. Karpen, Ulrich. "University Admission Criteria: Some German-American Comparative Observations." **International Review of Education**, 22 (1976), 203-21.

Admissions procedures and criteria for access to higher education in the U.S. and West Germany are examined.

933. Kiehn, Ludwig. "Alternative Paths to the University--Germany." **Year Book of Education**, (1959), 475-83.

Discusses the "second educational path" to the university.

934. Kloss, Guenther. "More Arts and Social Science Places Proposed for Universities." **Times Educational Supplement**, 345 (June 23, 1978), 6.

935. Massey, A. J. "The Dimensions of Achievement Measured by a Placement Test." **Assessment in Higher Education**, 2 (1976), 118-34.

Implications of achievement tests are considered as well as a factor analytic study of an English placement test made of incoming students of universities.

936. Menacker, Julius. "Democracy and College Admission Policy: The German Perspective." **College and University**, 55 (Fall, 1979), 27-40.
Describes the way in which the German university has attempted to democratize, but facing inordinate demand for places it has instituted a limited admission policy.

937. Merritt, Richard L. "The Courts, the Universities and the Right of Admission in the Federal Republic of Germany." **Minerva**, 17 (Spring, 1979), 1-32.
Merritt outlines the legal rights of all citizens regarding choice of professions and traces the increasing federal power regarding admissions policies. He maintains the courts have exceeded their proper jurisdiction at least in this matter.

938. OECD. **Individual Demand for Education: France, Germany, Greece, United Kingdom**. Paris: OECD, 1979.

939. Perkins, James A. and Barbara B. Burn. **Access to Higher Education: Two Perspectives**. New York: International Council for Educational Development, 1978.
A culmination document of a three year project on access to higher education in the United States and West Germany. The report deals with the two systems, equal opportunity, educational articulation and access, access and employment and the role of government.

940. Phillips, Celia M. **Changes in Subject Choice at School and University**. London: London School of Economics and Political Science, 1969.
The author identified subject options available at different levels of grammar school education and assessed the connection between them and the university faculty entered in Great Britain, the Netherlands, West Germany, and France.

941. Renschler, Hans E. "Federal Republic of Germany." In Barbara B. Burn (ed.). **Admission to Medical Education in Ten Countries**. New York: International Council for Educational Development, 1978. pp. 64-91.
An overview of the educational system is given in ten countries, including West Germany, by a discussion of medical students and faculties, curriculum and examinations, selection procedures, waiting time, and results.

HIGHER EDUCATION AND EMPLOYMENT

PRE-WORLD WAR II

942. Winkleman, G. G. "Education of Heino Leopold von Goehde." **Peabody Journal of Education**, 53 (Jan. 1976), 131-35.

Through the experiences of one man, the author attempts to show us that pragmatic career considerations should maintain a significant place in higher education.

EAST GERMANY

No references found.

WEST GERMANY

943. Becker, Helmut. "Access, Higher Education, and Employment." In **Higher Education: Crisis and Support.** New York: International Council for Educational Support, 1974.

944. "Expansion of Higher Education and Employment Opportunities in the Federal Republic of Germany." **Higher Education in Europe**, 4 (July-Sept., 1979), 22-27.

945. Huefner, K. and others. **Higher Education and Manpower Planning in the Federal Republic of Germany.** Geneva: ILO, 1977.

946. Schramm, Jurgen. "Development of Higher Education and Employment in the Federal Republic of Germany." **Higher Education**, 9 (Sept., 1980), 605-17.

The Article gives a short account of the quantitative development of the German universities and the labor market in the last two decades. It also describes the organizational transformation which followed the 1976 law.

947. Teichler, Ulrich. "Higher Education and Employment in the Federal Republic of Germany: Trends and Changing Research Approaches from the Comparative Point of View." In Henry Wasser (ed.). **Economics of Higher Education: A Comparative Perspective of Policy and Dilemma**. New York: Center for European Studies, Graduate School, City University of New York, 1978. pp. 32-66.

STUDENT SERVICES: HEALTH, EATING, AND HOUSING

EAST GERMANY

No references found.

WEST GERMANY

948. Augenstein, Heinz. "A Model for Student Counseling and Guidance Based on German Experience." **International Journal of Institutional Management in Higher Education**, 3 (May. 1979), 127-40.

The author describes guidance and counselling practices generally in West Germany, but focuses specifically on a test model being implemented at the University of the Saarland.

949. Chase, Philip B. "The Student Health Scene in Europe in the Mid 70's." **Journal of the American College Health**, 24 (June, 1976), 313-17.

Personal observations at made of health services in higher education in five countries, including West Germany.

950. Holzmann, Albert A. "Placement Service of the University of Cologne." **German Quarterly**, 25 (May, 1952), 164-69.

Description of a placement service operated solely by the students themselves.

STUDENT SUPPORT

EAST GERMANY

No references found.

WEST GERMANY

951. Woodhall, Maureen. **Review of Student Support Schemes in Selected OECD Countries**. Paris: OECD, 1978. pp. 53-61.

STUDENT LIFE

PRE-WORLD WAR II

952. Arnold, Thomas James. "Recollections of a Goettingen Student." **New Monthly Magazine and Literary Journal**. 18 (1830), 245-48, 342-44.

953. Bork, Uwe and Manfred Klee. "**Studentenwerke**: Their Work and Their History." **Western European Education**, 11 (Fall-Winter, 1979/80), 21-33.
Student organizations at the German universities are described and placed in historical context.

954. Howitt, William. **The Student-Life of Germany**. London: Longman, Brown, Green and Longmans, 1841.
A comprehensive account of student life is given, including chapters on fraternities, ceremonies, duels, songs, drinking, special celebrations, seasonal amusements, and political participation.

955. Mayhew, Henry. **German Life and Manners as seen in Saxony at the Present Day. Illustrated with Songs and Pictures of the Student Customs at the University of Jena**. London: W. H. Allen, 1865.

956. Ticknor, George. "German Student Life at Goettingen." In Stewart E. Fraser and William W. Brickman (eds.). **A History of International and Comparative Education**. Glenview, Ill.: Scott, Foresman and Co., 1968.
A Letter to E. T. Channing in Boston, on April 19, 1816.

EAST GERMANY

No references found.

WEST GERMANY

957. Hartung, B. "University Life in Germany." **Teachers College Journal**, 38 (Dec., 1966), 115-19.

958. McNamee, Lawrence F. "Life at a German University." **Texas Outlook**, 41 (Aug., 1957), 12-15.
Gives a glimpse of student life, including how the student gets to the university, student expenses, tuition, course of studies, and a typical day.

959. Stengel, Rudolph F. "Munich Student: Chronicle of his Day." **Clearing House**, 23 (Feb., 1949), 355-56.

960. Thompsen, J. A. "No Duels, no Beer." **Spectator**, 185 (Aug. 11, 1950), 175.
Account of a British student in Germany--student life highlighted.

961. "Who Finances Students in Germany?" **Higher Education**, 10 (Jan., 1954), 87.

962. Ziman, Naomi. "Life in the **Studentenbunker**." **Spectator**, 187 (Oct. 26, 1951), 534.
Student life is described in what was once an air-raid shelter in Bonn.

STUDENT ACTIVISM

PRE-WORLD WAR II

963. Donohoe, James I. "Munich Student Revolt." **Pacific Spectator**, 41 (1950), 49-59.
Account of student struggles at Munich from January, 1942 until February, 1943.

964. Eyck, F. Gunther. "The political theories and activities of the German Academic youth between 1815 and 1819." **Journal of Modern History**, 27 (1955), 27-38.
Deals with the legend that the original **Burschenschaften** constituted a powerful and dangerous force, providing evidence that there was no far-reaching, serious conspiracy among students and fraternities.

965. Giles, Geoffrey J. "The National Socialist Students' Association in Hamburg, 1926-1945." Ph.D. dissertation, Cambridge University, 1975.

966. Jarausch, Konrad H. "The Sources of German Student Unrest, 1815-1848." In L. Stone (ed.). **The University in Society**. Princeton: Princeton University Press, 1974. Vol. 2, pp. 533-569.
Jarausch attempts to refine present explanations of student unrest, especially as they pertain to the breakdown of a sense of psychological and emotional community, by assessing student unrest in Germany from 1815 to 1848.

967. Robertson, Priscilla. "Students on the Barricades, Germany and Austria, 1848." **Political Science Quarterly**, 84 (1969), 367-79.

968. Utley, Philip Lee. "Radical Youth Generation Conflict in the 'Anfang' Movement, 1912-Jan., 1914." **History of Education Quarterly**, 19 (Summer, 1979), 207.
Discusses what is claimed to be the first left-wing movement concerned with the rights of youth as such. The author uses psychoanalytic theory to explain the fervor of the generational conflict involved.

969. Zorn, Wolfgang. "Student Politics in the Weimar Republic." **Contemporary History**, 5, 1 (1970), 128-43.
Zorn compares the present student movement with student political action in the Weimar period.

EAST GERMANY

970. Whiting, Charles H. "Where Students Refuse to participate." **Times Educational Supplement**, 2786 (Oct. 11, 1968), 745.

Analyses why the East German student does not engage in protest activities.

WEST GERMANY

971. Buschbeck, Malte. "The Politicization of the University." **Western European Education**, 3 (Winter, 1971/72), 329-48.

The account of recent events regarding the inclusion of students in all decision-making and voting bodies. Buschbeck explores the extent to which the university ought to be involved in the ideological struggle over social reform.

972. "Germany's Student Revolt." **School and Society**, 96 (Oct. 26, 1968), 373-76.

973. Goldschmidt, Dietrich. "West Germany." In Margaret Archer (ed.). **Students, University and Society: A comparative Sociological Review.** London: Heineman, 1972.

Discussion of the role of student activism in university reform.

974. Hunnius, F. C. **Student Revolts: The New Left in West Germany.** Pamphlet published by War Resisters International, London, 1968.

A pamphlet sympathetic to student activities in West Germany.

975. "Irreconcilables and Fumbling Reformers in West Germany." **Minerva**, 7 (Autumn-Winter, 1968/69), 153-77.

Chronicles events at various universities, especially regarding student activism and professorial politics.

976. Levitt, Cyril. "The New Left, The New Class and Socialism." **Higher Education**, 8 (Nov., 1979), 641-55.
The author interviews former student activists in Canada, West Germany, and the U.S.A. and finds many have retained a political commitment, but the movement was ambivalent due to the relations of a specific generation to the deterioration of the condition of intellectual labor in society.

977. Merritt, Richard L. "The Student Protest Movement in West Berlin." **Comparative Politics**, 1 (July, 1969), 516-33.
Merritt gives background data about the emergence of student activism, stressing the political bias and socio-cultural facets of student protest.

978. Seabury, Paul. "Student Freedom and the Republic of Scholars: Berlin and Berkeley." **Comparative Education Review**, 10 (June, 1966), 350-58.

979. Stern, J. P. "Student Disaffection and the German Professor." **Times Educational Supplement**, 2764 (May 10, 1968), 1559.

980. "Towards University Reform and Political Action by the Students in the Federal Republic of Germany." **International Bureau of Education Bulletin**, 42, 4th qtr. (1968), 244-47.

981. Webler, Wolf-Dietrich. "The Sixties and the Seventies: Aspects of Student Activism in West Germany." **Higher Education**, 9 (March, 1980), 155-68.
The fundamental differences between the student movement in West Germany in the 1960's and 1970's are analysed and the personal, social, political, and organizational factors influencing these changes are described.

STUDENT EXCHANGES

EAST GERMANY

No references found.

WEST GERMANY

982. Institute of Education of the European Cultural Foundation. "The Intra-European Mobility of Undergraduate Students." A study carried out on behalf of the Commission of the European Communities, Paris, 1977.

The report deals with the motivations underlying student exchange, the less than satisfactory level of exchange, obstacles to free circulation of students and organized mobility.

983. Littmann, Ulrich. "Perspectives from Bonn." **International education and Cultural Exchange**, 10 (Feb., 1974), 24-28.

The author describes the various exchange opportunities between the United States and West Germany.

984. Neumeister, Hermann. "Germany's Language Assistant Exchanges." **Educational Exchange**, (Spring, 1969).

985. Roehrs, Hermann. "Facilities for Study Abroad as a Contribution to the Expansion of Education in Developing countries. Problems and Proposals with Special Reference to Germany." **World Year Book of Education**, (1965), 283-88.

PROFESSORS

GENERAL

PRE-WORLD WAR II

986. Perry, Walter. **German University Education**. London: Longman, Brown, Green, and Longmans, 1845.

The study focuses on the professors and students of Germany.

987. Ringer, Fritz K. **The Decline of the Mandarins: The German Academic Community, 1890-1933**. Cambridge: Harvard University Press, 1969.

988. Ritter, Gerhard. "German Professor in the Third Reich." **Review of Politics**, 8 (Apr., 1946), 242-54.
Ritter gives a personal account of his experiences as a professor and explains that even though the Nazis worked for total control, the machinery was so gigantic that it was extremely clumsy and allowed for many activities to go on that were subversive.

989. Thomas, R. Hinton. **Liberalism, Nationalism, and the German Intellectuals, 1822-47**. Cambridge: W. Heffer and Sons, 1952.
This study is an analysis of the academic and scientific conferences that took place over a 30 year period in the nineteenth century.

990. Turner, R. Steven. "University Reformers and Professional Scholarship in Germany, 1760-1806." In L. Stone (ed.) **The University in Society**. Princeton: Princeton University Press, 1974. Vol. 2, pp. 495-531.
Turner challenges the tendency to regard the period after 1806 as the only fruitful period of study since the period of the Enlightenment began. He finds the professorate in relationship to the advance of scholarship to be quite fruitful during the period in question.

991. Unfug, Douglas A. "Gauss, Humboldt and the University of Berlin: The Academic Marketplace in 1810." **AAUP Bulletin**, 48 (Dec., 1962), 344-45.
The paper shows copies of correspondence indicating the hard bargaining that took place when Humboldt offered Gauss a position at the University of Berlin.

EAST GERMANY

992. Kiel, Siegfried. "Further University Level Training for Lecturers in Higher Education in the German Democratic Republic." **Higher Education in Europe**, 6 (Jan.-Mar., 1981), 53-55.

WEST GERMANY

993. Ben-David, Joseph. **The Scientist's Role in Society.** Englewood Cliffs, N. J.: Prentice-Hall, 1954.
Ben-David attempts to describe the emergence and development of the social role of the scientists as well as the organization of scientific work. In this context he looks at the German scientific hegemony in the last century and its contribution to organized science.

994. Capelle, Jean. **Mobility of Postgraduate Students, Academic Teachers, and Research Workers.** Strasbourg: Council of Cultural Cooperation, Council of Europe, 1977. pp. 57-60.
One of a series of statements on Council of Europe countries.

995. Eckstein, Brigitte. "The Socialization of German University Teachers: Some Observations on Role Acquisition in an Academic Context and the Consequent Institutional Effects." **Higher Education**, 6 (May, 1977), 135-38.
Eckstein looks at the norms, values, and attitudes of university teachers. Her focus is on the impact of the power of the head of departments and she suggests ways of counteracting this influence.

996. Elsterman, Gert. "On the Aging of Scientific Personnel in Higher Education and Research." **International Journal of Institutional Management in Higher Education**, 2 (May, 1978), 21-29.
Elsterman calls attention to the collective aging of academic staff in higher education and suggests policies to palliate its negative effect.

997. Fuhrig, Wolf D. "Professor Emeritus in West Germany." **Journal of Higher Education**, 34 (Dec., 1963), 511-13.
Part of a round-table on using the talents of retired faculty members.

998. Goldschmidt, Dietrich. "Teachers in Institutes of Higher Learning in Germany." In A. H. Halsey, J. Floud, and C. A. Anderson (eds.). **Education, Economy, and Society**. Glencoe Ill.: Free Press, 1961.
A study is included in this book which is based on the findings of an investigation undertaken in 1953-54.

999. Kidd, Charles V. "New Academic Positions: The Outlook in Europe and North America." **Science**, 212 (April, 1981), 293-98.
Kidd looks at the shortage of academic positions in West Germany, France, the U.K. and the U.S.A. His projections were that only one percent of new positions would be open each year in West Germany. He describes the proposed programs to deal with this problem.

1000. Mann, Golo. "The German Intellectuals." **Encounter**, (June, 1955), 42-49.
Mann traces the place and status of the German intellectual during the past two centuries, the tensions between the humanists and the nationalists. He sorts out the role of the intellectual today in the middle of the economic miracle.

1001. "Question of West Germany's Professors." **Times Educational Supplement**, 2657 (Apr. 22, 1966), 1206.

1002. Science Council. "Recommendations of the Science Council on the Reorganisation of University Teaching Staffs in Western Germany." **Minerva**, 4 (Winter, 1966), 246-253.
A summary of **Wissenschaftsrates** recommendations.

ACADEMIC FREEDOM

PRE-WORLD WAR II

1003. Beall, Lewis L. "Academic Freedom in the Third Reich: Can It Happen Here?" **Clearing House**, 43 (Apr., 1969), 483-87.
Reflecting on the recent curbs on freedom to learn, teach and use resources, Beall looks at the German tradition and its abuse by Hitler as an object lesson for Americans.

1004. Brown, Cynthia Stokes. "Academic Freedom at Goettingen Before 1815." **School and Society**, 100 (Mar., 1972), 173-78.
Brown discusses the role of **Lernfreiheit** and **Lehrfreiheit** at Goettingen prior to 1815.

EAST GERMANY

No references found.

WEST GERMANY

1005. Fuhrig, Wolf D. "Academic Freedom and Political Conformity: West German Scholars in Conflict with the State." **Journal of Higher Education**, 34 (Feb., 1963), 61-66.

1006. Oppenheimer, Martin. "Academic Freedom in the Federal Republic of Germany." **AAUP Bulletin**, 63 (April, 1977), 45-49.
The author discusses the general development of banning people from access to civil servant positions if their loyalty to the state is suspect. He concentrates specifically on the negative impact of these provisions on academic personnel.

1007. Shils, Edward. "Stanford and Berlin: The Spheres of Politics and Intellect." **Minerva**, 10 (July, 1972), 351-361.
Shils uses the dismissal of Bruce Franklin at Stanford and the rejection of the candidacy of Ernest Mandel for a position at the FU in Berlin to raise special concerns about freedoms of university teachers.

UNIVERSITY INSTRUCTION

EAST GERMANY

1008. Borm, Reinhard and Sigrid Borm. "Use of Educational Television by the Institutions of Higher Learning in the German Democratic Republic." **Higher Education in Europe**, 5 (July-Sept., 1980), 18-19.

WEST GERMANY

1009. Burn, Barbara B. "Learner-Centered Education in German Universities." **International Education**, 5 (1975), 21-29.
Burn points out how learner centered higher education is in conflict with the German higher education tradition; however, it seems to be inevitable requiring traditions to be changed.

1010. Hoffman, Bjorn. "Individualized Instruction at German Universities." **Journal of College Science Teaching**, 11 (Sept., 1981), 12-14.
Various forms of individualized instruction at West German universities are discussed, with details of the University of Cologne, which is serving as a model for other institutions.

1011. Kotowski, Georg. "German Universities' Pending Problems of Teaching Systems," **Educational Forum**, 22 (Mar., 1958), 279-87.
Kotowski expresses optimism that the academic tradition in Germany is still productive and that with adjustments, teaching at the university can expect to recover some of its lost status.

1012. Strozier, Charles B. "Role Playing Successfully Provides Perspectives on Life in Nazi Germany." **Simulation/Gaming**, 4 (Mar./April, 1977), 13-4.
A university history course has made use of role playing to provide perspectives on life in Nazi Germany. These are video-taped and discussed.

WOMEN

PRE-WORLD WAR II

1013. Stephenson, Jill. "Girls' Higher Education in Germany in the 1930's." **Journal of Contemporary History**, 10 (1975), 41-69.
Provides evidence that the Nazi party took considerable interest in girl students who were admitted to higher education in relatively large numbers. Women were distinguished not by intellect but by womanliness.

1014. Lange, Helene. **Higher Education of Women in Europe** (trans. by L. R. Klemm). New York: Appleton and Co., 1890).

Lange includes Germany in her study of women in European higher education. She finds the cause for failure in Germany to be from adverse circumstances, men's unwillingness to aid the cause, and women's indifference.

EAST GERMANY

No references found.

WEST GERMANY

1015. Cassara, Beverly B. "Career Patterns of Female Professors in West Berlin Institutions of Higher Learning." **Higher Education,** 24 (Summer, 1979), 22-30.

1016. Cassara, Beverly B. The Academic Woman: West Germany and Washington." **Change,** (Mar., 1978), 46-7, 64.

Reports on a Fulbright stay in Berlin and data she collected demonstrating that the four institutions of higher learning in that city remain male dominated.

1017. Schmarsow, Christine. "Women in Higher Education--Some Information on the Situation in the Federal Republic of Germany." **Higher Education in Europe,** 6 (Oct.-Dec., 1981), 50-54.

Chapter 10

TEACHER EDUCATION

GENERAL TEACHER EDUCATION

PRE-WORLD WAR II

1018. Alexander, Thomas. **Training Elementary Teachers in Germany.** New York: Teachers college, Columbia University, 1936.

1019. Brown, John F. **The Training of Teachers for the Secondary Schools in Germany and the United States.** New York: Macmillan, 1911.
Brown describes the standards and institutions in Germany for the training of secondary school teachers, providing historical treatment in the previous century and a plan and standard for American high school teachers.

1020. Dunkel, Harold B. "Herbart's Pedagogical Seminar." **History of Education Quarterly,** 7 (Spring, 1967), 93-101.
Outlines Herbart's secondary school teacher training program in the first half of the nineteenth century at Koenigsberg.

1021. Kandel, Isaac L. **The Training of Elementary School Teachers in Germany.** New York: Teachers College, Columbia University, 1910.
The study is based on visits to German normal schools in the summer of 1909. Kandel finds the schools to be successful in doing what they are intended to do, but they also illustrate the dangers of applying bureaucratic methods in education.

1022. Rust, Val D. and David Starr. "Personalized Teacher Education: The Example of Herbart." **Educational Studies,** 8 (1977), 221-29.
This is an assessment of the pedagogical seminar conducted by Herbart at Koenigsberg for secondary teacher candidates. Implications for contemporary education are drawn.

1023. Smith, Benjamin M. "Education in Prussia and the Training of Teachers." (Published originally as "Report on the Primary School System of Prussia, Jan. 15, 1839), House Journal of the Viriginia House of Delegates, No. 26, 1839.) In Stewart E. Fraser and William W. Brickman, **A History of International and Comparative Education**. Glenview, Ill.: Scott Foresman, 1968.

1024. Williams, Emily. **Report of Observations Made During a Three Month Visit to Training Colleges and Schools in Prussia and Saxony**. London: Odmans, 1981.

OCCUPATION AND REEDUCATION

1025. Abraham, Karl. "Why I Teach Sociology in a German Training College." **New Era**, 28 (Nov., 1947), 180.
This is a personal declaration by the author that German education cannot continue where it left off in 1933, and that educators must understand the relation between the state and society as exemplified in the teacher training program at Solingen.

1026. Edman, Marion. "Quality of Teacher Training." **Educational Leadership**, 6 (Oct., 1948), 16-17.
Points up significant factors in the reorganization of the program in teacher training.

1027. Henderson, James L. "A Comparative Survey of Teacher Training for Primary and Secondary Schools in the Four Zones of Germany between 1945 and 1950." M.A. Thesis, University of London, Institute of Education, 1952.

1028. **Teacher Education for Wuerttemberg-Baden: The Esslingen Plan**. International Workshop on Teacher Education. Stuttgart: E. Klett, 1949.
This is a report of a workshop intended to lay out a design for teacher education in one German state. Participants were from a number of countries.

EAST GERMANY

1029. Bar, Siegfried and others. **Initial and Further Training of Teachers in the GDR**. Berlin: Ministry of Education and the UNESCO Commission of the GDR, 1973.

1030. Wollner, Mary B. "Encounter with Communist Teacher Training." **Education**, 78 (April, 1958), 480-85.
Impressions of a brief visit to the East Berlin "Central Institute of Pedagogy."

WEST GERMANY

1031. Buckley, Dennis L. "Diverse Applications of the Unifying Principles of Lifelong Education to Teacher Preparation." **Western European Education**, 10 (Spring, 1978), 40-56.
Reports on teacher preparation for lifelong education programs in West Germany and four other countries. These programs were part of a research project employing principles of lifelong education.

1032. Ford, Boris. **Institutions Responsible for Teacher Training: Issues and New Trends in Some European Countries and in North America**. Paris: OECD, 1975.
The study includes specific discussion of proposals for integration of teachers colleges in West Germany with universities.

1033. Grittner, Frank. "Teacher Education in Germany." **Wisconsin Journal of Education**. 97 (Dec., 1964), 11.
After a month tour of Germany, he presents some observations.

1034. Hahn, Walter. "West Germany's Secondary-School Teacher Preparation." **Comparative Education Review**, 9 (Oct., 1965), 346-55.
Hahn examines the present status of secondary teacher preparation in West Germany and raises the issues and problems in this field. He looks at university preparation, professional studies, the state examination, and the **Studienseminar**.

1035. Hilker, Franz. "Organization and Structure of Teacher Education in the German Federal Republic." **Year Book of Education**, (1963), 256-73.

1036. Mohr, B. "Teacher Training in the Federal Republic of Germany." **Bildung und Wissenschaft**, (1977), 5-77.

1037. Muller, Peter. **Teacher Education in the Federal Republic of Germany**. Paris: UNESCO, 1977.

RELATIONS WITH UNIVERSITIES

EAST GERMANY

No references found.

WEST GERMANY

1038. Ford, Boris. "Changing Relations between Universities and Colleges of Education in West Germany, Sweden, and Denmark." **Universities Quarterly**, 28 (Autumn, 1974), 404-36.
Discusses the proposals of integration of teachers colleges and universities in West Germany, and assesses the political struggles involved, including the adoption of the **Gesamthochschule**.

1039. Ford, Boris. "The Emancipation of Teacher Training? Changing Relations between Universities and Colleges of Education." **Universities Quarterly**, 29 (Winter, 1974), 7-43.
This is a follow-up article on the changing relations between universities and colleges in the previous issue of the same journal. It is more general in scope but makes references to West Germany.

TEACHER EDUCATION IN SPECIFIC SUBJECTS

EAST GERMANY

A. Science Teacher Education

1040. "Botany at Potsdam: Botanical Institute of the Pedagogical Academy." **Times Educational Supplement**, 2209 (Sept., 20, 1957), 1220.
The article consists of a picture essay of an academy that trains secondary school biology teachers.

A. Preschool Teacher Education

1041. Pause, Gerhard. "Cooperation between Parents, Preschool and the Community: The Training of Pre-School Teachers with a View to Co-operation with Parents (Federal Republic of Germany)." Paper prepared by the Committee for General and Technical Education, Council of Europe, Strasbourg, 1977.

B. Art Teacher Education

1042. Barkan, Manuel. "Education of European Art Teachers." **Art Education**, 18 (June, 1965), 9-15.
The professional preparation of English, Danish, Swedish, French, and West German art teachers is described. In Germany, the art academies do most of the training, but there are differences in the various academies.

1043. Otto, Gunter. "Germany: Art Education and the Education of the Teacher of Art." **Art Education**, 18 (May, 1965), 12-16.
Otto provides a substantial contextual base for discussing the education of art teachers. His major point is the changing sense of what art is and how it has moved away from the idea of fine arts toward muse oriented art.

C. Mathematics Teacher Education

1044. Fehr, Howard F. "Education of a Mathematics Teacher for the German **Gymnasium**." **Mathematics Teacher**, 55 (May, 1962), 337-42.

D. Science Teacher Education

1045. Minssen, Mins. "'Analysis of the Evolution of a Science Concept: Macromolecules'-- A Case Study to Introduce New Trends in German Teacher-Training." **European Journal of Science Education**, 2 (July-Sept., 1980), 285-93.
Describes the use of a model curriculum in teacher training in West Germany. The model curriculum focuses on the evolution of the macromolecule concept.

1046. Nachtigall, Dieter. "Physics Teacher Education in Dortmund." **Physics Teacher**, 18 (Nov., 1980), 589-93.
The author describes attempts to revitalize physics teacher training at Dortmund in West Germany. He provides a detailed account of the program now under way.

1047. **Tendencies and Problems of the Training of Mathematics Teachers.** Bielefeld: Institut fuer Didaktik der Mathematik, Universitaet Bielefeld, 1975.
The document is a statement by a working group that addresses the issue of training mathematics teachers.

E. Social Science Teacher Education

1048. Brutz, George G. "Social Science Teacher Training in West Germany." **Social Education**, 23 (Jan., 1959), 17-18.
A brief account of social science teacher training.

1049. van den Hazel, B. J. "Environmental Education and Field Studies Programs in Three Selected N. W. European Areas." Faculty of Education, Nipissing University, North Bay, Ontario, Canada, 1976.
Two German centers, which conduct environmental studies, are described. These are part of teacher education programs.

1050. Hartig, Paul. "New Directions in the training of Teachers of English as a Foreign Language." **English Language Teaching Journal**, 29 (Oct., 1974), 2-8.
After discussing how teachers of English as a Second Language have traditionally been trained, the author lays out plans to revamp the system.

1051. Kroll, Barry W. "A German Model for Teacher Education." **English Education**, 8 (Summer, 1971), 225-28.
The author claims the West German **Studienseminar** is a superior system of training English teachers.

G. In-Service Teacher Education

1052. Frey, Karl. **Innovation in In-Service Education and Training of Teachers: Federal Republic of Germany, Switzerland**. Paris: OECD, Centre for Educational Research and Innovation, 1976.
Section I discusses INSET in the two countries. Section II includes a case study of INSET and scholastic reform in Berlin. Secton III examines some theoretical perspectives.

1053. "German Education Service Center." **Institute of International Education News Bulletin**, 28 (May, 1953), 24.

1054. Gray, Dorothy. "Experiences in Group Planning for German Teachers." **Educational Leadership**, 6 (Oct., 1948), 10-12.
Outlines work with social studies teachers using the group approach and democratic participation.

1055. "History in German Schools: Teacher's Course at Brunswick." **Times Educational Supplement**, 1785 (July 15, 1949), 482.
Describes an inservice program conducted by Georg Eckert for history teachers.

1056. Jessen, Klaus. "Evaluation of Teacher Training on Student-Centered Behavior." **Studies in Educational Evaluation**, 1 (Summer, 1975), 95-108.
The author reports that West German teachers who took a training course in classroom behavior were observed by external raters as more emotional, warm, and appreciative than those who were not trained.

1057. Klinzing-Eurich, Gisela and Hans Gerhard Klinzing. "Adaptation and Evaluation of Mini Courses in West Germany." Tuebingen: Institute fuer Erziehungswissenschaft, Universitaet Tuebingen, 1979.
Describes the adaptation of an American in-service teacher education training package in Germany put together by the Far West Regional Laboratory. Conclusions indicate it was effective.

H. Media and Teacher Education

1058. Howard, A. "Teaching Teaching by TV; Heidelberg Shows How." **Times Educational Supplement**, 2619 (July, 1965), 200.

1059. Ziefuss, Horst. "An Evlauation/Implementation Plan for Media Programs in Teacher Training." **Studies in Educational Evaluation**, 4 (Winter, 1978), 217-21.
This is an evaluation of a program in Munich to increase the effectiveness of the application of media for the training of teachers.

Chapter 11

EDUCATIONAL RESEARCH

EAST GERMANY

1060. Klein, Helmut. "Educational and Psychological Research and Decisions on Educational Policy." **Prospects,** 6 (Winter, 1974), 453-60.
Klein discusses how East Germany uses educational and psychological research in formulating educational policy. He stresses the link between theory and practice.

1061. Neuner, G. "Unity of Present and Future Educational Research." **Yearbook, 1971.** Berlin: Academy of Educational Research in the German Democratic Republic, 1972.

WEST GERMANY

1062. Carelli, M. Dino and Peter Sachsenmeier. **Educational Research in Europe.** Hamburg: UNESCO Institute for Education, 1978.
Report of an all-European conference for directors of educational research institutions in Hamburg.

1063. Hameyer, Uwe. "Sociological Aspects of Educational Change." **Studies in Educational Evaluation.** 4 (Spring, 1978), 47-53.
The author analyses 42 projects on educational research and curriculum development in West Germany, Austria, and Switzerland to get some idea of the general problems involved in the processes curriculum innovation.

1064. Mueller-Wieland, Marcel. "Educational Research in Countries other than the U.S.A.; German Speaking Countries: Austria, the German Federal Republic, and German Speaking Switzerland." **Review of Educational Research**, 27 (Feb., 1957), 57-74.
Reports on about one tenth of all articles published on the subject since 1950. The article touches on administration, curriculum, educational measurement, educational sociology, guidance and counseling, mental and physical development, language arts, fine arts and history, math and science, special programs, teacher personnel, and orientation in educational theory.

1065. OECD. **Classification of Educational Systems in OECD Member Countries: Finland, Germany, Japan**. Paris: OECD, 1972.

1066. Rust, Val D. **German Interest in Foreign Education Since World War I**. Ann Arbor: University of Michigan, 1967. Comparative Education Dissertation Series No. 13.

1067. Schaefer, Gerhard "Institute for Science Education." **Studies in Science Education.**
The functions of the IPN at Kiel, West Germany, are described.

1068. Schultze, Walter. "Educational Research in the Federal Republic of Germany." **School Review**, 66 (Sept., 1958), 298-312.
This is a survey of various educational research specialties in West Germany.

1069. Standing Conference of Ministers of Education and Culture. **Educational Research in the Federal Republic of Germany, 1971/72**. Bonn: Secretariat of the Standing Conference of Ministers of Education and Culture, 1973.
A compilation of projects in the field of educational research in West Germany, given at the Third Council of Europe.

1070. "UNESCO Institute for Education, Hamburg." **Nature**, 170 (Nov. 8, 1952), 789-90.
Account of the establishment of the Institute for Education, its purposes, governance and initial programs.

1071. von Friedeberg, Ludwig. "West Germany." **Review of Educational Research**, 32 (June, 1962), 308-19.
Reviews the literature from 1957-1962 in educational research. He discusses empirical surveys of the country's political and social development.

Chapter 12

ADULT EDUCATION

GENERAL

PRE-WORLD WAR II

1072. Pritle, Wayne, G. "German Adult Education following the Unification of 1871." **Adult Education** (U.S.A.), 23 (Winter, 1973), 99-114.
Describes the failure of adult education centers to attract the working class following German unification in 1871. Through the work of people such as Robert von Erdberg, programs of intensive individualized education for the working classes brought them into the education process and revolutionized adult education in the country.

OCCUPATION AND REEDUCATION

1073. Cook, A. H. **Adult Education in Citizenship in Postwar Germany**. New York: Fund for Adult Education, 1848.

1074. Davis, Hubert J. "Films at Work in Occupied Germany." **Educational Screen**, 32 (April, 1953), 156+.
Explains how films are being used as an adult education tool in West German reeducation efforts.

1075. Deming, Robert C. "Adult Education in the U. S. Zone of Germany." **Adult Education Bulletin**, 12 (Dec., 1947), 37-43.

1076. Hopman, A. N. "Adult Education in Occupied Germany, U.S. Zone." **School and Society**, 66 (Dec. 27, 1947), 505- 07.

1077. Huebener, Theodore. "Adult Education in Germany." **High Points**, 32 (Nov., 1950), 5-9.
Describes the activities of the Voice of America, **Die Neue Zeitung**, and the **Amerika Haus** in reorienting the attitudes of the Germans.

1078. Stadler, K. "**Volksbildung** in the Russian Zone of Germany." **Adult Education**, 20 (Dec., 1947), 54-60.

1079. Stadler, K. "Education for Democracy in Germany." **Adult Education**, (Sept., 1947), 17-24.

EAST GERMANY

1080. Fleischhauer, Karl-Heinz and Gerhard Pogodda. **Adult Education in Europe: Adult Education in the German Democratic Republic**. Paris: UNESCO Studies and Documents No. 5, 1978.
Full discussion of the system of adult education in the GDR, personnel engaged in adult education, and theory and research in the field.

1081. Schneider, Gottfried. "Adult Education in the German Democratic Republic." **Society and Leisure**, 8 (1976), 105-120.
Descriptive account of adult education.

1082. Schneider, Gottfried. "Adult Education in the German Democratic Republic." **Prospects**, 7 (1977), 263-71.
Schneider explains how adult education is a part of the total educational system in East Germany and he also discusses its scientific character, its relationship to vocational qualifications, and its attempts to give women greater equality.

WEST GERMANY

1083. "Adult Education Legislation in Ten Countries of Europe." **Notes and Studies**,62-64 (1974). A special issue of the European Bureau of Adult Education.

1084. Blaug, Mark and John Mace. "Recurrent Education--The New Jerusalem." **Higher Education**, 6 (Aug., 1977), 277-99.
Authors review recurrent education policies in six OECD countries, including West Germany, and conclude that the concept requires clarification and that the costing of proposals for recurrent education should be undertaken.

1085. Carlson, Robert A. "Liberal Adult Education Adapts to the Technological Society: A Study of West Germany's Adult Education Centers." **Adult Education**, (U.S.A) 27 (Feb., 1976), 3-12.
The study discusses developments now underway in West Germany's adult education centers and focuses on recent attempts to break from the liberal arts tradition and offer practical education, including certificates of competence.

1086. Cook, R. J. "Adult Education in England and Germany: A Comparative Study." M.A. Thesis, University of London, Institute of Education, 1954.

1087. Council of Europe. **Developments in Adult Education Structures: Five National Studies.** Strasbourg: Council of Europe Committee on Out-of-School Education and Cultural Development, 1976.
One of the five national studies is that of North-Rhine-Westphalia, which has undergone plans to adopt a credit system.

1088. Dolff, Helmuth. "The Situation of Adult Education Legislation in the Federal Republic of Germany." **Notes and Studies**, 60-61 (May-June, 1974), 3-5

1089. Ebbighausen, W. C. "Short Statement on the Ideas and Practice of the Integration of Adult Education in the Formal System of Education." **Notes and Studies**, 53-54 (May-June, 1972).

1090. Godfrey, Eve. "Self-directed People in Organizations. Part II: What about the Factual Realization of the Philosophy." **Industrial Training International**, 10 (March, 1975), 88-9.
The major focus is on personal impressions of the International Summer School in West Germany.

1091. Hedwig, Rudolph and others. **Recurrent Education Policy and Development in OECD Countries: Recurrent Education in the Federal Republic of Germany.** Paris: OECD, 1972.
Looks at recurrent education in the overall West German education system as well as plans for the reconstruction of that system. Focus is on the legal provisions, agreements, and regulations.

1092. Kaplan, Abbott. "Adult Education in Germany." **Adult Education**, 5 (1954), 22-29.
Reviews the coming of age of adult education giving some attention to evening school, **Arbeit und Leben**, universities, worker's education, and other agencies.

1093. Knoll, Joachim-Hans. "New Approaches to Post-Secondary Education in Germany." In **Learning Opportunities for Adults: New Structures, Programmes and Methods**. Paris: OECD, 1980. Vol. II, 7-37.

1094. Kulich, Jindra. "Adult Education in West Germany." **Adult Leadership**, 10 (Oct., 1961), 99-100+.
Summary of a report on adult education by the West German Commission for Learning and Education, published in Jan., 1960, chaired by Helmut Becker.

1095. Lawson, Robert F. "Contrasting Conceptions of Further Education in North America and Some West European Counties." **International Review of Education**, 14 (1968), 3-23.
Concentrates on the U.S.A., Canada, England, and West Germany.

1096. Lenhardt, Gero. "Problems in Reforming Recurrent Education for Workers." **Comparative Education Review**, 22 (Oct., 1978), 452-63.
The author addresses several questions relevant to the relationship between capital, labor, and the state in West Germany. He shows that continuing training can hardly contribute to labor market chances of workers, and how labor market constraints limit the state's possibilities to protect workers against the dysfunctions of economic development.

1097. "The Planning of Further Education in two West German Educational Projects." **Notes and Studies**, 51-52 (Dec., 1971), 18-28.

1098. Robertson, A. G. "Adult Education in Theory and Practice--Some German Perspectives." **Studies in Adult Education**, 3 (Oct., 1971), 154-65.
The author discusses the series of paperbacks edited by Hans Tietgens on the theory and practice of adult education.

1099. Rudolph, H. and others. **Recurrent Education in the Federal Republic of Germany.** Paris: OECD/CERI, 1972.
This report is divided into three sections. Number one looks at legal provisions and regulations; number two focuses on plans for including recurrent education in the educational system; number three assesses the overall future of this activity in Germany.

1100. Striner, Herbert E. **Continuing Education as a National Capital Investment.** New York: Ford foundation, 1975.
The author looks at Denmark, France, and West Germany to see what steps these countries have taken to deal with problems of economic growth by reconceptualizing the role of adult education.

1101. Urbach, Dietrich. "Further Education in the Federal Republic of Germany." **Bildung und Wissenschaft,** No. 11/12(e), 1981, published by Inter Nationes.
After discussing history, state policy and the political discussion about further education, the author describes the participants, further training institutes, vocational further training, political education, and concludes with individual aspects of this training.

1102. UNESCO. **Adult Education in the Federal Republic of Germany.** Paris: UNESCO, 1955.

EAST AND WEST GERMANY

1103. Adamski, W. **Continuing Education in Western and Eastern European Societies.** Amsterdam: European Cultural Foundation, 1978.

1104. Knoll, Joachim-Hans. "Training Adult Educators in the Federal Republic and the German Democratic Republic." In Manfred Jourdan (ed.). **Recurrent Education in Western Europe.** London: NFER-Nelson, 1981. pp. 93-116.
A comparative analysis of adult education in the two Germanies. The author concludes that high industrialization is more important as a defining factor than ideological presumptions.

CORRESPONDENCE EDUCATION

EAST GERMANY

No references found.

WEST GERMANY

1105. Gunning, Robert. **Regulations and Legislation Regarding Correspondence Education. A Survey of Five Countries with Recommended Guidelines for Developing Countries.** Paris: UNESCO, 1981.
   Survey of France, India, U.K., U.S.A., and West Germany.

RESIDENTIAL ADULT EDUCATION

EAST GERMANY

No references found.

WEST GERMANY

1106. Borinski, F. "Value of Residential Institutions: Germany." In **Adult Education Towards Social and Political Responsibility**. Paris: UNESCO, 1979. pp. 95-102.

EAST GERMANY

1107. Moehle, Horst. "Progressive Changes in the Content and Methods of Extramural Studies at the Karl Marx University, Leipzig." **Convergence**, 52 (1972), 37-42.
Describes extramural studies at an East German University.

WEST GERMANY

1108. Allesch, Juergen. "Analysis and Perspectives of Academic Continuing Education Courses in the Federal Republic of Germany." **Higher Education in Europe**, 6 (Oct.-Dec., 1981), 16-21.

1109. Dickerman, Watson. "Adult Education in the German Universities." **Journal of Higher Education**, 24 (May, 1953), 241-48.
Descriptive account of public lectures, seminars, etc., of university personnel.

1110. Hahn, Walter. "Upward Academic Mobility for the Nonsecondary School Graduate: Some Avenues Open to Young Adults in West Germany." **Higher Education**, 9 (1980), 7-20.
Hahn reviews the adult education institutions designed to qualify young adults for academic studies. He also explores a number of issues related to upward academic mobility.

1111. Knoll, Joachim-Hans. "Adult Education with or without the Universities." **Convergence**, 5 (1972), 71-87.
Describes the fundamental structural change taking place in West German higher education and its growing involvement in adult education.

1112. Raapke, Hans-Dieter. "The Participation of the Universities in Adult Education in the Federal Republic of Germany." In Jindra Kulich and Wolfgang Krueger (eds.). **The Universities and Adult Education in Europe**. Vancouver: Centre for Continuing Education, the University of British Columbia, 1980. pp. 73-85.
Until now little has been done to foster continuing education in West Germany, although some continuing education departments have been established at universities.

1113. Vogts, H. "University in the Federal Republic of Germany in Relation to Adult Education." **International Journal of Adult Youth Education**, 13 (1961), 108-09.

VOLKSHOCHSCHULEN

EAST GERMANY

No references found.

WEST GERMANY

1114. Dolff, Helmuth. "West German Experience of 'Popular' Higher Education." **World Year Book of Education**, (1979), 159-66.
Looks at the role of the **Volkshochschulen** in German adult education.

1115. Dolff, Helmuth. "Can the **Volkshochschulen** of Today Answer the Requirements of Adult Education for Tomorrow?" **Convergence**, 5, 3 (1972), 31-36.

1116. Heinhardt, Harry. "The **Volkshochschulen**: Germany's Community College." **Community College Review**, 6 (Summer, 1978), 16-20.
Briefly traces the history of the VHS and then points out how costs are kept to a minimum, including the development of standardized courses.

1117. Mreschar, Renate I. "Adult Education in the Federal Republic of Germany: Additional Education Courses at Adult Education Centres and Other Similar facilities." **Bildung und Wissenschaft**, No. 6-76(e), 1976, published by Inter Nationes.

EAST GERMANY

No references found.

WEST GERMANY

1118. "Creating Mediators: Languages and Interpreters Institute (**Sprachen und Dolmetscher-Institut**) at Munich." **Times Educational Supplement**, 2364 (Sept. 9, 1960), 283.

1119. "Leisure-Time English." **Times Educational Supplement**, 2463 (Aug. 3, 1962), 133.

1120. Schmidt-Sinns, Dieter. "Adult Political Education Programs in the Federal Republic of Germany." In **Adult Political Education in West Germany and the United States**. Bloomington: Institute of German Studies, Indiana University, 1977.
Discusses the Federal Center for Political Education, its development, curricula, instructional approach and problems.

1121. Vogt, Peter. "Training Centre for Overseas Television Staff at the **Sender Freies Berlin**." **Educational Broadcasting International**, 6 (Sept., 1973), 143-144.
Describes the training at **Sender Freies Berlin**, including course content and how to apply for studies.

1122. von der Handt, G. "Presentation of Ongoing Work on the German Pilot Project." **Colloquy on the Language of the Host Country to Adult Migrants**. Strasbourg: Council for Cultural Cooperation, Council of Europe, 1979. pp. 18-19.

MASS MEDIA RELATED TO ADULT EDUCATION

EAST GERMANY

No references found.

WEST GERMANY

1123. Balzert, Helmut and Hartmut Hille. "A Standardized Curriculum in Informatics for Adult Education." **Computers and Education**, 4 (1980), 189-98.
A report of a 1976 conference on informatics for adult education taking place in Frankfurt. Four learning aims are discussed: problem solving using a computer, structure and function of a computer, social implications of EDP, and DP organization.

1124. Carlson, Robert A. "Adult Educators Seek to Influence the Television Networks." **Adult Leadership**, 24 (June, 1976), 324-26.
Describes the role of the Adolf Grimme Prize competition as a mechanism for influencing network televison by adult educators in West Germany.

1125. Cory, Genevieve H. "Television Experiences in Other Countries." **New Directions for Continuing Education**, 5 (1980), 65-78.
Looks at the potential of educational television, espcially for adult education in Japan, Britain, West Germany, Sweden, Denmark, India, and Canada.

1126. McNeill, Thomas J. "Films at Work in Germany." **Educational Screen**, 35 (Nov., 1956), 404-07.
Provides examples of how films are being used in German adult education programs sponsored by the U.S. Information Service.

1127. Porcher, L. "Society as Portrayed in Audio-Visual Courses of Language Teaching." **Educational Media International**, No. 3 (1974), 14-15.
Describes a study undertaken of adult beginners in German language courses.

EAST GERMANY

1128. Kulich, Jindra. "Training Adult Educators in East Germany." In Jindra Kulich (ed.). **Training of Adult Educators in East Europe**. Vancouver: Center for Continuing Education, 1979. pp. 27-48.

WEST GERMANY

1129. Council of Europe. **Workers in Adult Education: Their Status, Recruitment and Professional Training**. Strasbourg: Council for Cultural Cooperation, Council of Europe, 1966.

1130. Schlunder, G. and H. Schweisfurth. "The Training of Full-time Adult Educators in the German Federal Republic." **Adult Education** (Great Britain), 50 (July, 1977), 91-96.
Although no special pre-service general or professional education is presently compulsory, some policy recommendations indicate a shift away from this tradition. The authors discuss the findings of a questionnaire sent to adult educators asking about their own backgrounds and the qualifications they would like to see required.

Chapter 13

SPECIAL TOPICS RELATED TO SCHOOLS

LIBRARIES

EAST GERMANY

No references found.

WEST GERMANY

1131. Chaplan, Margaret. "Public Librarianship in the Federal Republic of Germany Since 1945." **Library Quarterly**, 36 (1966), 299-320.
Chaplan reviews the general history of the public library movement from its beginnings to 1945. Then she turns her attention to West Germany after 1945, giving the legal basis of libraries and laws affecting their operation, describing librarianship and the training of librarians, describing the character of the collections and their use, and she concludes with a statement of the problems libraries face.

1132. Stevenson, Gordon. "The Eppelsheimer Subject Catalog." **Library Resources and Technical Services**, 15 (Summer, 1971), 309-28.
Since 1945 a method of catalog classification, originally devised by H.W. Eppelsheimer for the Mainz city library, has found wide acceptance. It is a complex of catalogs which combines features of both subject classification and alphabetical subject indexing.

1133. Stevenson, Grace T. "Library Adult Education Abroad: Germany." **Adult Leadership**, 11 (Feb., 1963), 225-6+.
Focuses mainly on the public library service in Germany, giving a positive account of the work accomplished.

1134. von Busse, Gisela and Horst Ernestus. **Libraries in the Federal Republic of Germany** (trans. by J. S. Andrews and G. Walker). Wiesbaden: Otto Harrassowitz, 1972.
This is a full treatment of libraries. Chapter headings are: The General Background; Types of Libraries; Library Co-operation and Central Organization; Some Aspects of Library Administration and Services; Library Building; Bibliography and Information Science; Librarianship as a Career; Practical Information.

EAST AND WEST GERMANY

1135. Ernestus, Horst. **Developing Public Library Services: A German Outlook**. Pamphlet from the University of Toronto School of Library Science: The Bertha Bassam Lecture in Librarianship No. 2, 1969.
Ernestus recounts the story of the public library, discussing its place in both Germanies.

GUIDANCE AND COUNSELING

EAST GERMANY

1136. Denga, Daniel I. "Elementary School Guidance and Counseling: Some International Perspectives." **Elementary School Guidance and Counseling**, 15 (Apr., 1981), 324-28.
The author describes East Germany and Nigeria as examples of how nations are implementing elementary school guidance and counseling programs.

WEST GERMANY

1137. Froehlich, Clifford P. and Frank G. Davis. "Vocational Guidance in Germany." **Personnel and Guidance Journal**, 31 (Apr., 1953), 462-64.
Contrasts the 1952 situation with a report by Keller in April of 1948. The conditions had become very favorable and he sees progress having been made in vocational guidance.

1138. **International Workshop on Guidance: Proceedings: Findings and Recommendations for the German Schools.** Weilberg: U. S. Office of the High Commissioner for Germany, Dec., 1951.

1139. Menacker, Julius. "Guidance and Educational Opportunity: The German Perspective." **Personnel and Guidance Journal**, 57 (April, 1979), 408-11.

1140. Segel, David. "Evaluation and Guidance in German Schools." **School Life**, 30 (Oct., 1947), 15-19.
Report of the methods used for selection of students at various stages in German schools. The report provides some objective data on selection.

1141. United States High Commissioner for Germany. "Proceedings, Findings, and Recommendations for the German Schools: International Workshop on Guidance." Frankfurt, Office of Public Affairs, 1951.
This volume represents a compilation of reports, resolutions, and recommendations of a large number of committees having representatives from eight different nationalities concerning guidance in German schools.

AUDIO-VISUAL SERVICES

EAST GERMANY

1142. Dusz, Janos. **The Audio-Visual Services in Socialist Countries. Comparative Study on the Administration of Audio-Visual Services in Advanced and Developing Countries.** Paris: UNESCO, 1973.

WEST GERMANY

1143. "Film Education in Germany: Enjoyment and Discrimination." **Times Educational Supplement,** 2100 (Aug. 19, 1955), 869.
Provides samples of educational film endeavors in West Germany.

1144. Greiger, Stephan. "Media-Centre Steinfurt - Unveiling a Model." **Educational Media International**, 2, 2(June, 1973), 8-11.
Describes a new media center in West Germany.

1145. Keilhacker, M. "The Organization of Film and Television in the Schools of the German Federal Republic." **Year Book of Education**, (1960), 547-52.

1146. Neck, Reinhard and Johannes Balensiefen. "Loan System for Audio-Visual Media." **Educational Media International**, 3 (Sept., 1973), 28-31.
Discusses the loan system at the Rhein-Sieg local district's audio-visual centre.

1147. Schmid, Fridolin. **The Audio-Visual Services in Western European Countries. Comparative Study on the Administration of Audio-Visual Services in Advanced and Developing Countries**. Paris: UNESCO, 1973.

1148. "School Television Studio in the City of Frankfurt." **Sound and Image**, (April, 1973), 1-3.
Television studio facilities for schools in the city of Frankfurt are described.

1149. Valerien, J. "Coproduction Methods used in Cooperation between the Ofrateme and the Federal Republic of Germany." **Educational Media International**, 4 (Dec., 1973), 22-24.

1150. Wasem, Erich. "Audiovisual Media: Unused Potenial." **Western European Education**, 3 (Summer-Fall, 1971), 158-60.
Comments on the need for audio-visual media.

OTHER SPECIAL SERVICES

EAST GERMANY

No references found.

WEST GERMANY

1151. "File on the Computer in Education in Germany" Recherche, Lovain (Belgium), 1975.
This is a survey of special projects in computer applications to education in Germany.

1152. Greiger, Stephan. "Setting up an Educational Data Bank in the Federal Republic of Germany." **Educational Media International**, 3 (Sept., 1973), 22-28.

1153. Preston, Ralph C. "Recent Work in Objective Test Construction in Germany." **Educational and Psychological Measurement**, 14 (1954), 381-86.
Even though objective test construction is in its infancy some work is being done, which Preston describes.

1154. Whiting, Charles, H. "Dial Home for Homework." **Times Educational Supplement**, 2918 (Apr. 23, 1971), 15.
A homework answering service for students who have problems is described.

BUILDINGS

EAST GERMANY

No references found.

WEST GERMANY

1155. Ader, Jean. **Building Implications of the Multi-Option School**. Paris: OECD, 1975.
Describes a particular comprehensive school building in Froendenberg, West Germany (pp. 67-79) as a part of a general discussion of school building design.

1156. Allard, L. "New School in West Berlin." **Educational Leadership**, 15 (Dec., 1957), 154-56.
Brief description of a new elementary school building in West Berlin.

1157. Bush, G. "What's Needed for Schools in Germany." **Nations Schools**, 43 (April, 1949), 47-48.
Discusses the school building needs of West Germany.

1158. Hamon, Ray L. "School Plants in Germany." **School Life**, 30 (Oct., 1947), 20-22.
Outlines progress being made in restoring school facilities in Germany, especially in the American zone.

1159. "Rebuilding in the Rhineland." **Times Educational Supplement**, 2167 (Nov. 30, 1956), 1399.
Pictures of new schools in the Rhineland are shown.

1160. Werstler, Richard E. **The Schools of Europe**. Adrian, Michigan: Swenk-Tuttle, 1967.
Discusses the education program and its implementation in West Germany (pp. 27-38), but also school construction (pp. 93-100).

JOURNAL, NAME AND SUBJECT INDEXES

INDEX OF JOURNALS

Communication Education
Comparative Education
Comparative Education Review
Comparative Political Studies
Comparative Politics
Compare
Contemporary Education
Contemporary History
Convergence
CTA Action

Education
Education and Urban Society
Education Around the World
Education Canada
Education Digest
Educational Administration
Educational Broadcasting International
Educational Exchange
Educational Forum
Educational Leadership
Educational Media International
Educational Planning
Educational Record
Educational Review
Educational Screen
Educational Studies
Elementary English
Elementary School Journal
Encounter
English Education
English Language Teaching Journal
European Journal of Education
European Journal of Science Education
Exceptional Child

Foreign Affairs
Forum

German Quarterly
German Tribune Quarterly Review

Harvard Educational Review
High Points
Higher Education
Higher Education in Europe
Higher Education Review
History of Education Journal
History of Education Quarterly
History Teacher

Illinois Career Education Journal

Improving College and University Teaching
Industrial Arts and Vocational Education
Industrial Training International
Institute of International Education
Institute of World Affairs Proceedings
International Affairs
International Bureau of Education Bulletin
International Conciliation
International Education
International Journal of Adult Youth Education
International Journal of Institutional Management in Higher Education
International Journal of Physical Education
International Labor Review
International Review of Education

Journal of the American College Health
Journal of Central European Affairs
Journal of Chemical Education
Journal of College Science Teaching
Journal of Communication
Journal of Contemporary History
Journal of Education
Journal of Educational Administration
Journal of Educational Research
Journal of Epsilon Pi Tau
Journal of General Education
Journal of Higher Education
Journal of Home Economics
Journal of Legal Education
Journal of Library History, Philosophy, and Comparative Librarianship
Journal of Librarianship
Journal of Modern History
Journal of Moral Education
Journal of Negro Education
Journal of Philosophy
Journal of Physical Education and Recreation
Journal of Reading
Journal of Research in Music Education
Journal of Secondary Education
Journal of the Society of Public Teachers of Law
Journal of Teacher Education
Journalism Educator

Language Sciences
Library Journal
Library Journal
Library Trends
LIBRI
LIBER Bulletin

Mathematics Teacher
Medical Education
Michigan Education Journal
Minerva
Minnesota Reading Quarterly
Modern Languages
Modern Language Journal
Montana Education
Music Education Review

NALLD Journal
Nation's Schools Report
NASSP Bulletin
National Business Education Quarterly
National Education Association Journal
National Elementary Principal
Nature
New Directions for Continuing Education
New Era
New Monthly Magazine and Literary Journal
New Republic
New Statesman and Nation
North Central Association Quarterly

Occupations
Oxford Review of Education

Pacific Northwest Council of Foreign
Languages, Proceedings
Pacific Spectator
Paedagogica Historica
Peabody Journal of Education
Personnel and Guidance Journal
Phi Delta Kappan
Physical Educator
Physics Teacher
PMLA
Political Quarterly
Political Science Quarterly
Practical Home Economics
Programmed Learning and Educational Technology
Progressive Education
Prospects

Reading Teacher
Religious Education
Research in Librarianship
Review of Educational Research
Review of Politics

Scandinavian Journal of Educational Research
School Arts

AUTHOR INDEX

SUBJECT INDEX